PANGS

OF

PROXIMITY

PRIO is an independent international institute of peace and conflict research, founded in 1959 as one of the first of its kind. It is governed by an international Governing Board of seven individuals, and it is financed mainly by the Norwegian Ministry of Education, Research and Church Affairs. The results of all PRIO research are available to the public.

International Peace Research Institute, Oslo
Fuglehauggata 11, N-0260 Oslo, Norway
Telephone: 472–557150
Cable Address: PEACERESEARCH OSLO
Telefax: 472–55 84 22

PANGS

OF

PROXIMITY

India and Sri Lanka's
Ethnic Crisis

S.D. MUNI

 PRIO
International Peace Research Institute, Oslo

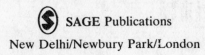 SAGE Publications
New Delhi/Newbury Park/London

First published in 1993 by

Sage Publications India Pvt Ltd
32-M Greater Kailash Market-I
New Delhi 110 048

Sage Publications Inc
2455 Teller Road
Newbury Park, California 91320

Sage Publications Ltd
6 Bonhill Street
London EC2A 4PU

Published by Tejeshwar Singh for Sage Publications India Pvt Ltd, photo-
typeset by Pagewell Photosetters, Pondicherry, and printed at Chaman
Enterprises, Delhi.

Library of Congress Cataloging-in-Publication Data

Muni, S.D.
    Pangs of proximity: India and Sri Lanka's ethnic crisis / S.D. Muni.
      p.   cm.
    Includes index.
    1. India—Politics and government—1977– 2. Sri Lanka—Politics and
government—1978– 3. India—Ethnic relations. 4. Sri Lanka—Ethnic relations. 5. India—Relations—Sri Lanka. 6. Sri Lanka—Relations—India.
I. Title.
    DS480.853.M85 305.8'00954–dc20   1993   93–12317

ISBN: 81–7036–338–1 (India)
        0–8039–9112–6 (U.S.)

Contents

Preface

This study began as a joint effort by myself and Dr. Kumar Rupe-singhe, Director, Project on Ethnic Conflicts at the International Peace Research Institute in Oslo (PRIO). The idea was Kumar's and it was at his initiative that we decided to critically examine Indian and Sri Lankan responses to Sri Lanka's ethnic conflict between the Tamils and the Sinhalese. I was asked to examine India's role and Kumar decided to write about the Sri Lankan side of the story. The study was launched in 1990 and in right earnest, both of us got on with the job. However, Kumar's expanding and unavoidable institutional and professional obligations at PRIO did not let him concentrate on this work. Therefore, I had to change the thrust of my study a little to prepare it as an independent work. This not only led to some delay in its completion but also left the Sri Lankan component of discussion and analysis far from being adequate and intensive.

There has been a tendency to look at India's approach to the consequences of Sri Lanka's ethnic crisis as being synonymous with the role of the Indian Peace Keeping Force (IPKF), sent to Sri Lanka to help implement the Indo-Sri Lankan Agreement of July 1987. This is not correct. IPKF was only a part, however significant, of the overall policy. Further, even though the role of the IPKF did not end in success, Indian policy as a whole cannnot be described as a disaster. Obviously, success has many suitors, and failure no mourners. This is inherent in human nature. One can, therefore, understand the compulsion on the part of some of the IPKF officers and police officers in India to wash their hands off the discredit and embarrassment that India's role in Sri Lanka's ethnic crisis resulted in. This pressure of conscience on the part of involved actors has been evident in some of their writings published recently. These writings offer valuable insights and some interesting information, but they are essentially partisan accounts seeking to absolve the authors of their respective lapses and laying the blame at the doors of other agencies or actors. Until the latter come up with their versions, no objective evaluation of and judgement on the events is possible.

In this study, an attempt has been made to look at India's involvement in Sri Lanka's ethnic conflict in the wider and long-term perspective of India's Sri Lankan policy. A careful scrutiny of the developments since the early 1980s in India's approach to Sri Lanka does suggest that this approach was flawed on a number of counts; but it also suggests that the policy was not without its strong points. India's policy was based on a sincere and abiding commitment to Sri Lanka's unity and territorial integrity on the one hand and genuine concern for the interests and rights of the Tamils. A number of difficulties in evolving and pursuing the policy arose because there existed, in Sri Lanka, a gap between these two objectives. Notwithstanding that, the fact remains that the Indo-Sri Lankan Agreement of July 1987 still provides the most appropriate and viable basis for resolving the Tamil question amicably.

There is no doubt that the induction of IPKF was not the only and the best way to ensure the implementation of the 1987 Agreement. But in the given context, it was accepted by most in the two countries. Moreover, not many of the IPKF's critics have come out with better, more effective and feasible alternatives. Further, the failure of the IPKF would not have looked as massive and grotesque as it was made out to be, if the IPKF issue had not been exploited politically, both in India and Sri Lanka in the altered context and changed correlation of political forces. After all, Sri Lankan armed forces are nowhere near containing the LTTE menace more than two years after the withdrawal of the IPKF. In the wider global context, peace-keeping operations even under the UN flag have not achieved desired goals in such situations as prevailing in former Yugoslavia and in Cambodia.

This study has been carried out with the full awareness that we are still too close to the events to take a really dispassionate look at the issues involved. We are further constrained by the fact that a good deal of critical and sensitive information is still buried under the stone-slabs of official secrecy and individual reticence of the in-service and retired civil servants and military officers. Due to these limitations, the study may raise more questions than it answers. But if the questions raised are pertinent and provocative enough to stimulate and encourage further enquiry and analysis, this study would have served its purpose. Also if this study can contribute towards shifting the thrust of debate on Indo-Sri Lanka relations and the Sri Lankan ethnic conflict from politically motivated polemics to cool and careful scrutiny, my effort will not be a waste.

I am extremely thankful to the International Peace Research Institute in Oslo, particularly Dr. Kumar Rupesinghe for getting me involved in this study and extending financial support for six weeks in Oslo to use PRIO's data base on Sri Lanka. Help and cooperation extended by the research and administrative staff of Kumar's unit in PRIO was very valuable in the progress and completion of this study. No less important a role in the completion of the study was played by the PRIO Director, Sverre Lodgaard, who extended all possible facilities to help me complete my work. The credit for language editing the manuscript at PRIO goes entirely to Ms Susan Höivik.

In the course of completing this study, I met several Indians, Sri Lankans and others. In Sri Lanka, I had the rare privilege of meeting President Premadasa (thrice); former President J.R. Jaye-wardene (once) and the SLFP leader Mrs. Bandaranaike, besides many other Sinhala political leaders, Sri Lankan civil servants, military officers, and intellectuals. Immensely rich and vital insights into the Tamil perceptions of ethnic conflict and India's role have been provided to me by leaders like late Amrithalingam, late Padmanabha, late Uma Maheswaram, Krishna Kumar Kittu (in London), Vardharaja Perumal and many other Tamil activists who would not like to be named. They all may kindly forgive me if I have misunderstood, misinterpreted or not accepted their views. Learning is a difficult process, more so at an advanced age like my own.

New Delhi   S.D. MUNI
August, 1992

1

A Framework of India's Approach towards its Neighbours

Introductory Remarks

Sri Lanka's ethnic crisis has been primarily of its own creation and is, as such, an internal phenomenon. However, the implications and consequences of this crisis were not to remain, or perhaps could not have remained, confined to the national borders of the Island Republic. They have spilled over beyond these boundaries and sucked into them the interests and involvement of external factors and forces, thus constituting a formidable external dimension to Sri Lanka's ethnic crisis. We should bear in mind that the external dimension has come to stay as a major theoretical and policy challenge in the study and eventual resolution of ethnic crisis throughout the Third World.[1] It cannot be overlooked or underestimated in studying the Sri Lankan situation. Of all the external forces and factors in the Sri Lankan case, India's involvement has been pervasive, significant and even decisive. Above all, it has been a major complicating aspect. Without taking this factor into account, the Sri Lankan crisis cannot be understood properly, perhaps, nor can any effective attempt be made towards its resolution.

Any discussion of India's involvement in Sri Lanka should take place within the comparative context of India's overall behaviour in the region. Sri Lanka is not the first case of India's deep, direct and even armed involvement in the internal crisis of a neighbouring country. Nor could it be the last, as seen in India's prompt military support to suppress the coup attempt on President Gayoom's government in the Maldives in November 1987. Varying degrees and patterns of such involvement have been witnessed since India's independence, as Table 1 indicates.

Table 1
India's Involvement in the Internal Crises in Nearby Countries

Country	Year	Nature of Crisis	Nature of India's Involvement
Burma	1948–49	Tribal (Karen/Kachin) Insurgency	– Supply of arms to the Burmese government – Mobilisation of support from Commonwealth countries – Offer of mediation between U Nu's government and Karen insurgents (*a*)
Indonesia	January 1949	Dutch action against the Republican government	International conference to mobilise support (*a*)
Nepal	November 1950– February 1951	Anti-Rana Revolution	Support to the King and the democratic forces and establishment of a tripartite government
	1951–53	Dr. K.I. Singh's armed revolt against the Delhi Agreement	Police action to contain the revolt
	1960–62	King's dimissal of Parliamentary system of elected government of Nepali Congress	– Sympathy and support for democracy – Urge King to restore status quo ante (*b*)
China/ Tibet	September/ October 1950	Chinese military action in Tibet	– Expressions in favour of Tibetan autonomy, caution China to favour a peaceful settlement
	1956–59	– do –	– Refugees accepted – Support for Tibet's autonomy – Increased tension leading to Chinese

Table 1 (Continued)

Country	Year	Nature of Crisis	Nature of India's Involvement
			aggression in October 1962
Pakistan	1971	Crisis in East Pakistan	Support for Bangladeshi movement; military intervention and creation of Bangladesh
Sri Lanka	1971	JVP Insurgency	Support for Sri Lankan government; despatch of troops
	1983–87	Tamil Struggle for Eelam	(Subject of this study)
Maldives	November 1987	Coup attempt by mercenaries	Military help to foil the coup attempt

Sources: (a) S. Gopal, *Jawaharlal Nehru: A Biography*, vol. II, 1947–56, Oxford, 1983, p. 55. Also, Bandana Misra, 'India's Military Help to Neighbouring States: A Case Study of Burma (1948–49), Nepal (1951–53) and Sri Lanka (1971)', M.Phil. Dissertation, Jawaharlal Nehru University, New Delhi, 1975.

(b) S.D. Muni, *Foreign Policy of Nepal*, National, New Delhi, 1973.

It is clear from the Table that Indian involvement has featured in various crises precipitated either by tribal/ethnic insurgency or political upheaval to change a given system. India has promptly and actively responded, frequently playing a decisive role in the outcome. Therefore, as we look at India's involvement in Sri Lanka, a wider regional perspective on India's objectives and behaviour in the overall neighbourhood should also be kept in mind.

At the root of this perspective is the gradually growing autonomous capitalist state of India, highly sensitive to its security concerns and to its ideological preferences in the region. This sensitivity has been displayed in its various policies and actions ever since India came into being as an independent sovereign entity in 1947. These two aspects—the security consciousness and ideological structure of the Indian state—explain a good deal of India's behaviour in the region. Therefore, they need to be understood properly.

Security Perceptions

India perceives its security interests as coterminous with those of the region as a whole. Accordingly, any threat to the security or stability of neighbouring countries has been viewed as a direct threat to India's security as well. This perception has been articulated by persons like Nehru, Menon and Panikkar, on whom fell the early responsibiiity of defining India's security concerns in relation to such neighbouring countries as Pakistan, Nepal and Sri Lanka.[2] Subsequent generations of Indian leaders as well as India's strategic community have reiterated it.[3]

In a way, this perception is a continuation of the British legacy in India's strategic thinking, since its roots and even the manner in which it has been articulated can be traced to the records of the East India Company and the British Colonial Office on the one hand, and the writings and speeches of British strategists like Lord Curzon and Olaf Caroe on the other. During those times, Pakistan did not yet exist; Sri Lanka and Burma were still parts of the British Expire; Nepal was a wilfing accomplice, if not a formal colony, in the British security management of the subcontinent. This reflection of the British legacy in the Indian security perception has often led critics and observers in India and abroad to attribute to Indian leaders imperial motives and hegemonic, expansionist tendencies in South Asia.[4]

India's leaders have perceived their country as a major Asian power, destined to play a dominant role in regional and global affairs. Not long after independence, India's first Prime Minister Nehru, in a January 1949 letter to the then US Ambassador in India Loy Handerson, compared India's position with that of the USA and said:

> Fate and circumstances have thrust a tremendous responsibility on the United States. Fate and circumstances have also placed India in a rather special position in Asia, and, even though those of us who happen to control to some extent India's destiny today may not come up to the mark there can be no doubt that the new India will go ahead. It may stumble often, but it has the capacity to stand up again and take some more steps forward.[5]

This role-perception led them to propound ideas and visions of a wider federation of Asian states, to contain the forces of imperialism, domination and control at the global level. Long before India's independence, Nehru said at one stage:

> If there are to be federations, India will not fit into a European Federation where it can only be a hanger-on of semi-colonial status. It is obvious that under these circumstances there should be an Eastern Federation not hostile to the West but nevertheless standing on its own feet, self-reliant and joining with all others to work for world peace and world federation.

> Such an Eastern Federation must inevitably consist of China and India, Burma and Ceylon and Nepal and Afghanistan should be included. So should Malaya. There is no reason why Siam and Iran should also not join, as well as some other nations. That would be a powerful combination of free nations joined together for their own good as well as for the world good. Power would not be merely material power but something else also which they have represented through these long ages. It is time, therefore, that in this fateful period of the breakdown of empires that we thought in terms of this Eastern Federation and worked for it deliberately.[6]

As India's independence drew closer, Nehru refined this idea; and in 1945, he asked for a South Asian Federation of 'India, Iran, Iraq, Afghanistan and Burma'. In the same year, the All India Congress Committee in a resolution on Asian cooperation said: 'A free India will inevitably seek the close and friendly associations with her neighbouring countries and would specially seek to develop common policies for defence, trade and economic and cultural development with China, Burma, Malaya, Indonesia and Ceylon as well as other countries of the Midde East'.[7] It is therefore, erroneous to take, as many in the neighbouring countries have done, the idea of federation and closer relations that India sought with its neighbours, as being motivated by independent India's desire to recreate the 'British Empire' or show any disrespect for the independence, sovereignty or freedom of action of smaller neighbouring countries. Where the Indian leadership erred was in taking it for granted, and in good faith, that its neighbours were also thinking along these lines, and that their enlightened interests as perceived by their respective leaderships, were looking forward to closer association with India.

Most of India's enthusiasm in this respect vanished with the partition of the subcontinent and the social and cultural holocaust precipitated by the creation of Pakistan. The emergence of a Communist China and its military assertion in Tibet caused a further setback to Indian visions for Asia and the neighbourhood. The Bandung Conference of 1955 on Afro-Asian affairs, therefore, proved to be the end and not the beginning of India's moves towards Asian resurgence.

In operational terms, India's security perception was rooted deeply into the geostrategic make-up of the Indian subcontinent, which, without doubt, had been evolved and nursed by the British.[8] Accordingly, the natural security perimeters of the subcontinent were defined by the high mountainous ranges to the north and northwest; and the continental shelf and territorial waters in the Indian Ocean, including the Bay of Bengal, to the south. Historical experience as well as geostrategic commonsense made it abundantly clear to anyone in power in Delhi—whether the British or the Indians—that any external power capable of penetrating either the deep-sea or the mountainous cover of the subcontinent had easy access to the Indian heartland.[9] Accordingly, India could not but perceive its security as closely tied up with the security of its neighbours and the neighbouring regions in Southern Asia.[10] Importantly, India could ensure its security by keeping itself and its neighbouring regions out of great-power conflicts and rivalries, and also free from the military presence or strategic influence of extraregional powers. This again, was a part of the British legacy, wherein every attempt had been made to keep other imperial and great-power influences away from the Indian subcontinent.

Independent India's desire to have the subcontinent free of extraregional strategic influences found expression in many ways. To begin with, there was India's resistance to the Cold War, particularly the policies of 'containment' pursued by the Western powers. This was clearly shown in Nehru's denunciation of such US-led military pacts as SEATO, CENTO and the Baghdad Pact.[11] India has consistently maintained its opposition to great-power military presence in or around South Asia. Indira Gandhi came down rather heavily against such presence during the 1970s.[12] India's strong support to the movement for the Indian Ocean as a

Zone of Peace since 1971 has been another clear manifestation of this policy.

Specifically, India reacted very strongly to US efforts to establish a strategic relationship with Pakistan. As early as in May 1950, Nehru wrote to Mrs. Vijay Laxmi Pandit, his sister and India's Ambassador to the United States:

> It does appear that there is a concerted attempt to build up Pakistan and build down, if I may say so, India. It surprises me how immature in their political thinking the Americans are! They do not even learn from their own or other people's mistakes; more especially in their dealings with Asia, they show a lack of understanding which is surprising.[13]

Nehru's reaction grew in strength as the establishment of the US-Pak military alliance became imminent. Writing to Pakistan's Prime Minister Mohamed Ali in late 1953, Nehru said:

> If such an alliance takes place, Pakistan enters definitely into the region of Cold War. That means to us that the Cold War has come to the very frontiers of India. This is a matter of serious consequence to us, who have been trying to build up an area of peace . . . . It must also be a matter of grave consequence to us, you will appreciate, if vast armies are built up in Pakistan with the aid of American money . . . . All our problems will have to be seen in a new light.[14]

Similarly, in the case of Nepal, when India learnt of the possibility of Western support, to the autocratic Rana regime during the anti-Rana revolution of 1950–51, Nehru said:

> Frankly, we do not like and shall not brook any foreign interference in Nepal. We recognise Nepal as an independent country and wish her well, but even a child knows that one cannot go to Nepal without passing through India . . . . We would like every other country to appreciate the intimate geographical and cultural relationship that exists between India and Nepal.[15]

Subsequently, developments in China and its relations with Tibet were to deepen India's security concerns in Nepal and the other

Himalayan kingdom, Bhutan. India tightened its mutual security arrangements with these kingdoms and obtained explicit written undertakings from them, in the form of treaties, agreements and exchange of official letters, that they would not develop strategic/ military relationships with China.[16] Nepal even assured India that Chinese-aided development projects would not be allowed to operate in Nepal Terai, contiguous to the Indo-Gangetic plain.[17]

India also was uneasy about the growing Chinese influence in Pakistan since the early 1960s and in Bangladesh after the over-throw of Mujibur Rahman's regime in 1975.[18] However, viewed from the perspective of the smaller neighbouring countries, this Indian desire to keep external and adversarial strategic forces out of the subcontinent appeared as a strategy for establishing India's hegemony and dominance, so as to secure the region as its own area of influence and dominance. As such, the Indian proposition was not acceptable to them. In operational terms, the neighbours found it a strong constraint on their independence and freedom of action, particularly such actions through which they wanted to mobilise countervailing forces to balance India in the region. In turn, such policy moves were seen in India as acts of invitation, facilitation or consolidation for undesirable extraregional strategtic influences in the subcontinent. Thus there existed a clear divergence in India's regional security perceptions on the one hand, and those of its neighbours on the other. At root was the fact that while India appeared preoccupied with the geostrategic reality of the sub-continent, its neighbours tended to ignore or underplay this thrust. Moreover, while India's security perception was extrovert, meaning that the major security challenge seemed to be coming from outside the region, that of its neighbours was introvert, i.e., among their perceived sources of threat to their respective securities, India itself constituted a major factor. Therefore, for the neighbours, any security approach that ignored this perceived threat from India and did not take measures to meet it by mobilising and cultivating the countervailing extraregional forces was unrealistic.

True, the strategic divergence between India and its neighbours has been a persistent theme in intraregional relations in South Asia, but the intensity and expression of this divergence has de-pended upon a number of other factors. Two of the most important of these need at least brief mention. One relates to the nature of regimes and ruling elites in South Asia. There have been instances

when, between a certain regime in the neighbouring country and
India, strategic divergence has either faded out or remained an
easily manageable factor in bilateral relations. Examples include
India's relations with Nepal during the regime of King Tribhuwan
after the overthrow of the Rana System (1951–55) and also during
the brief interval of parliamentary democracy (1959–60); with
Bangladesh during the regime of Sheikh Mujibur Rahman (1972–75);
with Sri Lanka generally (during the pre-1987 period) when the
SLFP has been in power; and brief periods of democratic rule in
Pakistan. Similarly, the periods of the non-Congress regimes in
India (1977–79 and 1989–91) have also been considered as 'soft' in
strategic terms, with regard to relations with India's neighbours.[19]

The second factor relevant in this regard concerns the nature of
strategic equations between India on the one hand and the extraregional major powers on the other. The divergence between
India and its neighbours has been less pronounced during periods
of reduced discord between the extraregional powers and India.
The period from 1947 to 1950–51 may be seen in this light; at that
time, Soviet relations with the South Asian countries were almost
non-existent and the USA was still formulating its containment
strategy in Asia. Things soon started changing, though the role of
China still remained a low-key factor in intra-South Asian relations
as a result of the understanding struck between India and China
within the framework of the famous 'five principles' of peaceful
co-existence (the *Panchsheela*). After the late 1950s, this framework lost much of its significance due to developments in the Tibet
region of China, including the flight of the Dalai Lama with
thousands of his followers to India, and the implications of these
developments on Sino-Indian relations. The Sino-Indian border
issue aggravated seriously in the wake of these developments,
eventually precipitating the Sino-Indian conflict of October 1962.
From then onwards, India became security-sensitive towards any
warming of relations between any of its neighbours on the one
hand and China or the USA on the other, as mentioned above.
There have been exceptions and nuances, however, such as the
periods of Janata rule (1977–79) in India and the current phase
(starting since the mid-1980s) when a considerable effort in India's
policy towards improving relations both with the USA and China
could be seen. The Janata government even tried to downgrade
India's close and extensive security relationship with the former

Soviet Union, though without much success. Notwithstanding these exceptions, India has maintained its basic perception about securing the region from the penetration of extraregional strategic presence and influence. Some observers even see the divergence between India and its neighbours as being responsible for the entry and consolidation of the extraregional strategic presence in the subcontinent, and not the reverse.[20] But then these observers either ignore or seriously underestimate the role of the Cold War(s) and the Sino-Soviet rivalry which led the extraregional powers to seek a foothold in the subcontinent, so strategically located. Such attempts by the extraregional powers served to reinforce the strategic divergence within South Asia: enough evidence is available now to substantiate this contention.[21]

The extension of extraregional great-power rivalry and conflict into the subcontinent gave India a sense of weakness and vulnerability in the regional context—a fact often forgotten in analyses of the regional situation. For instance, Nehru protested strongly against the extension of the Cold War to South Asia, because in this he saw a move to contain India in the region as well as Asia. He considered this an attempt to build up Pakistan against India— his fears were not so unfounded, in view of the pro-Pakistani stance of the Western powers on the Kashmir question, followed by the establishment of the US-Pak military alliance. This sense of vulnerability came out clearly in what Nehru said on the eve of US military assistance to Pakistan: 'In effect Pakistan becomes practically a colony of the United States . . . . The United States imagine that by this policy they have completely outflanked India's so-called neutralism and will thus bring India to her knees. Whatever the future may hold, this is not going to happen . . . .'[22]

The arms that Pakistan obtained under this alliance forced India to build up its arsenals as well. India had to bear the brunt of Western and Chinese arms in its encounters with Pakistan in 1965 as well as 1971. There is a persistent fear in India that the new and sophisticated arms supplied to Pakistan by the USA during the second Cold War period (Soviet intervention in Afghanistan) in the 1980s have not only added to Pakistani intransigence towards India, but also provided a technological edge over India in any possible future encounter.[23] This explains much of India's sensitivity towards any of its neighbours establishing a security or strategic relationship with the USA, China, indeed even the former Soviet

Union or any other extraregional power of consequence, or Pakistan.

To this factor of national weakness and vulnerability evident during the Nehru period, was added another factor of political and regime vulnerability during Indira Gandhi's period. This was when she seriously feared a covert Western attempt (through the CIA) to oust her from power in the mid-1970s, particularly in the aftermath of the violent coup that eliminated Sheikh Mujibur Rahman of Bangladesh.[24] Indian suspicions regarding internal threats to India from covert external actions have also been activised in the context of such developments as the assassination of Indira Gandhi in October 1984, as well as whenever doubts are cast on the unity of diverse cultures and ethnic groups within the Indian state.[25]

There is also an economic dimension to India's sense of weakness and vulnerability towards extraregional great-power presence in the region through its neighbours. The Indian bourgeosie fear that the extraregional powerful economies of the West, Japan and the Newly Industrialised Countries (NICs) may find ways of penetrating the protected but huge Indian markets for their consumer goods through the neighbouring countries. The liberal import policies of India's neighbours are seen as a powerful facilitating factor in this respect. As a consequence, considerable tensions often arise in trade relations between India and its neighbours, especially on the question of unauthorised flow of third-country consumer goods or raw material-based products into India.[26] The powerful economic presence of extraregional powers is also seen as a major hurdle to improving regional economic interaction and cooperation, which could in turn facilitate expansion of regional market for Indian products. Here again, India's neighbours fear that any weakening of their economic links with third countries may eventually lead to Indian economic domination in the region.[27]

Thus we see an economic reinforcement of the strategic divergence between India and its neighbours. One example of this is India's insistence—and the neighbours' reluctance—to expand the framework of regional cooperation under the South Asian Association for Regional Cooperation (SAARC) by including on its agenda such core economic issues as trade, industry and finance.

The argument as regards India's perceived weaknesses and vulnerabilities in shaping strategic approach to its neighbours may not sound very persuasive to many, in view of India's size, population, resources and military capabilities. Even if India's felt weaknesses and vulnerabilities may have been a factor during the 1950s and the 1960s, this would no longer seem true from the 1970s onwards. In 1971 India decisively defeated Pakistan militarily and was instrumental in creating a new nation, Bangladesh, in the subcontinent. Furthermore, India exploded a nuclear device in 1974; it incorporated Sikkim into the Indian Union in 1975; and since the 1980s, it has emerged as a major economic and military factor on the South Asian scene. How far then is this sense of weakness and vulnerability relevant in India's approach towards its neighbours now?

To answer this question we must look at the dilemma suffered by an aspiring and emerging regional power which is continuously confronted by greater global forces in the pursuit of its own aspirations. In a way this is a dilemma typical of any major power in its adjacent region.[28] Neither the great powers like the USA, the former Soviet Union and China, nor the 'regional influentials' like Iraq, Iran, Saudi Arabia, Egypt or Indonesia have escaped this dilemma. The growing capabilities of a regional power like India do give it a greater sense of confidence and lead to greater initiative, risk-taking and push in its policies, but without really resolving this dilemma for good. Similarly, better strategic rapport and understanding with the extraregional great powers can soften its persecution psyche in regional conduct, but inherent fears and suspicions linger on.

The Role of Ideological Coordinates

As mentioned initially, for any broader perspective on India's behaviour in the region, we must bear in mind not only the factor of security perception, but also India's ideological coordinates. The nature of socio-cultural contiguities in the South Asian region can provide a vital backdrop here. The societies of South Asia—particularly India on the one hand and each of its neighbours on the other—are intermeshed, with cultural contiguous ties across national boundaries. Accordingly, intervention of one society into the other is a fact of life, not a matter of conscious or planned decisions taken occasionally to suit specific interests. This operates both ways: not only from India to a particular neighbouring country, but vice versa as well. Any social turmoil in one country is bound to affect the other in terms of refugees, displacement of life and property of the kith and kin, or other cultural affiliates. In such situations ethnic, religious and other sympathies and support get mobilised for the victims across the border irrespective of the nature of relations between the neighbouring governments. If the social turmoil in one country is serious, the socio-cultural constituency in the other country can become a significant pressure group, influencing the relations between the two countries.[29]

This factor of social and cultural intermeshing has played a critical and persistent role in India's relations with its neighbours. A telling example could be seen in the struggle for the emergence of Bangladesh in what was then East Pakistan, which led to more than 10 million Bengali refugees coming to India. More recently, thousands of Chakma refugees (Buddhist tribal people) from Bangladesh have come to India to escape discrimination and repression by the now ousted military regime there, resulting in tensions between the two governments. The case of Tibetan refugees from China during the 1950s which has already been mentioned, continues to remain an important irritant in Sino-Indian relations. Yet further instances of social and political turmoil in the neighbourhood could be cited, with the Sri Lankan situation being the latest one. The frequent reference to the Tamil Nadu factor in Indo–Sri Lankan relations is in fact a reference to the socio-cultural constituency of the Sri Lankan Tamils in India.

There have likewise been cases of such socio-cultural constituencies being exercised in the neighbouring countries as a result of socio-political turmoil within India. The Assam turmoil and Gurkha trouble in India's north-Bengal area of Darjeeling, with respect to Indo-Nepalese relations during the 1970s and early 1980s, respectively, and the effect of the Kashmir uprising on Indo-Pak relations during early 1990s are among recent examples. The problem of Nepalis in Bhutan similarly threaten to vitiate bilateral relations between Nepal and Bhutan, Bhutan and India and even India and Nepal.[30]

However, the activisation of such social constituencies is perceived in India as different and far less ominous in comparison to that perceived in the neighbouring country, precisely because of India's size and dimensions. The social constituency of a neighbouring country in India will mostly be confined to one or two of its provinces, and the pressures generated by these constituencies will generally play only a limited role in the overall structure of federal policy-making in India. This limited role may at times become more powerful than what its actual dimension may demand, depending on the nature of the crisis in the neighbouring country or on a conscious decision on the part of the central government to attribute to it an extended role for specific political and strategic purposes.

As against this, the activisation of a social constituency within India in sympathy to a particular issue may be viewed with much greater concern and alarm in the affected neighbouring country because of its small size and perceived weakness. It is the size (both territory and population) factor that helps us understand the much talked-about 'minority psyche' of the majority Sinhalese community in Sri Lanka: there is a vast socio-cultural constituency of nearly 60 million Tamils in India, ever-sympathetic to the Tamils of Sri Lanka. Similarly, Pakistan remains conscious of the fact that despite its own identity as a Muslim nation, there are nearly as many Muslims in India as in Pakistan. Again in Nepal, though more than 80 per cent of the population is of Indian origin, those in the Terai, who constitute half of this number are later arrivals who are viewed by the rest in the kingdom as the Indian fifth column in Nepal. Even in Bhutan, persons of Nepali origin who are concentrated in the narrow plains of southern Bhutan are viewed more as an extension of Indian Nepalis than those of Nepal proper.

Social turmoil is part of the political process, and more so in developing countries as in South Asia. The socio-political dynamics of intraregional relations in South Asia is rooted in the characters of the various states of South Asia and the nation- and state-building strategies adopted by them. All the South Asian countries began by aiming at a secular and democratic state, on the basis of experiences during the colonial period. Even Jinnah of Pakistan was thinking along secular lines once Pakistan came into existence as an independent and sovereign state.[31] The Nepalese monarchy, after its revival in 1951 from century-old Rana domination, also pledged itself to a democratic, representative, people-oriented and secular polity. Bangladesh was also born amidst secular and democratic political ideals. India, because of its size and population diversity, chose to become a federal state in addition to being democratic and secular. Thus there existed a broad harmony in the politico-ideological coordinates of state structures in South Asia.

Gradually, however, each of India's neighbours drifted into strategies of building a more sectarian state—with increasing emphasis on the domination of one language, one religion and even one community, on the one hand, and centralisation of authority and political power on the other. Thus, for example, developed the dominance of Punjabis in the Islamic state of Pakistan. In addition, the democratic aspirations of Pakistan also came to be suppressed for long periods since the mid-1950s, in favour of military dictatorship. Similarly we can note the dominance of the Sinhalese population, Buddhism and the Sinhala language in Sri Lanka; of Islam and the Bengali language in Bangladesh; of the monarchy, Hinduism and the Nepali language in Nepal; and of the monarchy, Drukpas and Buddhism in Bhutan. Also within India, strains and aberrations have developed with regard to the secular and federal components of its polity. For a brief period in the mid-1970s (June 1975 to December 1977) India also diluted the democratic content of its polity under the emergency provisions of its Constitution. But on the whole, India has persisted with democratic, secular and federal ideals and structures in its polity. Notwithstanding the noticeable rise in sectarian and fundamentalist forces, India may have to keep its secular and progressive ideals in the foreseeable future as well, because otherwise it might prove impossible to retain the unity and integrity of the huge and diverse Indian state.

Thus there arose a strong divergence between India and each of its neighbours with regard to state-building strategies along lines similar to the divergence in the strategic field. This divergence in socio-political process has had unfortunate consequences on intra-regional relations. Secretarian state-building strategies in India's neighbouring countries have led to the alienation of democratic political forces and minority ethnic groups, frequently precipitating massive uprisings, armed conflicts and socio-political crises of the type witnessed in East Pakistan and Sri Lanka on the ethnic front and in Nepal, Pakistan and Bangladesh on the question of the restoration of democratic rule. To this has been added the complicating factor of social conflicts precipitated by the uneven development and unequal distribution of economic growth as well as political mismanagement of problems at the initial stages, of which India has been as much guilty as any of its neighbours. This uneven development and political callousness have significantly contributed to internal conflicts in India's Assam, Northeast, Punjab and Kashmir regions.

Conflicts arising out of socio-political processes in the region have not remained confined to their respective countries of origin. Instead, they have tended to spill over into the neighbouring countries, mostly into India, due to the presence of large socio-cultural constituencies and ideological affinities there. Indeed, in the field of ideology, affinities have at times taken precedence over democratic aspirations. Even Communist and extremist militant groups in a given neighbouring country may have found sources of support and sympathies in India due to socio-cultural linkages and geographical contiguity. For example, from Nepal not only the Nepali Congress, but the Communist and Left-extremist groups have found support and sustenance in India. So is the case with Bangladesh. From Pakistan also, besides members of the Pakistan Peoples Party, various political groups from Sindh and Frontier Province (including Wali Khan's National Awami Party) have sought support and protection in India in their struggle against the military regime. Thus we find a wide spectrum of sympathies in India for alienated and struggling social and political groups of people in neighbouring countries. Political activisation of these sympathies, at the social and popular levels, has generated pressures on the Indian state to respond to these conflict/crisis situations in the neighbouring countries. Here it is important to note that such pressures have mostly been generated in those provinces and regions of India that are adjacent to the respective neighbouring country. Accordingly, the roles played by Bihar, Uttar Pradesh and parts of West Bengal and Assam in relation to Nepal and Bhutan; by Tamil Nadu in relation to Sri Lanka; by West Bengal, Assam and the Northeastern region in relation to Bangladesh and Burma, assume significance in India's policy towards it neighbours. The case of Pakistan is different, as it affects all the North and Central India almost entirely where the Pakistan movement was strong during the independence struggle. Further, Kashmir occupies a critical position in the whole gamut of Indo-Pak relations. As a result of the role of these adjacent Indian provinces, the dynamics of Indian federalism—i.e., relations between the centre and the states—become an important factor in India's neighbourhood policy. Likewise, the behaviour of the

Indian state has been influenced by the socio-cultural bases and ideological profiles of agitating groups and/or the state in the given neighbouring country.

India has generally cooperated with the neighbouring states in dealing with any political challenges posed by the Left and extremist forces, but has been more reluctant to lend support for the suppression of democratic movements and struggles. India has also been extremely reluctant to endorse separatist tendencies and movements of alienated ethnic groups in the neighbouring countries, notwithstanding its expression of support for such groups for their being discriminated and suppressed on account of their respective ethnic identities—largely because of the presence of a strong and politically assertive social constituency in India.

Broadly speaking, India's ideological coordinates as a multi-ethnic, multi-religious, secular, democratic and plural state have guided its behaviour. Within the parameters of these coordinates, India has remained a strong, stabilising, status quo-oriented force in regional affairs. Particularly so, because experience in the region suggests that situations of political and social conflict in the neighbouring countries have created conditions for the penetration of undesirable extraregional and adversarial forces into those countries, and hence into the region. At times of course, the Indian state has made use of such socio-political conflicts to put pressure on the state in the neighbouring country so as to pursue its own security and strategic goals in the region, as could be seen in the emergence of Bangladesh. There have likewise been attempts on the part of the neighbouring countries to take advantage of India's internal turmoils and conflicts in pursuing their own objectives in relation to India and the South Asian region. Pakistan's support to extremists in the Punjab and Kashmir provinces of India may be mentioned as an example here. Even Nepal, Bangladesh and Sri Lanka have not desisted from exploiting India's internal difficulties in pursuance of their respective interests.

With its security perceptions and ideological coordinates as the cornerstone of its behaviour in the region, India has tried to maintain harmony between them. From India's viewpoint, the ideal situation in this respect was during the emergence of Bangladesh, when India saw its support for the emergence of a new nation as a move towards mitigating its own security concerns in relation to the military capabilities of Pakistan on the one hand, and as a contribution towards the victory and consolidation of democratic and secular political values in the subcontinent on the other. But regional situations have not always allowed that harmony to be maintained. There have been several instances in relation to a neighbouring country where India has found its specific security interests in conflict with the ideological coordinates. In such situations, Indian policy has opted to advance its security interests at the cost of seeking ideological harmony in the neighbourhood.

A typical example of this was India's withdrawal of support to the democratic forces struggling against the autocratic reassertion of the monarchy in Nepal after October 1962. China launched an armed aggression against India at that time. The security costs of the Nepali king's political alienation from and antagonism towards India (arising out of India's support for the democratic forces) became too costly. King Mahendra's use of the China card to hurt India's security sensitivities went too far when he agreed to open a strategic road connection between Kathmandu and a Tibetan border town. Subsequently, the logic of the policy ploy led Nepal in 1989–90 to purchase arms from China which led to the creation of a serious crisis in Indo-Nepalese relations. This crisis, quite unintendedly, gave spurt to democratic forces and resulted in the collapse of the King-dominated panchayat system.[32]

Whether an India more confident of handling its security concerns in the region, either because of enhanced military capabilities or because of better strategic rapport with the extraregional great-powers, will be an ideologically assertive state in regional affairs pressing for the cause of democracy, secularism and federal political structure, remains to be seen. However, the chances are that due to growing military and economic capabilities combined by external pressures and internal turmoil, India may gradually drift into becoming a national security state (and there are already some indications of this). Then the ideological component of India's regional concerns would become increasingly subordinated to its new security profile. India's ambiguous and vacilliating attitude towards the struggles for democracy in Nepal (1989–90), Bangladesh (1990), and Burma (1990–92) underlines this tendency. It may not be out of place here to mention that changes in the political structures of the neighbouring countries, if compatible with stated ideological preferences of the Indian state may result in lessening India's dilemma of choosing between security interests and ideological preferences while evolving policy responses to critical developments in the neighbouring countries. In general, the ideological character of the Indian state and its compatibility or otherwise with the characters of polities in its neighbourhood is a vital factor to be taken into account in understanding India's approach towards its neighbours.

Notes to Chapter 1

1. Jonathan Wilkenfeld (ed.), *Conflict Behaviour and Linkage Politics*, David McKay: New York, 1973; Astri Suhrki and Lela Noble (eds.), *Ethnic Conflict in International Relations*, Praeger: New York, 1977; Fredrick L. Shields (ed.), *Ethnic Separatism and World Politics*, University Press of America, 1984.

2. Jawaharlal Nehru, *The Discovery of India*, Oxford: London, 1944; also his, *The Unity of India: Collected Writings, 1937–1940*, Lindsay Drummond: New York, 1942; K.M. Panikkar, *Problems of Indian Defence*, Asia Publishing House: New York, 1960; also his, *Geographical Factors in Indian History*, Bharatiya Vidya Bhawan: Bombay, 1955; *India and the Indian Ocean*, Allen and Unwin: London, 1945.

3. K. Subrahmaniyam, *Our National Security*, Birla Institute: New Delhi, 1972; also his 'Subcontinental Security', *Strategic Analysis*, vol. 1, nos. 5 & 6, August–September 1981; 'India and its Neighbours: A Conceptual Framework of Peaceful Coexistence', in U.S. Bajpai (ed.), *India and Its Neighbourhood*, Lancer: New Delhi, 1986; Rohit Handa, *Policy for India's Defence*, Chetana: New Delhi, 1976; D.K. Palit, 'India as an Asian Military Power', *India International Centre Quarterly*, vol. 2, no. 1, January 1975; U.S. Bajpai (ed.), *India's Security*, Lancer: New Delhi, 1983.

4. See for instance, a series of articles by the late Gen. A.I. Akram, President, Institute of Regional Studies, 'Islamabad', in *Muslim* (Islamabad), January 1984; S.U. Kodikara, *Strategic Factors in Inter-State Relations in South Asia*, Australian National University: Canberra, 1979; Imtiaz Ahmed and Abdur Rob Khan, 'India's Policy Fundamentals, Neighbours and Post-Indira Developments', *BIISS Papers 3*, Bangladesh Institute of Strategic Studies: Dhaka, July 1985.

5. S. Gopal, *Jawaharlal Nehru: A Biography*, vol. II, 1947–1956, Oxford: New Delhi, 1983, p. 56. For a recent American view of India's strategic perspective, see George Tanham, 'Indian Strategic Culture', *Washington Quarterly*, Winter 1992, pp. 129–49.

6. As cited in Stanley Jayaweera, 'The Ethnic Crisis and the Indo-Sri Lankan Peace Process, July 1983–July 1987', a seminar paper presented at BMICH, Colombo, January 1990, p. 4 (mimeo).

7. As cited in S.D. Muni and Anuradha Muni, *Regional Cooperation in South Asia*, National: New Delhi, 1984, pp. 10–11.

8. Auspex, 'India's Strategical Future', *U.S.I. Journal*, vol. 75, no. 319, April 1945. Writings of Lord Curzen and Olaf Caroe adequately reflected this British strategic perspective for India.

9. Panikkar, *Problems of Indian Defence* 1960; Pendaral Moon, *The Future of India*, London, 1945.

10. Lorne J. Kavic, *India's Quest for Security: Defence Policies, 1947–1965*, University of California Press: Berkeley, 1967, pp. 27–30; also see, Raju G.C. Thomas, *Indian Security Policy*, Princeton University Press: Princeton, 1986.

11. Jawaharlal Nehru, *India's Foreign Policy*, Selected Speeches, September 1946–April 1961, Publication Division, Government of India: New Delhi, 1961, pp. 87–98, 182–236; Gopal, *Jawaharlal Nehru*, vol. II.

12. Surjit Mansingh, *India's Search for Power: Indira Gandhi's Foreign Policy 1966–1982*, Sage: New Delhi, 1984; also V.P. Dutt, *India's Foreign Policy*, Vani: New Delhi, 1984; P.S. Jayaramu, *India's National Security and Foreign Policy*, ABC Publishers: New Delhi, 1987.

13. Gopal, *Jawaharlal Nehru*, vol. II, p. 63.

14. *Ibid.*, p. 185.

15. Nehru's Speech in *Lok Sabha*, India, Parliamentary Debates, Part II, vol. VIII, 6 December 1950.

16. S.D. Muni, 'India and the Himalayan Kingdoms: Security Interests and Diplomacy', Occasional Paper, Diplomacy Division, JNU: New Delhi, 1977 (mimeo).

17. *Ibid.*; also S.D. Muni, 'India and Nepal: Erosion of a Relationship', in *Strategic Analysis*, July 1984.

18. Mansingh, *India's Search for Power*, 1984.

19. I have discussed some aspects of this phenomenon in my 'India's Political Preferences in South Asia', in *India Quarterly*, New Delhi, vol. 31, no. 1, January–March 1975; and 'South Asia: Systemic and Strategic Divergences—Implications for India's Security', *Mainstream*, vol. XXII, nos. 29–30, 17 and 24 March 1984.

20. Pran Chopra *et al.*, *Future of South Asia*, Macmillan: New Delhi, 1986.

21. Baldev Raj Nayar, *American Geo-politics and India*, Manohar: New Delhi, 1976; Ramakant (ed.), *China and South Asia*, South Asian Publishers: New Delhi, 1988; also Y.I. Vertzberger, 'China's Diplomacy and Strategy Towards South Asia: From Benign Neglect to Prominence', *Jerusalem Journal of International Relations*, vol. 8, nos. 2–3, June 1986, pp. 100–41; Steven I. Levine, 'China and South Asia', *Strategic Analysis*, New Delhi, vol. XII, no. 10, January 1989; Steophan Yurkor, *Peking Plans for Asia*, New Delhi, 1982.

22. Gopal, *Jawaharlal Nehru*, vol. II, p. 185.

23. See for instance, Air Cmdr. Jasjit Singh, *AWACS: The New Destabiliser*, Lancer: New Delhi, 1987.

24. Pupul Jayakar, *Indira Gandhi*, Viking, Penguin India: New Delhi, 1992; Inder Malhotra, *Indira Gandhi: A Personal and Political Biography*, Hodder and Stoughton: London, 1990; Nalini Kant Jha, *Internal Crisis and Mrs. Indira Gandhi's Foreign Policy*, Janaki Prakashan: Patna, New Delhi, 1985.

25. A report by Robert Hardgrave had speculated about possible chaos in India if Mrs Gandhi were to be assassinated. This report, written before the assassination, was commissioned by the US State Department. Its publication raised an intense controversy in India, alleging a possible US hand in the assassination.

Earlier, J. Kirkpatrick, the U.S. Permanent Representative to the UN mentioned India's cultural diversity and fragile unity. This had led to fear that the US was aiming at the balkanisation of India. The support enjoyed by Punjab secessionists in the USA and other Western countries had been a point of serious irritation and concern with regard to India's internal security. Here we should note that an official US memorandum prepared on the proposed expansion of Voice of America facility in Sri Lanka mentioned 'promoting disaffection' in the region as one of its objectives. *Lanka Guardian*, 1 February 1985.

26. This question is often a central issue in trade agreements between India and Nepal as well as other neighbours, except Pakistan (with which there have only seldom been normal trade relations); Mahendra P. Lama, *The Economics of Indo–Nepalese Cooperation*, M.N. Publishers: New Delhi, 1985, chapter III.

27. P.R. Bhatt, 'Trade Flows in South Asia', *India Quarterly*, New Delhi, July–December 1984; Rahman Sobhan, 'Political Economy of Regional Cooperation in South Asia', *South Asia Journal*, vol. 1, no. 3, January–March 1988.

28. Stephen P. Cohen and Richard L. Park, *India: Emergent Power?*, National Strategy Information Centre Inc.: New York, 1978; John W. Mellor, *India: A Rising Middle Power*, Westview: Boulder, 1979.

29. I have touched on this point briefly in my 'Dimensions of Domestic Conflict', in Urmila Phadnis, S.D. Muni and Kalim Bahadur (eds.), *Domestic Conflicts in South Asia*, South Asian Publishers: New Delhi, 1986, vol. I; also Partha S. Ghosh, 'India's Relations with Its Neighbours: The Ethnic Factor', a paper presented at the International Centre for Ethnic Studies, Workshop in Colombo, 2–4 August 1989 (mimeo).

30. S.D. Muni, 'Bhutan in the Throes of Ethnic Conflict', *India International Centre Quarterly*, vol. 18, no. 1, Spring 1991, New Delhi, pp. 145–54.

31. Ayesha Jalal, *The Sole Spokesman: Jinnah, The Muslim League and the Demand for Pakistan*, Cambridge University Press: Cambridge, 1985; also her 'India's Partition and the Defence of Pakistan: An Historical Perspective', *The Journal of Imperial and Commonwealth History*, 1987, pp. 289–310.

32. S.D. Muni, *India and Nepal: A Changing Relationship*, Konark Publishers: New Delhi, 1992.

2

India's Concerns in Sri Lanka

The significance of security concerns and ideological coordinates (socio-cultural identities and characteristics of political systems) in guiding India's behaviour towards its neighbours has been under-lined in the previous chapter. Sri Lanka could not be an exception in this respect. Both the major preoccupations of India's regional policy (for example, its security concerns and its ideological factors) have been active and manifest in India's approach towards Sri Lanka since the two neighbours achieved independence during 1947–48.

Some scholars have also argued that fluctuations in the under-standing and cooperation between India and Sri Lanka have resulted from the changing context of 'economic compatibility' between them. The evidence of warmth between Mrs. Indira Gandhi's Congress regime in India and Mrs. Bandaranaike's Sri Lanka Freedom Party (SLFP) regime in Sri Lanka, both following similar state-controlled economic policies, is cited to support the conten-tion.[1] This argument is not very persuasive for various reasons. To begin with, the warmth between the two regimes was not consistent in its intensity, not to mention many areas of serious divergence between them. Further, at no stage could the economic factors take precedence over strategic or ideological ones. In fact whatever the areas of similarities in their respective economic outlooks, could be seen as subsumed under strategic and ideological factors. It is more persuasive to argue that economic compatibilities and cooperation between the two countries during Mrs. Gandhi's and Mrs. Bandaranaike's regimes might have been the consequence rather than the cause of overall harmony in their respective per-spectives.

We do not wish to undermine the importance of economic interests in India's neighbourhood policy, particularly in relation to Sri Lanka. But until the end of the eighties, India's economic interests such as those regarding trade and investments in the neighbouring region were not strong enough to play a decisive or predominant role. These interests may gain in significance in future, as there are indications in the early 1990s. But it is doubtful, looking at India's own market size and diversity and dimensions of its economy, if they would be able to override security and ideological factors in the foreseeable future.

Strategic Imperatives

Sri Lanka's geostrategic significance was sharply highlighted in India's security perception during the last phase of the Second World War, when Japanese bombs hit Colombo, Trincomalee and Madras. It was also felt at that time that a Japanese full-scale assault on Sri Lanka was round the corner. Such an assault did not occur but India's security planners, were sensitised to the vulnerability of its coastlines. Drawing attention to this aspect, Panikkar wrote:

> There has been an unfortunate tendency to overlook the sea in the discussion of India's defence problems. Until now, the discussion has proceeded on the assumption that the security of India is a matter exclusively of North-East frontier . . . . This is an entirely one-sided view of Indian history . . . ever since the sixteenth century . . . the future of India has been determined not on the land frontiers, but on the oceanic expanse which washes the three sides of India.[2]

Since countries like Burma and Sri Lanka were then parts of the British Indian empire, he pleaded for close defence links with these countries. Other Indian defence analysts continued to demand such links between India and Sri Lanka even after their independence.[3] The then Congress President Dr. Pattabhi Sitaramaya stated in 1949:

> India and Ceylon must have a common defence strength and common defence resources. It cannot be that Ceylon is in

friendship with a group with which India is not in friendship, not that Ceylon has no right to make its own alignments and declare its own affiliations—but if there are two hostile groups in the world, and Ceylon and India are with one or the other of them and not with the same group, it will be a bad day for both.[4]

The twin perceptions of India's coastal vulnerability and Sri Lanka being an integral part of India's oceanic defence led India to accept the continued presence of British naval and air bases (in Trincomalee and Katunayake respectively) in Sri Lanka. This presence had been legitimised under the U.K.–Ceylon Defence Pact of November 1947, which became a part of the colonial inheritance when Sri Lanka gained independence in February 1948.[5] India's endorsement of continued British military presence in Sri Lanka seemed contrary to India's general opposition to such military ties between any of its neighbours and any outside major power, particularly Western. Such opposition was to become more strident and pronounced subsequently in the context of Pakistan's security ties with the U.S. and Anglo-U.S. moves to set up military alliances with newly independent Asian countries. However, India had a number of considerations to look benignly at the British military presence in Sri Lanka. Strictly speaking, the U.K.–Ceylon Defence Pact was a continuation of a colonial arrangement that had proved its utility during the Second World War. It had nothing to do with the post-Second World War Cold War tensions and rivalry which accounted for the system of security alliances in Asia. This continued British military presence was an assurance for both India and Sri Lanka that naval defences of the region stretching up to Southeast Asia, in Malaya, Singapore, Burma and Island territories in the Indian Ocean, were looked after well.

It may be pertinent to keep in mind here that India's overall policy between 1947 and 1952–53 was in harmony with broad Western strategic interests in Asia in general and South Asia/Indian Ocean region in particular. After some initial hesitations (due to the concept of British Crown's supremacy in the Commonwealth which smacked of colonial stigma) India joined the Commonwealth as a Republic in 1949. This was hailed by the *New York Times* as 'a historic step, not only in the progress of the Commonwealth but in setting a limit to Communist conquest and opening the prospect of a wider defence system than the Atlantic Pact'.[6] There were even

British commanders leading Indian forces in the Kashmir conflict of 1947–48 and Britain was one of the principal sources of defence supplies to India throughout the 1950s. The Commonwealth Defence Committee was activised by Nehru to respond to regional security situations, such as the one precipitated by tribal insurgency in Burma. On various occasions, the Indian Prime Minister Nehru conceded the fact of India's strategic proximity to the West in various ways. While on the verge of India's independence, Nehru explained in a 'Note' on 18 January 1947 that India's world-view was to some extent 'a continuation of British foreign policy; to some extent a reaction against it. For the rest . . . benevolent intentions for all concerned'.[7] In 1949, while undertaking his first foreign visit to America as the Prime Minister, Nehru suggested to his close associate Krishna Menon, saying 'Why not align with the United States somewhat and build up our economic and military strength'.[8] On another occasion a year later, Nehru, cautioning his Ambassador in Moscow Radhakrishnan and Secretary-General in the Foreign Office Sir Girija Shankar Bajpai against considerations of a proposed Friendship Treaty with the former Soviet Union said:

> If there is a world war, there is no possibility of India lining up with the Soviet Union, whatever else she may do. It is obvious that our relations with the United States as with the United Kingdom in political and economic matters are far closer than with other countries.[9]

With this perspective guiding India's overall strategic outlook during the early years of her independence, India's quiet endorsement of the continuing British presence in Sri Lanka was no surprise. India also did not take any serious note of the Agreement of 1952 between U.S. and Sri Lanka on the facility of Voice of America transmission from Colombo.

However, by 1952–53, India became disenchanted with the West, specially its strategic approach to Asian issues, and had begun to perceive the extension of the Cold War to the subcontinent as a threat to its own and of the region's security. Subsequently, Pakistan's integration with the American sponsored military alliance systems in Asia was vehemently opposed by India, more so since the U.S. had chosen to ignore India's sensitivities and concerns in

this regard.[10] This was the time when divergence and discord
appeared between India's anti-West stance and Sri Lanka's pro-West
leanings. The then Prime Minister of Sri Lanka, John Kotelawala
did not share India's resentment on the U.S.–Pak military relationship.[11] Kotelawala was also inclined to get his country join the
South East Asian Treaty Organization (SEATO), the Asian counterpart of NATO, as he shared the thrust of the Western strategic
perception that the main threat to peace and security in the world
came from Communist powers like the Soviet Union.[12] Kotelawala
claimed that he was dissuaded from doing so by India.[13] There
were however other factors as well which restrained Kotelawala in
pursuing his desire to associate Sri Lanka with SEATO. Such
factors included opposition within the ruling UNP and also the
consideration that through its Defence Agreement with the U.K.,
Sri Lanka was already linked to the Western alliance system. At
one stage, Kotelawala, in order to justify his pro-West leanings
and the U.K.–Ceylon Defence Agreement even went so far as to
say that 'the day Ceylon did away with England, it would go
under India'. It may be noted here that the U.S. Secretary of
State, John Foster Dulles, who was the main architect of U.S. sponsored military alliances in Asia, visited Sri Lanka to persuade
Kotelawala in favour of Sri Lanka's membership for SEATO. Sri
Lanka had also permitted French fighter planes to refuel in Sri
Lanka while carrying out their military operations in Vietnam
during this period.

The divergence between India and Sri Lanka on the emerging
Cold War issues gradually became more clear and pronounced. It
was quite sharply expressed in the exchanges between Nehru and
Kotelawala whenever the two met and discussed these issues, as in
Colombo Prime Ministers Conference, Bandung Afro-Asian
Conference and the Commonwealth meetings.[14] Some observers
described the intensity of their differences as being the product of
their personal incompatibility with each other rather than being
the result of clash of interests between their two countries.

This divergence between India and Sri Lanka disappeared almost
overnight when S.W.R.D. Bandaranaike came to power in Sri
Lanka in 1956. He not only refused to treat India as a source of
threat to Sri Lanka, but also shifted the island's foreign policy
towards a more active non-aligned position and away from the
Westward leaning of his predecessor. He had very warm and

friendly relationship with India's Prime Minister Nehru and like
the latter, he denounced the relevance or efficacy of great-powers'
sponsored military alliances in Asia, preferring to keep clear of
East-West Cold War issues. The most impressive gesture of Sri
Lanka's independent foreign policy was the demand made by
S.W.R.D. Bandaranaike on Britain to withdraw its military (naval
and air) bases from Sri Lanka. This development underlined greater
harmony in the strategic perceptions of India and Sri Lanka and
resulted in the development of smoother bilateral relations between
the two countries.[15]

Such smooth relations continued when Mrs. Sirimavo Bandaranaike succeeded her husband after his assassination in 1959.
There were, however, two minor exceptions in 1963 and 1971. Sri
Lanka entered into a maritime agreement with China in July 1963
regarding cargo and passenger ships. By this time, India had
become sensitive to the growing Chinese influence in the subcontinent as a result of the Sino-Indian conflict of 1962, in which
China had occupied large parts of Indian territory as a result of
unprovoked and massive aggression in October. India expressed
serious concern on the Sino-Sri Lanka maritime agreement as it
suspected strategic underpinnings, at least from the Chinese side,
in this agreement. Mrs. Bandaranaike's government stoutly denied
that the agreement had any security dimension.[16] In the Sino-
Indian conflict, Mrs. Bandaranaike had played an important
mediatory role by holding a conference of Colombo powers and
evolving proposals for the resolution of territorial dispute between
the two Asian giants. Nehru had appreciated Sri Lankan role in
this regard.[17]

The second exception, in 1971, related to the refuelling in Sri
Lanka, of Pakistani planes carrying military personnel to suppress
the struggle for liberation of Bangladesh. India's sympathies and
support lay with the Bangladesh liberation forces. Accordingly, it
had refused permission to Pakistani planes to overfly Indian territory
to carry military men and materials as well as other supplies to its
then eastern wing in the process of suppressing the Bangladesh
uprising. Mrs. Bandaranaike's government in Sri Lanka justified
its action by stating that the Pakistani flights in question were
civilian, at least in appearance, since these were PIA flights carrying
people in civilian dress. This was, of course, merely a clever device
to circumvent the Indian objections. In effect, it provided the

much-needed facility to Pakistan, while also enabling Sri Lanka
not only to demonstrate its neutrality in the intraregional conflict
but also to make some money in the process.[18]

The strategic divergence as a major factor was not to re-enter
Indo-Sri Lanka relations until the 1980s as shall be discussed later.
Some Sri Lankan scholars associate this divergence with the UNP
governments in Sri Lanka, who have persistently pursued a pro-
West strategic policy, inviting Western strategic presence, particularly of the U.S., in the name of counteracting the perceived
'security threat' from India. Such a perception has naturally been
discounted and resented by India. The contention of a link between
the UNP regime in Colombo and a strategic divergence between
India and Sri Lanka might seem tenable on the basis of broad
generalizations but such generalizations may not stand a closer
scrutiny. For instance, there was no significant strategic divergence
between India and Sri Lanka during the early years of independence i.e., 1948–53, when the Senanayakes had led UNP governments in Colombo. This was also the case during the two UNP
regimes of Dudley Senanayake (1965–70) and J.R. Jayewardene
(1977–79). An important point to be noted here is that during
these two phases, there were strong elements of pro-West leanings
in India's policy as well. Between 1965 and 1970, the Congress
regimes of Shastri (1965–66) and Mrs. Gandhi (1966–70) were not
only weak but also under heavy Western pressures due to the
consequences of armed conflicts with neighbours (China in 1962
and Pakistan in 1965) on the one hand and food shortages and
economic difficulties on the other. India was in dire need of
Western strategic support and economic assistance to deal with
these developments. The U.S. support for India during this period
was so critical and visible that it even sought to alienate Pakistan
from the U.S. During 1977–79, there was a non-Congress government in power in New Delhi. The Janata government in India
shared a good deal of the strategic perceptions and the domestic
political experiences of the Jayewardene government in Colombo.

Ideological Considerations: The Political Aspect

The factor of ideological coordinates as discussed in the previous
chapter, has played a considerably effective role in India's approach

to Sri Lanka. Unlike other neighbours of India, Sri Lanka has always been a democracy and to that extent, this created an ideological bond and systemic sympathy between the two countries. An important demonstration of this political affinity was apparent during the April 1971 internal crisis in Sri Lanka. The crisis was precipitated by the attempt of an extremist Sinhala radical group called Jatiya Vimukthi Peramuna (JVP) to capture power through armed revolt. The SLFP government of Mrs. Bandaranaike was in power in Colombo and as soon as the revolt erupted, India, along with other countries, was approached for help.

India promptly responded by sending five frigates to seal-off approaches to Colombo. In addition, India's military assistance also included military equipment for 5,000 troops, six helicopters with pilots for non-combat duties and about 150 Indian troops to guard Bandaranaike Airport.[19] Other countries who joined in these efforts were the U.K., USA, Yugoslavia, the USSR and Pakistan. It was not only the regime rapport between Mrs. Gandhi and Mrs. Bandaranaike that prompted the Indian response. There were a number of other important considerations of India's perceived national interests that were taken into account while despatching prompt military assistance to Sri Lanka. The question of protecting democratic system and domestic stability was of the highest priority. Then it was suspected that the JVP uprising had the backing of Communist countries like China and North Korea, though China subsequently came out in support of Mrs. Bandaranaike's government. No less important was the fact that the JVP in its indoctrination lectures had clearly denounced India in various ways. The dominance of such a group in Colombo could not be in India's interests.[20] Thus a number of strategic and ideological factors combined to influence India's decision.

Notwithstanding the affinity between India and Sri Lanka on account of democratic systems, the two countries have pursued divergent strategies of nation-building, resulting in tensions between them. Both these countries launched the course of their developments in the post-British independent period with a clear thrust on secularism in their domestic politics. But while India had a federal structure of power devolution, Sri Lanka, being a small country, operated a unitary system. The secular thrust of Sri Lanka soon gave way to a sectarian approach to nation and state-building, with emphasis on the dominance of the Sinhala community, Sinhalese language and Buddhism as religion. This, as we shall see below, led to the alienation of Tamils in Sri Lanka and precipitated the Island's worst ethnic conflict between the Sinhalese majority and the Tamil minority. Not that India did not have its share of ethnic conflicts within its own cultural diversity, including the one involving the Tamils on the question of language (Hindi vs. Tamil) and greater autonomy in managing affairs of the state. But the Indian and the Sri Lankan approaches to their respective ethnic conflicts have been considerably different. Further, India has also had to face the problem of a spillover of Sri Lanka's ethnic conflict and not vice versa.

At this stage, we must be clear in our mind that there were two Tamil problems that impinged on India's relations with Sri Lanka. One was the question of 'Indian Tamils' or 'estate Tamils', who were seen in Sri Lanka as persons of Indian origin, working on Sri Lanka's tea and rubber estates. The citizenship status of these persons became a contentious issue between the two countries soon after they gained independence from British colonial rule. The presence of Indian Tamils in Sri Lanka's estate sector was the creation of British empire in the subcontinent when they were encouraged to migrate to Sri Lanka from India to provide cheap and disciplined labour to boost estate sector.

India's overall approach to such expatriates who had emigrated during the British rule was that these people now belonged to the country of their adoption and settlement; they should remain loyal to that country and India could not take them back from various former British colonies. However, these people had extensive socio-cultural and family ties in their respective regions (from where they migrated). Accordingly, it was in India's interest to see that these people enjoyed basic rights and were not unduly discriminated or victimised in their countries of adoption. In case of estate Tamils in Sri Lanka, socio-cultural and family ties with Tamils in India were very strong and their plight invoked spontaneous and strong emotional as well as political support in Tamil Nadu.

The Sri Lankan government did not consider the persons of Indian origin working on the estates as their responsibility and wanted India to take them back. India's refusal to do so turned these persons into, what was described as stateless persons. For various political and economic reasons, Sri Lanka subjected them to discrimination and hardships. They were denied franchise rights, settlement on land and a proper wage structure, the discussion of which is beyond the scope of this study. India protested and there ensued since the early 1950s, long and irritating negotiations between the two countries to resolve the issue. A major agreement on the question was concluded in 1964 between the Indian Prime Minister Lal Bahadur Shastri and Sri Lanka's Prime Minister Mrs. Bandaranaike. The implementation of this agreement ran into further difficulties necessitating further agreements and efforts to solve the problem. Final settlement of the question has come about even more recently—during 1989–91—leading to the hope that this irritation has finally been resolved.[2]

Historical Roots of the Ethnic Divide

While the problem of the Indian Tamils could be dealt through diplomatic efforts, it was the other component of India's socio-cultural constituency, the Sri Lankan Tamils, that really sucked India deep into its whirlpool. Before we take up the discussion of India's response to the ethnic conflict between the Sri Lankan Tamils and the Sinhalese community that flared up in 1983, which constitutes the main thrust of this study, it may be in order to understand the anatomy and dynamics of this conflict in its evolutionary perspective.

The roots of ethnic antagonism between the Sinahlese and the Tamils are traced to the myths woven around the origin and evolution of the two communities in the island. The Sinhalese are seen as the early migrants into Sri Lanka from those regions that constitute Bengal and Orissa today. The date of this migration is put at late 5th or early 6th century B.C. (i.e., 543 B.C. or 483 B.C.). This migration took the form of an Indian prince called 'Vijaya' who came to Sri Lanka with seven hundred of his Aryan associates. Being a grandson of the union between an Indian princess and a lion, he established a pure race Sinhala (related to the *lion* called *singh* in Sanskrit). This race adopted Buddhism as its religion when King Mahindra, son of the Emperor Ashoka, visited Sri Lanka about two and a half centuries after Prince Vijaya's arrival.[22]

The Tamils are considered late-comers, being the descendants of Chola Kings of south India who periodically invaded Sri Lanka during the second century B.C. However, there are Tamil historical chronicles that claim Tamils as the pre-Sinhala Dravidian indigenous inhabitants of the Island. By 12th century A.D. they had established a systematic polity of their own under the flourishing kingdom of Jaffna in the north of the island.[23]

There are two main approaches to look at the sharpening ethnic consciousness among the two communities and thus the growth of potential conflict between them. One is rooted in the historical process wherein mythical portrayal of wars between the Sinhala and Tamil kings for the control of the island are recounted with considerable enthusiasm and involvement. Credit is also given to the fact of separate developments of ethnic and religious consciousness of the two communities, through their literary and religious revivalist movements. The European colonisation, first Portuguese and later the British, brought the two communities to interact with each other, thus making them conscious and protective of their respective cultural specificities.[24]

The other aproach does not give much credibility to historical myths, and some of the recent analyses have strongly refuted the contention that Tamils or Sinhalese ever had any cultural conflict or incompatibility in the ancient and medieval periods. Instead, economic clash of interests occurred between them as a result of the rise of middle classes in both these communities. The protagonist of a pure Aryan Sinhala race, Anagarika Dharmapala (a Buddhist monk) is referred to indicate that there existed an economically based 'sons of soil' consciousness among the Sinhalese against Tamils, Muslims, etc. as early as in 1922. Kumari Jayawardene, emphasising the role of a weak Sinhala middle class in the communalisation of the island's social and political life says:

There was no 'national bourgeoisie' with basic contradictions with imperialism. . . . This weak bourgeoisie was thus incapable of creating among the people a national consciousness based on rationalism and scientific outlook . . . . They were thus more susceptible to the traditional ideologies and superstitions that were dominant among the other classes. In this situation, where a Sri Lankan consciousness could not arise, the need of the new class for an identity . . . was met by a revival of older identities based on familiar traditional categories of religion, caste and ethnicity. Rather than being swept away by the winds of nationalism and national unity, the older forms of identity were given a new lease of life resulting in communalism, casteism, a distortion

of history, a revival of myths of origin and hero-myths along
with the creation of visions of a past golden age.[25]

Notwithstanding the cultural distortions and the sharpening of
ethnic incompatibilities, to which the colonial rule of the British
contributed in no small measure, the Tamils and Sinhalese co-
existed in Sri Lankan society and polity without much overt antagonism. There is no evidence of any conflict in violent form.
There were communal riots involving the Sinhalese but the other
party was either the Catholics (1883, 1903) or Muslims (1915).
This violence in a significant way, was the manifestation of the
Sinhalese self-perception of being economically and politically
deprived vis-à-vis the Muslims and the Christians. The Sinhalese
also nursed a sense of insecurity and deprivation vis-à-vis Tamils,
who were perceived as a cultural extension of a huge Tamil population in India. This sense of insecurity led the Sinhalese leadership in
the post-independence period, to initiate moves and policies to the
detriment of the Tamils. This provided economic and political
content to historically nursed ethnic antagonism, resulting in the
worst explosion of ethnic violence.

Since Sri Lanka's independence in 1948, various Sinhala dominated governments have systematically pursued policies to dis-
criminate against Tamils in the areas of land, language and
economic opportunities. The land colonisation policies of the first
UNP regime in the Tamil dominated regions of northeastern and
eastern Sri Lanka sought to gradually alter demographic balance
in these regions to the disadvantage of the Tamils. The motive was
to change electoral balance by habitating Sinhalese in these areas.
The UNP governments have consistently favoured such settlement
policies with political objectives in mind. Even in the thick of the
ethnic conflict, the then National Security Minister, Lalit Atulath-
mudali justified this approach and asserted that the Sinhalese
being settled in the Tamil areas were given 'four months military
training' and that despite protests and opposition, 'the government
will go ahead with these settlement plans'. Referring to the Malay-
sian example of solving its ethnic problem, he added: 'Gerald
Templer had suppressed terrorism in Malaysia by settling 600
thousand people in terrorist troubled areas in that country but in
Sri Lanka only 200 thousand will be settled in terrorist strongholds'.[26]
The process of politicisation of the ethnic divide and conflict

formation was speeded up when the leader of the UNP breakaway group (in 1954), S.W.R.D. Bandaranaike of the Sri Lanka Freedom Party brought his coalition to victory on the slogan of 'Sinhala only' in the 1956 elections. This marked the beginning of the sectarian approach to nation and state-building at the cost of the island's multi-ethnic, multi-religious and secular character of the polity. 'Sinhala only' with emphasis on Buddhism was definitely in violation to Article 39 of the Soulbury Constitution. This policy precipitated the first Sinhala–Tamil communal riots in 1958. Though S.W.R.D. Bandaranaike was considered a friend of India, the development on the ethnic front in Sri Lanka could not go unnoticed. There were protests in India on the question of Bandaranaike's language policies. An astute Indian statesman from the southern Tamil state, C. Rajagopalachari said: 'We in India are not quite uninterested in our neighbour's welfare; nor are events there without their effect across the narrow and shallow waters that divide us, and I beg of the leaders of Ceylon not to treat us quite as alien and strangers.'[27]

At the time, this question did not assume conflict dimensions. In one respect, S.W.R.D. Bandaranaike's 'Sinhala only' policy aimed at reducing the influence of the English language and of Christian missionary education.[28] Moreover, he was still sincerely trying to meet the grievances of the Sri Lankan Tamils, as was evident in the evolution of the Bandaranaike–Chelvanayagam Pact in 1957.

Notwithstanding S.W.R.D. Bandaranaike's personal orientation and long-term intentions, the political forces unleashed by his 'Sinhala only' proved detrimental to the island's ethnic peace and harmony. He prompted his rivals, the UNP leadership, also to exploit Sinhala sentiments and encourage fundamentalist and chauvinist forces for political expediency. Bandaranaike was assassinated by a fanatic Buddhist monk in 1959 on the suspicion that he was compromising Sinhala interests in favour of Tamils. From then, the mainstream Sinhala political parties, the UNP and the SLFP, have been championing the cause of majority Sinhalese to harness electoral and political gains. In the process, disadvantages in education, government jobs and even business and industrial enterprises have been inflicted on the Tamils driving them gradually to desperation.[29] When a Tamil enthusiast raised the slogan of a separate Tamil state in 1972, he was ignored as an extremist and cynical, but only four years later in May 1976, the main Tamil party, the Tamil United Liberation Front (TULF) committed itself to the goal of a separate sovereign state for Tamils, the Eelam. The militancy of the Tamil ethnicity and the militarisation of the Tamil movement was an inevitable logical course to follow.[30] More so because electoral promises made to the TULF by the UNP in 1977 elections were not honoured. Recall the UNP election manifesto in 1977:

> There are numerous problems confronting the Tamil speaking people. The lack of solution to their problems has made the Tamil speaking people support even a movement for the creation of a separate State. In the interests of national integration and unity so necessary for the economic development of the whole country, the Party feels such problems should be solved without loss of time.

The UNP failed to deliver its manifesto promise, however. Not only this, within a month of the UNP's electoral victory in 1977 ethnic violence erupted in the North, with Tamils mostly at the receiving end. Tamil militant groups were still mostly in their infancy; many innocent lives were lost and valuable property (including the famous Jaffna library) was destroyed. To this day, no one has assessed how this chain of violence between 1977–81 contributed to shattering Tamil hopes from the UNP regime and encouraging Tamil militancy.

India and the Emerging Conflict

By the early 1980s, the ethnic situation had reached the point of major explosion when a number of Tamil militant leaders and their associates left for Madras to carry on with their struggle against the Sri Lankan state. Their presence in Tamil Nadu no doubt activised the Tamil social constituency in India and many Tamil public figures, media organizations and even local politicians started sympathising with them. On the other hand, it is extremely difficult to say with certainty whether there was any involvement, and if so, to what extent, of either the government of Tamil Nadu or the central government in New Delhi. One well-placed Sri Lankan source, asserting that the militant leaders organised military training for themselves and their cadres in Tamil Nadu through underworld connections and by employing retired Tamil military personnel of the Indian army also concedes: 'It must be emphasised that this training was done surreptitiously and without the knowledge of the Government of India or the Government of the State of Tamil Nadu'.[31]

Sri Lankan analysts also cite instances to show that the Indian intelligence outfit RAW (Research and Analysis Wing) had become involved with the Tamil guerrillas and was helping them even before the anti-Tamil violence of July 1983. But this is based upon the assessment of a former US intelligence analyst, Tom Mark, who was rather close to the Sri Lankan security establishment, as is evident from his writings.[32] It is difficult to know just how seriously such reports should be taken. Because even the LTTE documents released subsequently claim contacts between India's RAW and the Tamil militants for providing assistance and military training to the latter, *not before September 1983*.[33] At any rate, this particular report clearly indicates that the purpose behind the RAW's involvement at that stage was to gather intelligence about movements of Western ships at the port of Trincomalee in Sri Lanka, with the help of members of Tamil militant groups. This gave Indian intelligence sources an additional opportunity to gather information about the nature of these Tamil militant groups and their activities. Corroboration of this version can be found in other Sri Lankan sources as well.[34] This would all seem to be a legitimate activity for any intelligence organisation. There was nothing to suggest in Tom Mark's report that the involvement with Tamil militants at that stage was aimed against the Sri Lankan state, or that there was any supply of arms to these militants by the Indian agency. RAW did become heavily involved with the militants, but that was to come later, after the July 1983 ethnic violence in Sri Lanka.

While the state government in Tamil Nadu and the central government in New Delhi were keeping a close watch on developments in Sri Lanka, they scrupulously refrained from doing anything that could be construed as interference in its affairs. The state Chief Minister M.G. Ramachandran, addressing the Tamil Language Research Conference in Madurai in 1981, objected to even a reference to the 'Tamil Problem' in Sri Lanka, asserting that Tamil Nadu did not want to interfere in the internal affairs of the neighbouring country.[35] The ruling All India Anna DMK party of M.G. Ramachandran stayed away from the all-party conference called by the opposition DMK leader M. Karunanidhi in June 1983, to express solidarity with the Tamil militants of Sri Lanka, and pleading that asylum be given to the struggling Tigers (Tamil militants). However, in view of the gradually emerging atmosphere of support and sympathy for the Tamil militants in Tamil Nadu, Indira Gandhi, on the eve of her visit to the state on 20 July 1983, through quiet diplomatic channels, expressed her concern 'for the safety of the Indian citizens' to the Sri Lankan government. She further assured Colombo that India had no intentions of interfering in Sri Lankan affairs. But this 'sensitive' message was leaked by interested persons to the media in Colombo, which in turn heaped accusations of interference on Mrs. Gandhi's government. A senior Sri Lankan foreign service officer later had this to say:

> When messages such as this are communicated through diplomatic channels, professional etiquette demands that it be treated as strictly confidential. Over and above . . . this message was of a sensitive nature and it was handled accordingly by the Ministry of Foreign Affairs in Colombo. As such it was acutely embarrassing to those of us who handled this communication both in Colombo and New Delhi, when somehow the media in Colombo got wind of it and insulted the government of India for interfering in the affairs of Sri Lanka. Such news items were reproduced in the media in India thereby creating unpleasantness and further tension in Tamil Nadu.[36]

In conclusion both the appearance and reality of India's involvement in the Sri Lankan question prior to July 1983 need to be scrutinised carefully and evaluated accordingly. Any attempt to portray this involvement must distinguish clearly between India's concerns for persons of Indian origin i.e., estate Tamils, and India's guarded response to the gradually swelling popular sympathies in Tamil Nadu for the Sri Lankan Tamils of the North and the Eastern regions. To ignore this distinction and argue that Sri Lanka's ethnic crisis was the result of India's moral and material support to militant Tamil groups is nothing but a manifestation of political motivation and distorted historical understanding.

Notes to Chapter 2

1. Ravinath P. Aryasinha, 'Post-Independence Indo-Sri Lanka Relations (1948–88): The Relevance of the Economic Dimension', M.A. Dissertation, University of Colombo, Sri Lanka, March 1990.
2. K.M. Panikkar, *India and the Indian Ocean*, George Allen and Unwin: London, 1945, p. 7.
3. P.R. Ramachandra Rao, *India and Ceylon: A Study*, Orient Longman: Bombay, 1954; K.B. Vaidya, *The Naval Defence of India*, Bombay, 1949. As cited in S.U. Kodikara, *Indo-Ceylon Relations Since Independence*, Ceylon Institute of World Affairs: Colombo, 1965, pp. 32–33.
4. As cited in *ibid.*, p. 33.
5. For details of the UK-Ceylon Defence Pact see H.S.S. Nissanka, *Foreign Policy of Sri Lanka Under Bandaranaikes*, Vikas: New Delhi, 1984.
6. S. Gopal, *Jawaharlal Nehru: A Biography*, vol. II: 1947–56, Oxford University Press: Delhi, 1983, p. 54.
7. *Ibid.*, p. 43.
8. *Ibid.*, p. 59.
9. *Ibid.*, p. 64.
10. S.D. Muni, 'Indo-US Relations: The Pakistan Factor', *Man and Development*, vol. VIII, no. 3, September 1986, pp. 9–27.
11. Dhirendra Mohan Prasad, *Ceylon's Foreign Policy under the Bandaranaikes 1956–65*, S. Chand and Co.: New Delhi, 1973, p. 45 (n. 202).
12. *Ceylon and Kotelawala: A Selection of Speeches*, compiled and edited by GEP de S. Wickramaratne, Colombo, 1964, pp. 243–83; also Prasad, *Ceylon's Foreign Policy*, pp. 44–46.
13. Wickramaratne, *Ceylon and Kotelawala*, pp. 276–77.
14. John Kotelawala, *An Asian Prime Minister's Story*, Harper: London, 1956.
15. Nissanka, *Sri Lanka under Bandaranaikes*; S.U. Kodikara, *Sri Lanka's Foreign Policy: A Study in Non-alignment*, Vikas: New Delhi, 1984. Also his *Dilemmas in Indo-Sri Lanka Relations*, BCIS: Colombo, 1991.
16. Kodikara, *Indo-Ceylon Relations*, pp. 16–17; Anuradha Muni, 'Sri Lanka's China Policy', in *South Asian Studies*, vol. 8, no. 1, 1973; also Gamini Nawaratne, *The Chinese Connection*, Sandesa: Colombo, 1976.
17. Kodikara, *Indo-Ceylon Relations*, pp. 53–58; Gopal, *Jawaharlal Nehru*, n. 6, vol. III, 1956–64, p. 236; Nissank, *Sri Lanka under Bandaranaikes*, pp. 145–53.
18. See S.D. Muni and Urmila Phadnis, 'Emergence of Bangladesh: The Responses of Ceylon and Nepal', *Economic and Political Weekly*, vol. 7, no. 8, 19 February 1972.
19. These details were disclosed in Indian Parliament, *Lok Sabha Debates*, vol. 2, no. 1, 25 May, 1971, p. 30; for Mrs. Bandaranaike's version of this assistance, see *Indian Express*, 18 May 1971. Also see Vincent Coelho, *Across the Palk Straits: India-Sri Lanka Relations*, Palit and Palit: New Delhi, 1976, p. 96; G.S. Bhargava, 'Ten Days that Shook Ceylon', *The Hindustan Times*, 16 May 1971.
20. Coelho, *Across the Palk Straits*, pp. 96–97; Urmila Phadnis, 'Insurgency in Ceylonese Politics: Problems and Prospects', *Institute for Defence Studies and Analysis Journal*, vol. 3, no. 4, April 1971; Bandana Misra, 'India's Military

Help to Neighbouring States: A Case Study of Burma (1948–49), Nepal (1951–53) and Sri Lanka (1971)', M.Phil. dissertation, JNU, New Delhi, 1975, pp. 76–80.

21. For a historical background to this problem see Dharmapriya Wesumperuma, *Indian Immigrant Plantation Workers in Sri Lanka: A Historical Perspective 1880–1910*, Sri Lanka, 1986. For Indo-Sri Lankan relations and Indian policy on the question of Indian Tamils in Sri Lanka, see Lalit Kumar, *India and Sri Lanka: Sirimavo–Shastri Pact*, Chetana: New Delhi, 1978; S.U. Kodikara, *Indo-Ceylon Relations Since Independence*, Ceylon Institute of World Affairs: Colombo, 1965; H.P. Chattopadhyaya, *Indians in Sri Lanka*, O.P.S. Publishers: Calcutta, 1979; P. Sahadevan, 'India and the Overseas Indians: A Case Study of Problems of the Indian Tamils of Sri Lanka, 1964–1987', Ph.D. thesis submitted at JNU, 1992.

22. The history of evolution of the Sinhala race is portrayed in a Buddhist chronicle, *The Mahavamsa*; see H. Parker, *Ancient Ceylon*, Marwah: New Delhi, 1982; Angarika Dharmapala, *History of An Ancient Civilization*, M.D. Gunasena and Co. Inc: Colombo, 1902; R.A.L.H. Gunavardana, 'The Kinsmen of the Buddha: Myth as Political Character in the Ancient and Early Medieval Kingdoms of Sri Lanka', *Sri Lanka Journal of Humanities*, Colombo, vol. 2, no. 1, June 1976; Coelho, *Across the Palk Straits*, chapter II, pp. 7–16.

23. Dagmar Hellmann–Rajanayagam, 'Ethnicity and Nationalism—The Sri Lankan Tamils in the Late Nineteenth Century: Some Theoretical Questions', in Diethelm Weidemann (ed.), *Nationalism, Ethnicity and Political Development in South Asia*, Manohar: New Delhi, 1991, pp. 25–50.

24. *Ibid.*; Coelho, *Across the Palk Straits*, chapters III and VII.

25. Kumari Jayawardena, 'Some Aspects of Class and Ethnic Consciousness in Sri Lanka in the late 19th and early 20th Centuries', in the Social Scientists Association Seminar, *Ethnicity and Social Change in Sri Lanka*, Colombo, 1984, pp. 86–87. Also Neil Kuruppu's contribution entitled 'Communalism and the Labour Movement in Sri Lanka', in the same volume, pp. 93–106.

26. *Indian Express*, 16 March 1985. On the details of settlement policy during the ethnic conflict, see Malinga H. Gunaratna, *For a Sovereign State*, Sarvodaya: Colombo, 1988. Also, Robert N. Kearney and Barbara Diane Miller, *Internal Migration in Sri Lanka and Its Social Consequences*, Westview Press: Colorado, 1987 (specially Chapter 4, pp. 91–115).

27. *The Hindu*, 25 September 1958.

28. K.M. de Silva, 'Nationalism and the State in Sri Lanka', in K.M. de Silva *et al.*, eds., *Ethnic Conflict in Buddhist Societies: Sri Lanka, Thailand and Burma*, Westview Press: USA, 1988.

29. I have discussed some of the economic and educational consequences for the Tamils briefly in my 'Sri Lanka's Ethnic Crisis' in Kalim Bahadur, ed., *South Asia in Transition: Conflicts and Tensions*, Patriot Publishers: New Delhi, 1986, pp. 273–87.

30. For the evolution and various dimensions of the conflict between Sinhalese and Tamils, see Satchi Ponnambalam, *Sri Lanka: National Conflict and the Tamil Liberation Struggle*, Zed Books: London, 1981; Committee for Rational Development, *Sri Lanka: The Ethnic Conflict (Myths, Realities and Perspectives)*, Navrang: New Delhi, 1984; S.J. Tambiah, *Sri Lanka: Ethnic Fratricide*

and the Dismantling of Democracy, I.B. Tauris & Co.: London, 1986; K.M. de Silva, *Managing Ethnic Tensions in Multi-Ethnic Societies: Sri Lanka, 1880–1985*, Lanham: Maryland, 1985.

31. T.D.S.A. Dissanayaka, *The Agony of Sri Lanka*, Swastika: Colombo, n.d. (approximately, 1984).

32. Tom Mark, 'Peace in Sri Lanka: India Acts in Its Own Interests', *Daily News*, Colombo, 6 July 1987; also see P.S. Suryanarayana, *The Peace Trap: An Indo-Sri Lankan Political Crisis*, Affiliated East West Press Pvt. Ltd.: Madras, 1988, pp. 56–57.

33. 'Political Committee', 'Liberation Tigers of Tamil Eelam', 'India and the Eelam Tamil Crisis,' as cited in Rajesh Kadian, *India's Sri Lanka Fiasco: Peace Keepers at War*, Vision Books: New Delhi, 1990, pp. 101–2. For details of RAW's involvement with Tmil militants' training see *India Today*, 31 March 1984, and 15 July 1987.

34. Gunaratna, *For a Sovereign State*.

35. Stanley Jayaweera, 'The Ethnic Crisis and the Indo-Srilankan Peace Process, 1983–87', in S.U. Kodikara, ed., *Dilemmas in Indo-Sri Lankan Relations*, Colombo, 1991, p. 62.

36. Dissanayaka, *The Agony of Sri Lanka*, p. 67.

3

Responses to the Ethnic Crisis:
July 1983–July 1987

The July 1983 Violence

In the last week of July 1983, massive ethnic violence broke out in Sri Lanka, with its epicentre in Colombo. But in dimensions and in magnitude, it was without precedent in Sri Lankan history, and indeed had not many parallels in contemporary Asian experience. The violence was directed at Tamil life and property. It was perpetrated in a systematic and organised manner with the involvement of influential sections of the Jayewardene government, Buddhist clergy and Sri Lankan security forces (both police and armed forces). The gruesome details of this violence which took Sri Lanka by storm for four days from 24 July, have already been discussed elsewhere. The background causes and the roles of the main agencies and actors involved have also been analysed.[1]

India was directly affected as a result of this violence. The victims of the ethnic holocaust included not only the Sri Lankan Tamils but also estate workers of Indian origin, Indian nationals—both among estate Tamils and casual visitors—and members of the Indian High Commission. A senior Sri Lankan diplomat who witnessed the events wrote later:

> Another distressing feature that day in terms of the Vienna convention, was the damage suffered by the staff of the High Commission of India. The clerical staff of this Mission lives in Wellawatte and many of them have Tamil names or Tamil sounding names. Their homes were subjected to mob fury when the slums of the Canal Bank area erupted that morning. The High Commission evacuated these families to Hotel Taprobane.

Later when the homes of the diplomatic staff were threatened, they were evacuated to the Hotel Oberoi.

That evening when the new First Secretary Mr. M.J. Abrahams was returning home with his clerk Mr. K.V. Iyer, his car was set upon by hoodlums at Bambalapitiya and the vehicle set on fire. Mr. Iyer was hospitalized while Mr. Abrahams received out patient treatment.

The fire in Baillie Street near the President's House was still raging in the evening and some of the staff in the High Commission in the adjoining building feared that the Mission itself may be gutted. The Fire Brigade was taxed well beyond their resources but priority was given to the blaze in Baillie Street upon a request by the Ministry of Foreign Affairs. Once the fire was douched, I visited the staff of the High Commission, first those in hospital, then those in hotels and then my wife joined me in calling on those who were still in their homes. Even in the face of adversity they were truly gracious. Here was no recrimination on their part. In my knowledge of diplomacy they were truly worthy representatives of a great nation.[2]

It was in this fire that the Indian Overseas Bank was gutted and some of its employees injured. There was also commotion at the residence of the Indian Deputy High Commissioner, as one of the neighbouring houses was burnt and his wife became involved in putting out the neighbourhood fire.[3]

Under these circumstances no government in India could remain a silent spectator. More so because the consequences of this ethnic war, which erupted in its ugliest form in Sri Lanka, went far beyond affecting the Indian nationals and the Indian establishments there. They impinged on India's regional security concerns as well as its ideological sensitivities, including threats to internal stability and order in its own southern state of Tamil Nadu. Let us take the question of India's regional security concerns first, because that weighed more heavily on India's policy-making.

Consequences for India's Security Concerns

The warning shot was fired immediately after the outbreak of ethnic violence. The Sri Lankan government approached various 'friendly' countries—particularly the USA, the UK, China, Pakistan, Bangladesh and Malaysia—for military and political support. India was deliberately excluded, perhaps because of its obvious sympathies for the Tamils. Interestingly, there was no attempt to seek support from the Soviet Union, which a Sri Lankan commentator subsequently described as tactically unwise.[4] Perhaps, the Soviet Union's known identification with India on regional issues and the Sri Lankan government's pro-Western proclivities had decided the issue. In some Sri Lankan quarters (suspectedly sponsored by the ruling circles) it was also projected—quite inaccurately—that the violence had been precipitated through Soviet support to Leftist parties in Sri Lanka including the JVP, to overthrow the government. Such rumours were intended to facilitate the exclusion of India, a close Soviet friend, and to promote the mobilization of Western powers and their allies for security support.

As viewed from India, the implications of this move to seek outside help were that the Jayewardene government was out to seek a military solution to Sri Lanka's ethnic problem; furthermore, that in doing so, it wanted to isolate India in the region by facilitating the strategic presence of the forces inimical to India's perceived security interests. Accordingly, following reports from Colombo about these efforts to seek support from abroad, India's External Affairs Minister cautioned all outside powers to keep away from Sri Lanka's internal turmoil.[5] Mrs. Gandhi in her telephone conversation with President Jayewardene on 5 August also strongly disapproved of Sri Lanka seeking external military support.

India's caution signals, however, did not deter Colombo from going ahead. The Jayewardene government utilised both normal diplomatic channels as well as special missions to secure military and political support. These missions were led not only by his ministers, senior diplomats and special envoys, but also by his own son Ravi Jayewardene, his brother Harry Jayewardene and himself. Notable among these efforts were the visits of President Jayewardene to China, West Germany, the UK and the USA during May–June 1984; and those of his brother to the Philippines, Hong Kong, Indonesia, South Korea and Japan during August–September 1983. These missions emphasized the threat to Sri Lanka's unity and integrity posed by Tamil terrorism working with the support and encouragement of government and people in India. Also projected were scenarios of a direct military invasion by India for the creation of an independent and sovereign Tamil state à la Bangladesh to underline the seriousness of the crisis.

The achievements of these missions were many. The Sri Lankan government secured the assistance of the world famous Israeli intelligence agencies Mossad and Shin Bet to strengthen its own intelligence set-up and military training facilities.[6] Training facilities were further stepped up by British ex-SAS commandos who came in the name of a private mercenary agency called Keenie Minee Services based on a British Channel island and, according to a Sri Lankan account, 'reliably understood to be financed by the British Ministry of Defence'.[7] Here it is important to bear in mind that Sri Lanka was prompted to employ the Israeli agencies and the British mercenaries by the USA and the UK respectively, as these governments did not wish to openly support Sri Lanka, in deference to Indian sensitivities. Sri Lanka's intelligence connection with Israel was established following the visits to Colombo of the US Secretary of Defense Caspar Weinberger in October 1983, and General Vernon Walters, a former CIA officer, sent as President Reagan's special emissary in November 1983. In May 1984, an Israeli interest section was formally established in the US Embassy in Colombo.

Pakistan also promptly joined in helping Sri Lanka to deal with its ethnic conflict. Though initial reports of Sri Lankan request for arms to Pakistan were denied, Pakistan contributed rupees 10 million in August 1983, towards relief assistance and gave an option to the Sri Lankan government to utilise it for the purchase of rice, cloth, sugar, etc. Sri Lankan reporters claim that with these supplies also came military equipment, in Pakistani civilian planes to avoid any Indian suspicion and protest.[8] Sri Lanka's Army Chief, Major General T.I. Weeratunga, undertook a week long visit to Pakistan from 3–9 December 1983. He had extensive consultations with Pakistani military commanders and discussed matters of 'mutual interest' with them. A Pakistan Navy ship made a goodwill visit to Sri Lanka in the first week of August 1984, when the Commander of the ship made a courtesy call on the Sri Lankan Minister of Foreign Affairs and the Director of National Security. A year later, in August 1985, the Pakistani officials admitted that they were providing 'civil defence' training to Sri Lankans.

Pakistan's support for Sri Lanka was highlighted during the exchange of visits at the Summit level. President Jayewardene paid a week-long official visit to Pakistan in March–April 1985. During this visit, he went to the extent of equating Kashmir with 'Afghanistan', asking both to be 'allowed to decide about their future themselves'. He also supported the Pakistani proposal for South Asia as a Nuclear Weapons Free Zone.' In his return visit in December (10–13) 1985, General Zia promised to help Sri Lanka 'in any manner it was capable of'. Though Zia was politically constrained in promising any arms supplies to Sri Lanka in view of Israeli support for the latter which was resented within Pakistan, the anti-India tone of the two visits was absolutely clear even to a stray observer. Subsequently, Pakistani military officers of the rank of Brigadier, and ex-SAS commandos, were reported to be collaborating with their Sri Lankan colleagues in planning and executing battle tactics against the Tamil militants during the major assaults in late 1986 and early 1987. Sri Lanka also received sizeable and cheap military supplies from China. Later in the conflict, Malaysia, Britain, South Africa and even the USA supplied arms to Sri Lanka[10] through private arms dealers.

In return for this support, Sri Lanka had to agree to accommodate certain Western strategic interests, notably with regard to the USA. Three significant arrangements came to light. The first related to the visit of the US naval ships for refuelling and crew-rest. While on an important strategic mission in Colombo in November 1983, Special Envoy of the US President, General Vernon Walters, told a select group of the Sri Lankan journalists: 'As far as the US is concerned, we will be satisfied if Sri Lanka permits sailors some short-leave (crew-rest). The ships can remain out in the high seas for long periods'.[11]

To renovate and expand refuelling facilities at the strategic harbour of Trincomalee, the World War II vintage oil-storage tank-farm, international contracts were invited. But through a rather clear case of manipulation, the bids by India (in fact the lowest) and the Soviet Union were rejected, and the contract was awarded to a Singapore-based private consortium with suspected US links. India protested and eventually produced evidence to expose the phony nature of the consortium, forcing Sri Lanka to cancel the contract and reopen for tenders.[12] The most important deal in strategic terms between the USA and Sri Lanka was concluded in December 1983. This concerned the establishment of a powerful Voice of America transmission facility, expected to be the largest of its kind outside the USA. For this purpose, 1,000 acres of land were allocated by the Sri Lankan government near Katunayake airport. According to the agreement on this deal, there was to be no participation of Sri Lankan authorities or technicians at the top management level. The proposed facility had the provision for six transmitters, two of 250 KW each and four of 500 KW each. This led to fears in India that the facility could serve as a hi-tech outfit to monitor naval and land communications and movements in the region, including India. This facility could also be able to beam high frequency messages to US submarines deployed in the Indian Ocean region.[13]

Notable in the context of Sri Lanka's strategic relations with the West during this period was also President Jayewardene's assertion that his country's defence pact with Britain, entered into in 1947, still remained intact. This assertion was first made in 1981 and was repeated after the July 1983 violence.[14] Technically this position was correct because, in 1957 while requesting the closure of the British naval and air-force bases from Sri Lanka, the late S.W.R.D. Bandaranaike had not abrogated this agreement, as the bases in question were only a part of the executive arrangement between the two countries within the framework of the Defence Pact. This position had been maintained also during the SLFP regime (1960–65) by the then Deputy Minister for Defence and External Affairs, Felix R. Dias Bandaranaike.[15] What was important was not the correctness of the technical position but its reiteration by Jayewardene in the current context in Sri Lanka. In this way he conveyed the message that some sort of alliance in defence matters existed between his country and the United Kingdom, with all its implications in the bilateral and regional contexts. The political significance of this could be seen in the light of Sri Lanka's voting with Britain on the Falklands issue in the UN in 1981. Sri Lanka was one of about a dozen Third World countries, and the only one in South Asia, to do so.

A pertinent question arises here. With all this accommodation on the part of Sri Lanka, why were the USA and the UK not more forthcoming in helping the Jayewardene government openly and directly with military assistance? Jayewardene confessed to the Western reluctance to aid Sri Lanka in June 1984 after his visits to the USA and the U.K. Instead, Sri Lanka was directed to seek help from Western allies like Israel, South Africa and the private

British mercenaries mentioned earlier. This was applicable to
Pakistan as well although Pakistan had its own reasons for getting
involved in Sri Lanka—to counter India and expand its own
influence in the region. Moreover, since the early 1980s Pakistan
had established military training linkages with other South Asian
neighbours like Bangladesh and even Nepal.

The US hesitation was the result of new policy moves to build a
closer economic and strategic relationship with India during this
period. By 1983, the USA had emerged as India's principal trading
partner, outstripping even the Soviet Union. Prospects of improving
economic relations looked good, with the promised opening-up of
the Indian economy and the spurt in the demand for US hi-tech
items in Indian industry. India was also sounding the USA for
purchase of military equipment and dual-application technology,
such as the super computer, night vision equipments and radars.
The US response was positive but not yet decisive. Following the
personal rapport established between Mrs. Gandhi and President
Reagan in 1981 at the Cancun North–South summit, as also during
Mrs. Gandhi's official visit to the USA in 1982, the White House
became the chief advocate for building a positive cooperative
relationship between the USA and India. The State Department
was also coming round to this view, but the Pentagon and the
Technology Security agencies had strong reservations, not only
because of the history of close Indo-Soviet relations but also
because of the personality of Mrs. Gandhi, usually considered a
tough and difficult person to deal with.[16] In sum, however, the
USA had no desire to risk offending India's regional susceptibilities
in Sri Lanka at this juncture.

Besides the considerations of a newly developing approach
towards India, other constraints also explained the US reluctance
to get directly involved in Sri Lanka. One was that such a direct
US involvement was bound to provoke India into taking a more
aggressive and tougher stance on the ethnic situation. And if that
happened, a situation could be created to provoke Indian military
intervention in Sri Lanka, which the USA, in fact, wanted to avoid.
In the case of such an intervention, US help could be hardly of any
effective use—recall the 1971 experience of the futile US tilt in
favour of Pakistan during the emergence of Bangladesh—unless of
course, the US opted for direct military confrontation with India.

This was out of the question. On the other hand, it may be said here that the USA found Sri Lankan fears of Indian military invasion on the ethnic issue highly exaggerated and unrealistic.[17]

Yet another hurdle to direct US military assistance to Sri Lanka was the influence of the Tamil diaspora in the USA, which constituted a small but influential group. They were suspected of having links with the State Department and the White House—so much so that a senior Sri Lankan civil servant held this Tamil lobby responsible for making the US President write to Jayewardene seeking a negotiated solution of the ethnic problem.[18] Even some of Jayewardene's close Cabinet colleagues obliquely indicated to Congressman Solarz, during his visit to the Island in December 1986, that the Tamil guerrillas had links with the CIA.[19] There is no doubt that the Tamil diaspora was very active in the USA. They were instrumental in softening the State Department's references to Tamil militant groups and were also prepared to bargain with the USA for a Tamil Eelam.[20] In building up pressure on the Sri Lankan government the Tamil diaspora played an active role, not only in the USA but throughout the world, particularly in the countries giving aid to Sri Lanka. It mobilized human rights groups and created lobbies against the Sri Lankan state.[21]

Thus, while the factors of a shift in the US policy towards India, the constraints of practical efficacy and the role of the Tamil diaspora can explain the US hesitation towards rendering direct military assistance to Sri Lanka, why then was India so agitated about its regional security concerns arising out of the Western strategic involvement in Sri Lanka? The answer lies not so much in Indian fears about US military supplies to Sri Lanka, but in the possibility that this could form part of a process of Sri Lanka's integration into the Western strategic structure for the Indian Ocean. There were indications that such a structure was being put into operation since the early 1980s, to meet the exigencies of the second Cold War. Its initial signals could be seen in US efforts to evolve a strategic consensus in South Asia in the wake of the Soviet intervention in Afghanistan. India kept out of this consensus and even tried to break it, whereas Sri Lanka was an active participant. This had resulted in the US allocation for Sri Lanka of a small grant for arms sale in its 1981–82 budget. This remained unutilised until 1983 when it was withdrawn in view of the ongoing ethnic warfare. But this made Sri Lanka the second country in South Asia, after Pakistan, to have been granted such allocations and this was important from India's point of view.

Then came in 1984, the establishment of Central Command (CENTCOM) and proposals for setting up the Rapid Deployment Task Force attached to this newly raised command structure with the key base in Diego Garcia. Pakistan had been incorporated into the CENTCOM area of responsibility and given massive military and economic assistance from the US as a reward for its role. The developments discussed above such as agreements on ship visits, contract for the oil-tank farm on Trincomalee and the deal on a powerful VOA station between the US and Sri Lanka created a widespread impression that Sri Lanka was also being co-opted into the Western strategic structure for the region. There were reports of new strategic facilities and infrastructures in Sri Lanka being set up by the USA to take care of the contingencies, if and when created, as a result of the withdrawal or reduction of base facilities in the Philippines.

All this was sufficient to arouse India's concerns. More so because these developments were seen in the light of the high level US strategic visit to Sri Lanka (1983–84) including those of Defense Secretary Weinberger (1 October 1983) and special envoy General Vernon Walters (November 1983). Following these visits, in January 1984, a delegation from the US House of Representatives' Defense Appropriation Committee also visited Sri Lanka to discuss the possibilities of providing military assistance. In June 1984, President Jayewardene himself paid an official visit to the US where he explored the possibilities of moral and material support to his government. The positive shift in the US policy towards India did not concretise until towards the end of 1984, almost coinciding with the assassination of Mrs. Gandhi in October 1984. India's apprehensions about the possible US long and short-term strategic objectives in Sri Lanka were, therefore, not out of place.

It is obvious that there were mixed signals in the US policy. On the one hand was the felt need to develop military facilities in Sri Lanka and on the other, a growing desire to cultivate India without offending its regional sensitivities. This dilemma continued to dominate US policy even after the decision to build up a positive relationship with India. The consequent dilemma for India has been to harmonise its growing positive relations with the USA which include cooperation with its traditional fears in relation to the strategic presence of the extraregional powers in its neighbourhood. This is a dilemma likely to persist as it forms a part of India's perception of its legitimate aspirations and role in the South Asian region, underlined in the previous chapter.

India's concerns arising out of the involvement of Pakistan and China in Sri Lanka stood on a different footing, however. There is the perception of permanent adversarial relationship with these neighbours. The intensity of this perception was heightened during this period of ethnic conflict in Sri Lanka, because of the suspected Pakistani involvement first in the Punjab insurgency and then in the Kashmir problem. It is important to note that during his official visit to Pakistan in April 1985, President Jayewardene had even lent support to the Pakistani position on Kashmir.[22] Subsequently, he, along with other South Asian colleagues, had also endorsed a bilateral approach to the question of nuclear non-proliferation in South Asia, which besides being in line with the Western position on the issue, was also in conformity with the Pakistani position.[23]

As for China, the process of normalisation initiated by Mrs. Gandhi had still not gained momentum because of the absence of proper understanding on the border issue. During mid-1986 the border issue assumed importance as a result of skirmishes in India's Northeast sector, in the Sumdrongchu Valley region. The Chinese were also concerned about renewed disturbances in Tibet, and possible repercussions on relations with India. The growing Chinese desire to secure a naval reach to the Indian Ocean was also becoming a matter of deep concern to India. In January 1987 when Rajiv Gandhi was on a friendship visit to Vietnam, Chinese naval vessels were making port calls on India's neighbours, in Bangladesh, Pakistan and Sri Lanka. The Chinese were quite happy to denounce the 'regional bully' and affirm faith in Sri Lanka's unity and territorial integrity when President Jayewardene and other Sri Lankan dignitaries paid visits to their country. The supply of arms to Sri Lanka by China has already been noted earlier.

The Ideological Challenge

The ethnic violence in Sri Lanka posed a two-faceted challenge to the ideological coordinates of the Indian state. On the one hand was the complete breakdown of ethnic harmony in Sri Lanka as a result of the emergence of an assertive and intolerant Sinhala hegemonic state, which threatened to spill over and disrupt the internal Indian social and ideological balance, particularly in Tamil Nadu. On the other hand, was the antithesis of this Sinhala hegemonic state, in the form of demands for another sectarian and perhaps equally hegemonic state, the Tamil state, which in its potential was at least equally disruptive of the Indian state's ideological balance. India could choose neither.

There was a tendency in some quarters, particularly among the Sri Lankan Tamils fighting for a separate state, to compare their struggle with that of Bangladesh in order to invoke India's support, even to the extent of direct military intervention. We shall return to this question of direct military intervention subsequently; suffice it here to state that such a comparison with the Bangladesh situation was inept and untenable. From the ideological point of view of the Indian state, the struggle for Bangladesh was the struggle of secular Bengali forces against a state characterised by components both undemocratic (military dictatorship) and theological (the 'sole representative' of the Muslims of the Indian subcontinent and owing allegiance to Islamic religious tenets). In India, the breakdown of such a state was seen, as noted earlier, as a victory for the democratic and secular forces in the subcontinent. This meant, in a very significant way, the defeat of the ideological basis of Partition, since the Muslims of Pakistan had fallen apart and were searching for competing state manifestations. The linguistic identity of the newly emerging state of Bangladesh did reflect a sectarian connotation, but for India, this was not an antagonistic one. Because India, in its own structure of federalism, had long since recognized a political place for linguistic identity. Otherwise, the new Bangladeshi state swore by democratic and secular ideals.

None of this was the case with the professed Tamil state. Nor were there any other parallels between the Sri Lankan and the Pakistani states, not even with regard to the security threats posed. Pakistan, which had gone to war with India on three occasions, posed a persistent challenge. Against this, Sri Lanka was only aspiring to become a tool in the great-power strategic designs for the South Asian region. The Tamil leadership, and all those who suspected or expected Indian military intervene in Sri Lanka and help to create a state of sovereign Tamil Eelam, did not understand the nuances of ideological issues involved or the nature of the security concerns that had been aroused in India.

Consequent to the ideological challenge perceived, the way out for India lay in (a) folding back the adverse spillover on India, of the Sri Lankan ethnic violence, and, restoring, as far as possible, the democratic and secular attributes of the Sri Lankan state, through accommodation of legitimate Tamil aspirations for justice and equality; and (b) in diffusing the potential of a separate Tamil state by preserving the 'independence, unity and integrity' of Sri Lanka.[24] This Indian position was reiterated during the Sri Lankan crisis, in formal statements as well as informal discussions and negotiations with the contending Sri Lankan parties, the Sri Lankan government and the Tamil groups. Mrs. Gandhi in one of her early statements in the Indian Parliament immediately after the July 1983 outbreak of violence said:

We have made it clear . . . in every possible way that India does not pose any threat to Sri Lanka, nor do we want to interfere in their internal affairs . . . . We want the unity and national integrity of Sri Lanka to be preserved. At the same time . . . the developments in Sri Lanka affect us also. In this matter, India cannot be regarded as just another country. Sri Lanka and India are the two countries who are directly involved. Any extraneous involvement will complicate matters for both our countries.[25]

Nearly six years later, articulating India's internal concerns regarding the Sri Lankan situation that led to Indian involvement, the most controversial of the Indian High Commissioners in Sri Lanka during the period, J.N. Dixit, put the matter sharply and forthrightly:

So the first reason why we went into Sri Lanka was the interest to preserve our own unity; to ensure the success of a very difficult experiment that we have been carrying out ourselves. We claim to be the largest functioning democracy in the world. Despite what people like Galbraith, who say that India was the largest functioning anarchy in the world, we have succeeded in some measure. And what the Tamils in Sri Lanka were being compelled to follow in terms of their life, which would have affected our polity. Let us not forget that the first voice of

secessionism in the Indian Republic was raised in Tamil Nadu in
the mid-sixties. This was exactly the same principle of Tamil
ethnicity, Tamil language. So, in a manner, our interest in the
Tamil issue in Sri Lanka, Tamil aspirations in Sri Lanka, was
based on maintaining our own unity, our own integrity, our own
identity in the manner we have been trying to build our society
. . . .

Having said that, I would like to elaborate that we have to
respect the sentiments of the 50 million Tamil citizens of India.
They felt that if we did not rise in support of the Tamil cause in
Sri Lanka, we are not standing by our own Tamils and if that is
so, then in the Tamil psyche, Tamil subconscious the question
arose: is there any relevance or validity of our being part of a
large Indian political identity, if our very deeply felt sentiments
are not respected? So it was a compulsion, it was not a rationalized
motivation, but it was a compulsion which could not be avoided
by any elected government in this country.[26]

This statement clearly identifies the parameters within which the
Indian policy responded to the two ideological challenges posed by
developments in Sri Lanka. Before taking up the question of the
Indian policy, we shall need to have an idea of the nature of
ground realities that resulted from the Sri Lankan violence, on the
Indian side of the Palk Strait.

Firstly, there was the spillover of Sri Lankan violence in India.
As noted, the violence had seriously affected both Indian nationals
and estate Tamil workers of the Indian origin. The latter constitute
nearly one-third of the total Sri Lankan Tamil population and
about 5.6 per cent of the entire population of Sri Lanka. There
were another 0.6 million Tamils of Indian origin whose legal
status, as on July 1983, had to be decided. Of them 94,000 received
Sri Lankan citizenship in January 1986. The Jayewardene government sold this decision to the Buddhist clergy, by explaining that
this was to remove the possible pretext for India to invade Sri
Lanka.[27] Indian authorities in their briefs to the diplomatic community in New Delhi, while expressing their strong commitment to
non-interference in Sri Lanka's internal affairs, also underlined
their concern for the safety of the persons of Indian origin, including those that have been granted Indian citizenship but not yet
repatriated due to various administrative and rehabilitation hurdles.

Then there was the flow of Tamil refugees from Sri Lanka into the state of Tamil Nadu—officially acknowledged to be 150,000 by the end of 1987. There could, however, have been many others who remained unaccounted as they skipped the registration formalities and did not join the officially set up refugee camps. Maintaining the refugee camps with their regular inflow meant a great strain on the economic resources and administrative capabilities of the Tamil Nadu government. Even the law and order situation in the state was adversely affected as Tamil Nadu became a live playground, not only of the internecine conflicts and rivalries of the various Tamil militant groups but also of Indian and foreign intelligence agencies vying with each other to break into those militant groups. The Tamil Nadu underworld became active with the traffic of drugs and arms ferried across borders by Sri Lankan refugees spreading into the Bombay underworld.[28] One of the worst examples of Tamil Nadu's share of the internal disorder resulting from the spillover of the Sri Lankan crisis was the explosion at Meenambakam airport in Madras on 2 August 1984, with extensive damage to property and loss of life. The explosion was caused by detonation of two time-bombs hidden in Colombo-bound baggage. Of the 30 persons killed, 24 were Sri Lankans. The airport building also suffered heavy damage in its international section.[29]

India's Tamil social consituency had become activised. And as such, politics in Tamil Nadu could not remain unaffected, particularly because there has been a history of Tamil Nadu's cultural linkages with the Tamils of Sri Lanka. These linkages remained powerful, notwithstanding the contention of some observers that the two Tamil communities now constitute two distinct ethnic groups.[30] Here one may recall the examples of demonstrations and agitations in Tamil Nadu in support of Sri Lankan Tamils on developments adverse to the latter's interests in Sri Lanka, during 1958, 1961, 1977 and the early 1980s.

Political response to the Sri Lankan Tamil question also became inevitable in view of the Tamil militant groups' early linkage with Tamil Nadu politicians. With the competing groups of militants affiliating themselves with rival political parties in Tamil Nadu, the Sri Lankan issue necessarily became an important item on the political agenda in this sensitive Indian state. In this rival affiliation, while the TELO had become an ally of the DMK led by the then opposition leader M. Karunanidhi, the LTTE had chosen the then ruling party, the AIADMK, and the state Chief Minister M.G. Ramachandran (MGR) for patronage.[31] The general pattern of inter-party political rivalries on the Sri Lankan question suggested that while the party in power played a cautious role in projecting support for the Lankan Tamils, the opposition took a more hawkish and militant posture. The DMK's mobilisation of opposition opinion between 1983 and 1988, as against a cautious approach after coming to power in January 1989, may be mentioned here. The AIADMK on its part, while pledging support to the Sri Lankan Tamils, favoured a political and negotiated approach, avoiding any commitment to the demands for a separate, sovereign Tamil state. It confined its support for the Indian 'intervention' to a diplomatic intervention.[32] Once out of power, in 1989, the AIADMK hardened its stance on the Sri Lankan issue. It is also interesting to note that after MGR's/AIADMK's disenchantment with the LTTE and its supremo Prabhakaran, which started in late 1986, and exacerbated after the IPKF experience (1987–89), the AIADMK has lost much of its pre-1987 sympathy and support for the LTTE. No wonder then that the return of AIADMK to power under Jayalalitha's leadership in the aftermath of Rajiv Gandhi's assassination by suspected LTTE cadres led to Jayalalitha's strongest opposition to the LTTE. This question of the relationship between Sri Lankan Tamil militant groups and Tamil Nadu's political, socio-cultural and other vested interests is too complex to be even broadly discussed here. It deserves to be a subject of separate, full-length study.

The internationalisation of the Sri Lankan ethnic question in Tamil Nadu politics had a direct impact upon the policy which the central government in New Delhi was to adopt. There being a specific background to Tamil separatism in Tamil Nadu, led largely by the Dravida Kazhgam (DK) ideology and fanatic leadership, the centre had to be highly cautious in dealing with Tamil Nadu politics on this question, as was indicated in Dixit's statement cited earlier. It was also a question of managing the Indian federal structure so that states like Tamil Nadu would not be pushed to the point of alienation by setting up regional identities against national goals and priorities. Besides, the compulsions of power for the ruling party at the centre also dictated a careful nursing of its allies in Tamil Nadu, as the state accounted for 39 parliamentary seats.

Generally, however, the parties in power at the centre and the state have managed to harmonise their respective positions on sensitive regional issues, since both need each other in the interests of national unity and their own political survival. While the centre has tried to accommodate its ally in Tamil Nadu on the specificities of the regional issues, the ruling party in the state has also avoided embarrassing the centre in the conduct of its foreign policy. It has even cooperated with the centre in pursuing its foreign policy goals through the projection of regional issues. This could be seen in a reference to the USA, asking it to refrain from aiding the Sri Lankan government, in the resolution adopted by the Tamil Nadu Assembly on 25 October 1983.

In discussing the role of the Tamil social constituency and Tamil Nadu politics on the Indian approach towards the Sri Lankan ethnic issue, we should take note of the influence of Tamil militants and the separatist streak with powerful international, pan-Tamil connections. This streak cuts across the party lines in Tamil Nadu politics and emerges as an autonomous factor, not quite in control of either the state government of Tamil Nadu or the central government in New Delhi. The movement, its offshoots and the ideology represented by the DK symbolize this streak. Every now and then it is manifested in the defiant and agitational stances adopted against the centre on anti-Hindi issues (the latest outburst was in 1986) or by the DMK and the Kamaraj Congress leader Nedumaran to submit a petition signed by 10 million Tamils and lead a march of 50,000 Tamils to Colombo, on the Sri Lankan question. Similarly, the secret journeys of the DMK member of parliament to the Jaffna jungles to meet with the LTTE leader, reportedly against the wishes of his party leader M. Karunanidhi, may be recalled in this regard. This chauvinistic Tamil streak has constituted a major source of support to the LTTE in its uncompromising stance on the demand for a separate Tamil Eelam.[33]

It is hard to know the extent of external support for this separatist streak in the Indian Tamil movement, but we may safely assume that international forces looking for the rise of separatist forces in India and Sri Lanka might well have established links with this streak. It is interesting to note what a Sinhala nationalist and senior Sri Lankan civil servant indicated in this regard. Writing on the Sri Lankan crisis he said:

In addition to these daily broadcasts from Tamil Nadu, the terrorists also had a pirate TV station. They beamed various films on guerrilla warfare to viewers in Jaffna. These powerful transmitting stations could not have been set up without a large amount of money. Where did this money come from? Was a powerful foreign force manipulating the Sri Lankan terror dealers. What is the game of this outside agency? Is it the dominance of the Indian Ocean or the dismemberment of Sri Lanka and finally India?

On the other hand, how best can America which is also struggling for world supremacy destabilize India. The American Central Intelligence Agency must know that the Tamils in Tamil Nadu have for long been talking of seceding from India to form a Nation State of Tamils conjoining India and Sri Lanka. Is there a foreign hand placing a gun in the hand of the terrorist—a hand that may be even manipulating India. 'Awake ye Tamils; form a Nation State of your own in Sri Lanka'. The distant drumbeat of secession is being slowly thumped on South Indian drums. Are the drummers in the pay of a foreign power. Indeed, how best can India be destabilized other than by fanning the flames of dissension in Tamil Nadu and Punjab.[34]

It is in the light of such apprehensions that fragility of the Indian identity in the face of the challenge of Tamil separatism acquired a serious meaning in Indian perceptions. The autonomy of Tamil militant organisations, particularly the LTTE, from their Indian patrons and sources of support hinted at by other commentators also take on new meaning here.[35]

Thus we find that the most critical part of the spillover from Sri Lanka in India was the presence of Tamil militant groups. Besides the moderate and oldest Tamil United Liberation Front (TULF), there were various other militant groups. While the Sri Lankan National Intelligence Bureau put their number at 35, another source, closer to the Colombo establishment, claimed to have listed 42 of them.[36] Continuous infighting and rivalries among them, however, reduced their effective number to six or seven. Their mutual differences arose from their particular ideological orientations, personality factors and sources of support. They also differed in the specific aspects of their approach towards India, though each one of them appreciated the help received from India at one time or the other, and in one form or the other, and agreed that without India's active support, they would not manage to achieve their ultimate objectives.[37] It was only the PLOTE (Peoples Liberation Organisation of Tamil Eelam) first and the LTTE later who fell out completely with India. The PLOTE distanced itself from Indian connections by early 1985, when it struck a deal with the Sri Lankan government to collaborate in evolving a negotiated settlement of the problem as desired by Colombo. The PLOTE received both money and arms to liquidate any Tamil groups and their leaders who were pro-India and came in the way of Colombo's approach. This close identification with the Sri Lankan government, however, soon resulted in PLOTE's isolation from the Tamil movement. The LTTE always had sources of material support independent of India, as was claimed by leaders like Mahattaya (n. 35). They, however, also enjoyed support from diverse groups in India, like MGR and his government, DK and groups of smugglers. But by late 1986, the LTTE became disenchanted with the Tamil Nadu government and Chief Minister M.G. Ramachandran. This resulted in police searches on them in Madras, and the return of LTTE leader Prabhakaran to Jaffna. The LTTE, however, never completely severed its links with India. The degree of Indian support and encouragement to these Tamil groups had also changed from time to time, depending upon the scales of influence and power among them and the extent of their political support with the Indian policy-line on the Sri Lankan issue. Divisions among the militant groups were also intensified and their mutual relations vitiated by the role of Indian and external intelligence agencies that had penetrated them either to contain, make use of, or subvert the Tamil militancy.[38] The overall impact of this could be seen in the deteriorating law and order situation in Tamil Nadu and the intensification of party rivalries there.

India's Approach under Mrs. Gandhi

The foregoing survey of India's security and ideological concerns leads us to identify three principal objectives behind the Indian approach towards the Sri Lankan question. These were:

1. To reverse Sri Lanka's policy of cultivating extraregional and adversarial strategic interests perceived as a threat to India's immediate and long-term security interests.

2. To persuade the Sri Lankan government to seek a negotiated
   political solution of the ethnic crisis within the framework of
   unity and territorial integrity of Sri Lanka but based upon
   justice and equality for the Tamil minority.

3. As a part of point 2, India did not lend any legitimacy to the
   Sinhala hegemonic state in Sri Lanka and disapproved of
   Colombo seeking any military solution of the ethnic crisis
   through decimation or subjugation of the Tamil minority. In
   the same vein, India had no support for the Tamil militants'
   demand for the creation of a separate, sovereign Tamil
   Eelam.

In pursuing these objectives, there was no scope in Indian policy
for a direct military intervention in Sri Lanka, as mentioned earlier.
The possibility of such an intervention was indicated in many
statements by Sri Lankan policy-makers, both formally and informally, including at the highest levels by the President and the
Prime Minister, during Mrs. Gandhi's period.[39] Even some TULF
leaders believed that this was an option which Mrs. Gandhi was
keeping in reserve, should the Jayewardene government continue
with its violence against the Tamils and not respond to her call for
political negotiations with the Tamil leadership.[40] Subsequently,
some analysts of Indo-Sri Lankan relations of that period also
suggested that there were plans for an Indian military invasion of
Sri Lanka because the southern command of the Indian army was
alerted in July 1983 following the outbreak of ethnic violence. A
year later, in July 1984, an Indian publication *INDIA 2000* even
attributed, on the basis of allegedly leaked secret information, that
an airborne invasion was planned by a para-brigade located in
Agra.[41]

There is sufficient evidence to question these speculative con-
tentions. This was available in several of Mrs. Gandhi's assertions
that India posed no such threat to Sri Lanka; and in fact no such
adventure was undertaken by her, as the subsequent developments
underlined. Her principal policy adviser on Sri Lanka, G. Parthasarathy, confided (to his close Sri Lankan Tamil friend A.J. Wilson)
in October–November 1983, countering the hopes entertained by
the TULF leadership that 'Indian military intervention was more
or less impossible'.[42] This was indeed so, in view of the lack of
ideological rationale behind such an action, as we mentioned

earlier. Further, any such intervention would require adequate preparation of international political opinion, and this was nowhere evident in Indian diplomacy. Nor was the strategic environment of the region conducive to such an action in view of the situation created by the Soviet aggression in Afghanistan and the gradual consolidation of the US military presence in the Indian Ocean. We have already noted that the Indo–US relationship was then passing through a delicate phase of a gradually emerging desire for greater understanding and cooperation. Any precipitate military action by India in Sri Lanka would have seriously damaged the initiatives taken to improve the Indo-US relationship. Within India there was also the growing problem of Sikh insurgency in Punjab. Above all, there were no specific military targets to fight within Sri Lanka, except a war against the Sri Lankan armed forces to create an Eelam which was not in conformity with the Indian ideological position. All that which could have possibly been behind the alert and the so-called plans (if they were authentic) was to caution Colombo and to the Tamil militants that India would do all that was considered possible and desirable to advance their legitimate interests. It may, however, be possible now, since Indian policy has eventually failed in resolving the Sri Lankan problem, to discuss whether a better course to follow would have been for India to exercise this option and force the Sri Lankan government and the Tamil militants to sit down together to find out a political solution of the ethnic issue. We shall return to this question towards the conclusion of this study.

Mrs. Gandhi's policy operated at three principal levels. One was the bilateral level, that of diplomatic relations between India and Sri Lanka. Here, India expressed its concerns at the ethnic violence in Sri Lanka by sending her Foreign Minister within days, on 28 July, to make an on-the-spot assessment of the situation and discuss with the Sri Lankan authorities measures to protect the lives and property of Indian nationals and persons of Indian origin affected by the violence. This was followed by the visit of the Sri Lankan special envoy, brother of President Jayewardene, to India, where India offered its good offices for initiating direct talks between the Sri Lankan government and Tamil leadership, within the 'framework of a united Sri Lanka'.[43] Mrs. Gandhi nominated G. Parthasarathy for this purpose; he visited Sri Lanka on 25 August 1983 for preliminary talks with President Jayewardene.

Mrs. Gandhi also succeeded in persuading the Sri Lankan President and the TULF leadership to talk to each other without any pre-conditions to consider any other reasonable alternative to Eelam offered by the Sri Lankan side and to seek a solution to the Tamil problem within the framework of Sri Lanka's unity and territorial integrity.[44]

As a result of Parthasarathy's efforts, following his visit to Sri Lanka and President Jayewardene's visit to New Delhi on the occasion of the Commonwealth Summit (n. 44), a set of proposals, popularly known as Annexure 'C' emerged for consideration by the Tamils and the Sri Lankan government. These proposals aimed at devolution of power, with District Development Councils as the basic unit in a province. They envisaged merging the District Development Councils into Regional Councils. They also incor-porated provisions for the recognition of Tamil as a national language, proportional representation of ethnic minorities in the armed forces and police forces (in the regions) and asked for a national policy on land settlement which would not seek to alter the 'demographic balance' in ethnic terms. They further reiterated the objective of preserving Sri Lanka's 'unity and integrity'.[45] These proposals were put before the All Party Conference convened in Colombo in January 1984. Here we must say that this Conference worked in a manner that must be termed tardy and indeed devoid of seriousness and sincerity. All the same, the Indian side kept on pursuing this line, putting pressure even on the TULF leadership not to abandon the course of negotiations with Colombo.[46] The All Party Conference eventually ground to a halt in September 1984, a month before Mrs. Gandhi was assassinated; it was formally dis-solved in December 1984 without yielding any concrete results towards resolution of the crisis. Before looking into the causes of its failure, let us briefly go through the other two levels of Indian policy. Both these were secondary and aimed at reinforcing the bilateral level through which the Tamils and the Sri Lankan govern-ment were to be nudged towards arriving at a political understanding and solution. And also in the process, India's security interests were to be preserved.

The second level concerned dealing with Tamil militancy—mainly Sri Lankan but also Indian, in Tamil Nadu. This had two com-ponents: of expressing India's sympathies and support for the sufferings of the Sri Lankan Tamils, and second, of containing and

making use of the Tamil militant groups both in securing a reasonable political solution of the problem and preserving India's perceived interests. In every official statement and public speech
made by leaders up to the highest level, sympathies for Tamil
sufferings were expressed in a strong and unqualified manner. The
central government offices and the Congress (I) ruling party actively
joined the Tamil Nadu government's call for a general strike
organised to protest against Sri Lankan ethnic violence. India's
quiet diplomatic attempts to persuade the Sri Lankan President to
say a few words of sympathy for the damage to Tamil life and
property, however, did not succeed. Mrs. Gandhi also set up a Sri
Lankan Relief Fund Committee under her own guidance and with
a contribution of Rs. 1 crore (10 million) for providing humanitarian
relief, not only to the refugees coming to India, but also to the
Tamils affected by ethnic violence in Sri Lanka. Within days of the
violence, 'chartered civilian aircraft from India brought in supplies
of medicines and dry rations for the refugees. Chartered civilian
ships were made available for the transport of refugees from
Colombo to Jaffna'.[47]

The second component of dealing with the Tamil militant groups
was both sensitive and complicated, yet of greater significance for
the whole thrust of policy. We have noted earlier that the militancy
had to be contained in order to take the Sri Lankan Tamil movement away from the path of separatism and make it seek a political
and negotiated solution of the Tamil issue within the framework of
unity and territorial integrity of Sri Lanka. An equally powerful
reason for containing the Tamil militancy was the links that some
of the militant groups had established with international organisations—in Libya, Zimbabwe, Nicaragua, Syria, North Korea and
with the radical factions of PLO—as well as arms suppliers in
various Western countries. Initially India appeared acquiescent
towards such links as they kept India absolved of any charge of
involvement with the militants. Subsequently, however, such links
were seen as direct sources of danger to India, because the
militant groups were operating from Indian territory as a conduit
of foreign arms, money and influence. Further, links with third
parties weakened India's influence on the militant groups and
could consequently reduce its manoeuvrability in facilitating a
solution of Sri Lanka's ethnic crisis.[48] This could be done only by
winning their confidence and keeping them under Indian influence.

As noted earlier, the impression that India would not hesitate to intervene militarily in Sri Lanka to save the Tamils from ethnic violence, was created to make the militant groups rely more on India than any other source.

While Parthasarathy engaged the militant groups in political issues of finding an acceptable solution with the Sri Lankan government, the Research and Analysis Wing (RAW), the agency of the Government of India dealing with external intelligence, was asked to penetrate these groups to limit their militancy, erode their external linkages and bring them under Indian influence. In this task, the RAW secured the go-ahead signal to provide even military training, money and arms to the Sri Lankan Tamil militants as was subsequently exposed in several accounts.[49] An underlying consideration was also that in this way, the activities of the militants, while under India's control, could become an instrument in raising the costs of ethnic warfare for the Jayewardene government and thus in pressuring him, not only to desist from seeking a military solution to the ethnic crisis, but also to accommodate India's regional security concerns arising out of Sri Lanka's policy towards the West, China and Pakistan. This gave the RAW considerable leeway for operating with the militants, which eventually became a slippery zone of India's policy on the issue. The RAW lacked a political perspective on the policy; it also lacked accountability for many of its acts of omission and commission while supporting and monitoring the activities of militant groups or setting them up against each other.[50] As is well-known now, both the Indian policy and the Sri Lankan Tamil interests were to suffer because of disunity and internecine conflicts among the militant groups. And if the RAW's objective was to see that no single group should become dominant, then the emergence of the LTTE was a major failure. Subsequently came reports that some of the RAW agents involved with the Tamil militants were also in league with foreign intelligence agencies working on behalf of the Sri Lankan government in order to subvert the Tamil movement.[51] In 1989 the Indian Press ran several exposures regarding the indisciplined and scandalous life of RAW agents, which clearly suggest—with the advantage of hindsight—that the Agency was not yet mature to be assigned delicate operations. We shall come back to the failures of the RAW in the Sri Lankan situation.

The third level of Indian policy concerned international diplomacy. Through its various diplomatic missions throughout the world, particularly in the Western capitals, India drew the attention of host governments towards the atrocities being perpetrated by the Sri Lankan armed forces on the Tamils.[52] India also pleaded with the aid donors of Sri Lanka to exercise influence on Colombo for a political settlement of the ethnic issue. Following the employment of the Israeli intelligence agency (or agencies) by Sri Lanka and the establishment of an Israeli interest section in the US Embassy in Colombo, India activated its missions in the Arab capitals to put pressure on Sri Lanka. The issue of human rights violations in Sri Lanka against Tamils was raised in the UN General Assembly and the Human Rights Commission from 1983 onwards to focus attention on the plight of the Sri Lankan Tamils. India was, however, not in favour of any other government or international organisation getting directly involved in the Sri Lankan situation.[53]

Assessing the outcome of Indian policy during Mrs Gandhi's period in office, we find that except for persuading President Jayewardene to open the possibilities of negotiations with the Tamils, nothing much was achieved. There were several factors behind this unhappy outcome. To begin with, the period involved here was too short, only 16 months, after the July violence in Sri Lanka and up to Mrs Gandhi's assassination in October 1984. We are obviously not in a position to say what would have happened if Mrs Gandhi had been able to remain on the scene for a longer period. But perhaps, even then, not much could have been accomplished until international opinion, particularly in the West, turned in favour of a political solution of the Sri Lankan issue through Mrs Gandhi's good offices.

No less important than international opinion was the question of mutual trust and rapport between the regimes of Jayewardene and Mrs Gandhi. Each distrusted the other intensely, for personal as well as political reasons.[54] President Jayewardene distrusted even Mrs Gandhi's envoy G. Parthasarathy, not only for being Tamil and, therefore, suspected as partial to Tamils, but also because he was a tough negotiator.[55] Further, every time he was in Sri Lanka, he conveyed a message to the President from Mrs Gandhi that Mrs Bandaranaike's civic rights, taken away by the Jayewardene government should be restored. This plea was in fact issued in the interests of a broader national consensus on the Tamil issue, but was taken by the President as an expression of support for his political adversary.

It was because of this mutual distrust and suspicion that the proposals worked out by Parthasarathy in consultation with Jayewardene were not pursued seriously. The Lankan President even denied having had anything to do with these proposals. Some insiders allege that the concept of an All Party Conference and the way it was carried out were really aimed to kill the proposals listed in Annexure 'C'.[56] Even while the Annexure 'C' proposals were being formulated in November 1983, the Sri Lankan President announced that he did not 'propose to impose upon the people of this country a Jayewardene–Mrs Gandhi or a Jayewardene–Amrithalingam pact'. One week later, he also underlined the limited nature of the 'Indian good-offices'.[57] On 18 May 1984, talking to the delegates attending the All Party Conference in Colombo, Jayewardene emphasised the role of opportunities in education, employment and exercise of language rights rather than the devolution of power: this showed that he had not realised, or did not want to realise, the seriousness of the Tamil issue. From the very beginning Mrs Gandhi was sceptical to the advisability of putting the proposals to a body like the All Party Conference.[58] And after the first few sessions, it started becoming clear to the Indian side that the proposals so laboriously worked out, would not go very far. The Indian Foreign Minister Narasimha Rao blamed the Sri Lankan government on 9 May 1984, for 'failure to seize the opportunity provided', and said that he had little doubt that the 'APC may come to a grinding halt'.[59]

One possible factor behind the lack of will on the part of the Jayewardene government was deep divisions within his Cabinet on the nature and extent of accommodation to be shown towards Tamil demands and the good-offices' role of India. The President seemed neither willing nor capable of forcing decisions on his Cabinet. The July 1983 violence also showed that he had scarcely any control over the country's security apparatus or the members of his government who had actively participated in organizing and executing the July 1983 violence.[60] Nor was Mrs Gandhi's position very strong, as she was to face a general election by the end of 1984; due to internal developments in Punjab, she had become very controversial. But there could be no doubt as to her control over the government and also about her capacity to carry with her both the Sri Lankan Tamils and Tamil Nadu state on India's policy, particularly on the proposals of Annexure 'C'. As late as June 1984, after President Jayewardene's talks in New Delhi with

Mrs Gandhi, TULF leader Amrithalingam declared that he would abide by her decision.[61]

We have already discussed the distrust between the two regimes. On policy issues, this distrust was inherent in the strategies adopted by the two sides on key issues. Sri Lanka's strategy was to pretend to be talking, while in fact building its military capabilities to impose a solution on the Tamils from a position of strength. Thus, with the initial rush of supplies and training, and the increasing intensity of conflict in the North and the East, President Jaye-wardene's visits to the USA and the UK, as well as to China and other countries in mid–1984 (May–July), brought him back reassured, according to a first-hand impression,[62] though the two Western powers had refused to intervene directly to help his government. Around that time, a massive plan was speedily executed to settle Sinhalese in the Eastern Province and arm them so as to change the demographic composition of the area and thus deny a conti-guity (between North and East) to the Tamils in their claimed 'homeland'. This was carried out with the blessings of the President and with the direct involvement of his son, Ravi Jayewardene (who also happened to be Special Security Adviser to the President) and a senior minister, Gamini Dissanayake.[63]

As against this was India's double-track strategy of talking while pressurizing, through the arming of the Tamil militants. The extent of support to the militants varied with the intensity of the Sri Lankan army's operations and the failure on Colombo's part to advance the process of seeking a negotiated solution. This in turn was used as an argument by the Sri Lankan side, and rightly so, after the public exposure in March–April 1984 of the existence of training camps in Tamil Nadu for Sri Lankan militants. These exposures seriously eroded the credibility of India as an impartial mediator in the crisis and emboldened hardliners in the Sri Lankan establishment who wanted to put an end to Indian good-offices and instead give preference to a military solution. But it must also be said at this stage, that India was very sincere in pressing for a negotiated solution of the problem if the affected parties, i.e., the Tamils and the Sri Lankan government, could find one. It is common knowledge that India during this phase never let the militant leadership come to the forefront of the political process or gain the political clout and legitimacy they were to acquire sub-sequently. Even the training and arms provided to the militants were of a very moderate level, as explained by a US expert on Sri

Lanka in his Congressional testimony, prepared on the basis of extensive interviews in Sri Lanka, Madras and New Delhi.[64] Again, it was well-known that Mrs Gandhi had forced the TULF to scale down the ultimate Tamil demand for a separate state, to regional autonomy instead. If Colombo could clinch a satisfactory deal on this, India would have found it possible to sell the solution to the militant groups. Many keen observers of the Sri Lankan situation conceded that Mrs Gandhi's overall role was positive; further, that if a solution could be hammered out around the Annexure 'C' proposals, the problem could be solved with Colombo conceding much less than what it did subsequently, and lot of bloodshed could have been avoided.[65] This, however, was not to be. Mrs Gandhi was gunned down when her government was still in the midst of an uncertain policy towards Sri Lanka. Rajiv Gandhi received this uncertainty as a part of the political inheritance from his mother.

Rajiv Gandhi Phase: India Driven to Intervention

The basic objectives of Indian policy towards the Sri Lankan issue as formulated under Mrs Gandhi following the July 1983 violence remained valid for her successor, Rajiv Gandhi. There were, however, some tactical shifts that made a significant thrust on the manner of pursuing these objectives. Soon after coming to power, he conveyed to the Sri Lankan government his commitment to 'genuine and lasting' friendship between the two countries, indicating that his foreign policy style would be different from that of his mother.[66] This indication was sustained with the changes he brought about in his foreign policy team and a new emphasis on improving relations with India's immediate neighbours. The replacement of Parthasarathy with newly appointed Foreign Secretary Romesh Bhandari as chief negotiator was particularly welcomed in Colombo.[67]

In terms of the substance of policy, the most significant point in Rajiv Gandhi's departure from his mother's style of functioning was a softening in the attitude towards the Sri Lankan government and a consequent hardening of approach towards Tamil militant groups. This change was reflected in greater air and naval surveillance of the Palk Strait in cooperation with the Sri Lankan navy, to curb the militant traffic in arms and men. Indian customs became more strict in confiscating arms cargoes of Sri Lankan militants, and some cadres of militant groups were evacuated from their bases in Thanjavur.[68] Above all, India now conceded the priorities of the Sri Lankan government that any discussion of political issues should follow, rather than precede, an end to the violence. This in fact meant a total reversal of the priorities of Mrs Gandhi's regime. The official indication of this change became evident with the conclusion of Romesh Bhandari's first visit to Colombo in late March 1985.[69]

It was on this changed principle that Romesh Bhandari drew up a timetable for political negotiations between the Sri Lankan government and the Tamil militants (Appendix VIII E). This timetable was broadly endorsed at the Rajiv–Jayewardene summit meeting in New Delhi in the first week of June. Accordingly, a twelve week cease-fire was envisaged from 18 June during which first, the conflict between the Tamil and Sri Lankan forces was to be de-escalated (within three weeks), leading to an effective cease-fire (within five weeks) between them. This was, then, to pave the way for talks between the two sides in a third country, under India's good-offices. This initial timetable was, however, telescoped; after cease-fire, talks between Tamil militant groups and the Sri Lankan government took place in the Bhutanese capital of Thimphu on 13 July 1985.[70] By the time of the first meeting in Thimphu, Rajiv Gandhi made it clear that he did not favour the merging of the North and East provinces into one political unit, as was demanded by the Tamil organisations in fulfilment of their goal of a Tamil 'homeland'. He also underlined that there was no way in which India could endorse the demand that any proposed Tamil unit(s) be given more powers than those enjoyed by a state in the Indian federation.[71]

The change in the Rajiv government's position did not take matters very far. The Thimphu experiment collapsed, leading to a hardening of positions. The Sri Lankan delegation rejected the four 'cardinal principles'—Tamil nation, Tamil homeland, Tamil self-determination and fundamental rights of 'all Tamils in Ceylon'—advanced by the Tamil organizations for recognition. These organizations on their part rejected the proposals for provincial and District Councils tabled on behalf of the Sri Lankan government, as the latter would not recognize the above-mentioned 'cardinal' principles put forth by the Tamils.[72] In fact the collapse of the

Thimphu experiment could scarcely have come as a surprise to anyone. The two contending sides had joined the experiment for their own narrow reasons, not to make a success out of it. Each side wanted to demonstrate that it was the other party which did not mean business; each sought legitimacy for its respective reliance on military methods. As for the Sri Lankan side, it had, since the end of 1984, laid greater emphasis on military methods to combat the Tamil resistance. Now it was forced to have a show of political negotiations partly because of pressures arising out of the massacre of Sinhalese by the Tamil militants in Anuradhapur in mid-May 1985. There was also a need to rescue the regional image in South Asia after Sri Lanka's attempt to wreck the SAARC ministerial meeting in Thimphu in May 1985, on the rather flimsy grounds of taking exception to a statement by an Indian Minister of State on the Sri Lankan situation. After all, Rajiv Gandhi had by then established his regional credentials as one who was sincere in wishing to improve India's relations with its neighbours. No less important in Colombo's considerations was the pressure of the aid donors to initiate a political process. Otherwise there would be difficulties in continuing aid in view of pressures on human rights issues within these donor countries. The lack of seriousness on the part of the Sri Lankan government was evident in the composition of the delegation—lawyers who advanced legalistic arguments on issues that were essentially political.

The Tamil militants' search for legitimacy and recognition as those struggling for 'a nation' had become increasingly urgent. They found Thimphu an ideal occasion. That is why the LTTE leader Prabhakaran was persuaded to join, though reluctant on account of Indian officials' disrespect towards him and threats of putting curbs on the activities of his organization.[73] The militant organizations also got a chance to evolve a united stand, for the first time, on their cause and put it across forcefully in an international forum. Their statements tried to blame the Sri Lankan government squarely for the plight of the Tamils in a historical perspective.[74] Politically, the Tamil militant groups were pleased with the overall outcome of the Thimphu negotiations as they secured recognition (of the four groups—the LTTE, EPRLF, EROS and TELO) from the Sri Lankan and the Indian governments as legitimate parties with whom political settlement of the ethnic issue was to be worked out. Additionally, the Thimphu experiment also underlined the decline of the moderate TULF leadership's hitherto prominent role in representing the Tamil cause. This decline in the influence of the moderate TULF was a significant consequence of the shift in New Delhi's approach. Now the militant groups had graduated to the status of real parties in the conflict, instead of mere instruments of building pressure for a political settlement. It was for these tactical gains that the 'militants' had gone to Thimphu, and not to seek any meaningful negotiated settlement. That is also why they put forth propositions in the form of 'cardinal principles' which were non-negotiable and which the Tamil groups were certain would not be accepted by the Sri Lankan side.

Rajiv Gandhi government's initial hardline approach towards the Tamil militants and his desire to accommodate the Sri Lankan government raised serious questions about the handling of the Tamil militant component in India's Sri Lankan policy evolved during Mrs Gandhi's regime. It started a process of alienating at least some of the militant groups from Rajiv Gandhi's government. These groups in turn began exploring the possibilities of forging better ties with the opposition, both in Tamil Nadu and at the national level in India. They also started nursing and expanding their international contacts, a move that was eventually to make the LTTE independent of governmental (central and state) influence and provide it with a dominant position among all other militant groups. This is just what Mrs Gandhi's policy had so assiduously tried to avoid. This new stance of the LTTE initially included attempts to forge a greater unity with the other militant groups; as explained by its theoretician, Dr. Balasingham:

In general, a three-tiered 'unity move' can be observed: (a) within the expatriate Tamils, the moderates and the militants, the assorted guerrilla groups and the TULF and the in-between groups and personalities; (b) at the second level, there is a trend towards co-ordination, if not unity between political forces in Tamil Nadu led by the opposition DMK, but not excluding MGR's AIADMK; and (c) the attempted in-gathering of southern regional political forces in a broad move to confront the Delhi Centre on all the more crucial issues involving further Centre-State relations in India.[75]

The aim of this unity move and the changed strategy was also to step up military operations that had been quiet for some time, in

order to 'shift the balance of military power in our favour so that
we can negotiate with the government on our own terms'.[76] It
was clear, therefore, that an element of defiance vis-à-vis the
Indian government and the inclination to pursue an independent
line was developing among the militants. The main role in building
this defiance was played by the LTTE which, in April 1985, joined
the Eelam National Liberation Front (ENLF) set up by the EPRLF,
EROS and TELO (in April 1984), with some encouragement from
the Indian government. Perhaps the LTTE wanted to distance the
front from India's influence and eventually dominate it so as to
become the sole spokesman of the Tamil cause.[77] This also led to
the marginalization of the TULF so clearly evident during the
Thimphu talks. The ENLF, under LTTE influence, expressed its
apprehensions to the Indian Prime Minister that the proposals
being evolved by Romesh Bhandari and Hector Jayewardene following the Thimphu breakdown were not likely to satisfy Tamil
aspirations, and that such proposals should not be 'thrust down
their throats'.[78]

Here we can mention two factors that could have prompted the
Rajiv government to run the risk of attempting a solution of the Sri
Lankan issue even at the cost of alienating the militants. One was
the inherent impatience of the young leader with India's lingering
problems. Having secured an unprecedented electoral victory, he
was keen to resolve outstanding issues, not only with neighbours
but also within India, as in Assam and Punjab. Commentators in
India dubbed this as his 'pactomania'— to have quickly evolved
pacts for various problems. In the case of Sri Lanka, in view of his
mother's rapport with the militants and the re-election of his
party's ally, the AIADMK in Tamil Nadu, he thought that solving
the Lankan issue would not be difficult if only he could bring
Colombo around. There was a considerable amount of sincerity of
purpose in his thinking but his inexperience overlooked the
complexities of the issues and the actors involved.

The second important factor behind Rajiv's new approach was
the encouragement (and a certain amount of goading) provided by
the Western powers, the USA and the UK in particular. After
Rajiv and his government took office in December 1984, these
Western powers sought to bring New Delhi and Colombo together
to find a solution to the ethnic crisis. Both President Reagan and
his successor George Bush wrote and spoke to the two sides in this

regard as did many US officials at lower levels. In the case of
Britain, not only did Mrs Thatcher write to Rajiv Gandhi asking
him to work together with Jayewardene to find a solution to the Sri
Lankan ethnic problem, but even the British intelligence agency
MI6 was reported to have briefed the Sri Lankan government that
the new Indian government would be responsive to its concerns.[79]
However, we should note that while doing so, Britain was also
providing military assistance to Sri Lanka, almost on a grant
basis.[80] Subsequently there were reports of US arms merchants
being allowed private deals to sell arms to Sri Lanka on a cash-
and-carry basis, and of US mercenaries engaged in Sri Lanka's war
against the Tamils.[81] Might this perhaps have been due to the
Western perceptions of Rajiv Gandhi's government as soft and
accommodating unlike that of his mother?

Having realized that his responsive stance did not move Colombo
either to slow down military operations against Tamils or to show
reasonable accommodation towards Tamil demands even on the
lines of regional autonomy with adequate devolution of power,
towards the end of 1985, Rajiv reverted to the basic tenets of
Indira Gandhi's approach.[82] He asked Colombo to stop the killing
and come forward with concrete proposals to resolve the Tamil
problem.[83] This led to another round of negotiations, starting with
the visit of a high-level Indian delegation led by a Tamil Minister
of State in his Cabinet, P. Chidambaram, to Colombo in April/May
1986. The new proposals finalized in July were further improved
upon in November when an attempt was made to bring together
the Tamil leadership and President Jayewardene during the
Bangalore SAARC Summit. The LTTE leader Prabhakaran was
taken to Bangalore through the good offices of the Tamil Nadu
Chief Minister M.G. Ramachandran. This marked an implicit
recognition of the LTTE, even by Government of India, as the
dominant militant group. Prabhakaran however, refused to endorse
the proposals formulated.[84] This led to tensions between him and
MGR, which resulted in police raids in Tamil Nadu on LTTE
establishments and the return of Prabhakaran to Jaffna, as mentioned earlier. The Bangalore talks were pursued in Colombo
when the Indian Ministers of State of External Affairs and Home
Affairs, namely K. Natwar Singh and P. Chidambaram visited Sri
Lanka on 17 December 1986. As a result, a new set of proposals
emerged, known as 19 December proposals.[85] These proposals

meant a definite advance on the Annexure 'C' and the Thimphu stages as they tried to create a 'homeland' for the Tamils by slicing off the Sinhala-dominated Amparai district; they also sought a link-up between the North and the remaining parts of the East, i.e., Trincomalee and Batticaloa districts. The devolution of power to the Tamil areas envisaged under these proposals was not exactly the same as enjoyed by an Indian state in the federal set-up, but it was far ahead of what had been conceived so far. At a time when it was hoped that these proposals would eventually be accepted by the two sides, there emerged strong opposition to them in the Sri Lankan Cabinet, and President Jayewardene retracted from them in favour of a final and decisive military victory in North and East. The Tamil groups also had reservations on these proposals, but it was hoped that the Indian government would be able to secure their acceptance if only Colombo would come forward.[86]

The factors behind Jayewardene's reluctance were the same as those discussed in the previous section: namely, the inability of his weak government to face the pressure of Sinhala extremist opinion, and the weakness of a President to carry his hardliner Cabinet colleagues with him on an unpopular issue in a pre-election year. There was, of course, the enhanced confidence of the armed forces after having achieved organizational streamlining and an adequate supply of modern arms. The spurt in Sri Lanka's military operations added significantly to the legitimacy of the Tamil militants' reactive military operations, thus facilitating the further marginalization of the moderate Tamil leadership of TULF on the Tamil issue.

The resulting frustration led Rajiv Gandhi to suspend India's mediation efforts in early February 1987. On three previous occasions during 1986, he had decided to do so. Now India started thinking along different lines: direct intervention. Plans for such intervention were finalized by March 1987, and Colombo was warned repeatedly to desist from attempting military victory over Jaffna. However, when such warnings were not heeded, India intervened directly in June 1987, in the name of dropping relief supplies to beleaguered Jaffna: first through naval boats, and when these boats were stopped by the Sri Lankan Navy, then by air under the cover of Indian air force planes.[87] This intervention brought the Sri Lankan military operations in Jaffna to an end and led to the conclusion of the Indo-Sri Lanka Agreement nearly two months later.

Before we discuss the Indo-Sri Lanka Agreement and its antecedents in the next chapter, it may be pertinent to underline that the apparent success achieved by the Indian intervention was possible only in the context of a favourable international atmosphere at the time. Even more important is whether the intervention was motivated more by the alienation of India from both the contending parties on the key issues. The LTTE had also written to Rajiv Gandhi through M.G. Ramachandran in January 1987 that the 19 December proposals were not acceptable to them. Even as late as 27 March 1987, the LTTE and EROS refused to discuss the merits of these proposals with the two Ministers of State in Rajiv Gandhi's Cabinet and insisted only on the stoppage of Lankan military action.[88] Of course, as Sri Lankan military pressure mounted, the LTTE had to seek support from India. If this alienation of India from both the contending parties could be allowed to crystallise, then not only India's regional interests and status, but also the government's internal credibility would have suffered seriously for its incapacity to resolve the Tamil issue. In terms of the ideological challenge precipitated by the Sri Lankan crisis, it was clear that India could neither stand the victory of the Sinhala hegemonic state nor the establishment of a separate Tamil state. We may, therefore, argue that drastic Indian action along similar lines could have been predicted also if the military performance of the militant groups had been superior and the possibility of their victory to achieve Eelam could have been seen.

Notes to Chapter 3

1. T.D.S.A. Dissanayak, *The Agony of Sri Lanka*, Colombo, 1984; M.S. Venkatachalam, *Genocide in Sri Lanka*, Gian Publishing House: Delhi, 1987; S.J. Tambiah, *Sri Lanka: Ethnic Fratricide and the Dismantling of Democracy*, I.B. Tauris and Co.: London, 1986; L. Piyadasa, *Sri Lanka: The Holocaust and After*, Marram Books: London, 1984; Sri Lanka Coordination Centre, *Sri Lanka: Paradise in Ruins*, Kassel, 1983; Sinha Ratnatunga, *Politics of Terrorism: The Sri Lanka Experience*, International Fellowship for Social and Economic Development: Canberra, 1988; A.J. Wilson, *The Breakup of Sri Lanka—The Sinhalese-Tamil Conflict*, C. Hurst and Co.: London, 1988; Kumar Rupesinghe, 'Notes on Ethnic Violence in Sri Lanka', *PRIO Working Paper*, 7/86, Oslo.
2. Dissanayak, *The Agony of Sri Lanka*, p. 83.
3. Ratantunga, *Politics of Terrorism*, p. 21.

4. *Ibid.*, p. 165.
5. *The Times of India*, 3 August 1983; also *The Hindu*, 6 August 1983.
6. There is often some confusion as to whether it was Shin Bet (internal security service) or Mossad (anti-terrorist, external intelligence unit) of Israel that was involved in Sri Lanka by the Jayewardene government to fight Tamils. One Israeli source claims that both were present. Statements of Sri Lankan ministers are cited in support of the contention. Jane Hunter, 'Trouble-Shooter Walters Paves the Way for Mossad', *Israeli Foreign Affairs*, May 1986. As reproduced in *Lanka Guardian*, Colombo, 1986. Also see the recently published account of a former Mossad agent, Victor Ostrovsky, *By Way of Deception*, Bloomsbury Publishing Ltd.: New York, 1990.
7. Ratantunga, *Politics of Terrorism*, p. 164.
8. *Ibid.*, p. 161.
9. *Pakistan Times*, 5 April 1985; *Dawn*, 5 April 1985.
10. For details of military supplies and training support mobilised by Sri Lanka see Murlidharan, 'Armed Forces of Sri Lanka', M.Phil. dissertation, JNU, New Delhi, 1990; also Ratantunga, *Politics of Terrorism*; Wilson, *The Breakup of Sri Lanka*. An interesting report in *Asia Week*, 17 May 1987, indicated the variety and range of the supply sources. Tamil Information Centre, *Militarization in Sri Lanka*, n. d.
11. Ratantunga, *Politics of Terrorism*, p. 153; also Wilson, *The Breakup of Sri Lanka*, p. 201; J.N. Dixit's address to USI in India in March 1989, subsequently published in *Lanka Guardian* in January 1990, vol. 12, nos. 17 and 18; Praful Bidwai, 'Capitulation to US–Israeli Designs: The Bhandari Line on Sri Lanka', in *The Times of India*, 19 and 20 May 1987; 'Trinco, Wisky and Women: Price of Liberty', *Lanka Guardian*, vol. 4, no. 14, 1981; The visits of the US ships began in 1981. For a Sri Lankan political group's reaction, see a statement issued by Reggie Siriwardene, Ainsley Samarjiwa and Kumar Rupesinghe on behalf of Movement for the Defence of Democratic Rights, on 24 April 1981, Colombo.
12. On the oil tank-farm deal for Trincomalee, see V.P. Vaidik, *Ethnic Crisis in Sri Lanka—India's Options*, National: New Delhi, 1986; S.D. Muni, 'Sri Lanka's Strategic Connections', *Patriot*, 7 June 1984; Sreedhar, 'More than a Business Deal', *The Week*, 10–16 June 1984.
13. Jasjit Singh, 'The US Transmitters in Sri Lanka', *The Times of India*, 6 March 1985; Dixit in *USI Journal*; James Manor and Gerald Segal, 'Causes of Conflict, Sri Lankan and Indian Ocean Strategy', *Asian Survey*, vol. XXV, no. 12, December 1985; 'Spies in Sri Lanka', *Forum*, vol. 1, no. 15, 15 February 1985.
14. *The Times of India*, 9 April 1984.
15. See Felix R.D. Bandaranaike's statements in Sri Lankan Parliament on 4 November 1960; *Parliament Debates*, vol. 41, cols. 564; and 30 August 1963, *House of Representatives Debate*, vol. 53, cols. 1011–15.
16. These aspects have been discussed in my forthcoming study on *US Approach to South Asia: Reagan Years;* also see Maya Chadda, 'India and the United States: Why Detente Won't Happen', *Asian Survey*, vol. 26, no. 10, October 1986; Dilip Mukerjee, 'U.S. Weaponry for India', *Asian Survey*, vol. 27, no. 6, June 1987.
17. This was evident in most of the official discussions between the US and Sri

Lankan authorities. The transcript of discussions between Congressman Solarz and President Jayewardene along with his ministerial colleagues clearly brought out that point. *Transcript of These Discussions* (mimeo).

18. Malinga H. Gunaratna, *For a Sovereign State*, Sarvodaya Publishing House: Colombo, 1988, p. 283.

19. Discussions with Solarz, *Transcript*.

20. Interviews with members of the Tamil Association in the US in late 1986 and early 1987. I also personally witnessed the Congressional Committee hearings on Sri Lanka in early 1987 where the impact of the Tamil lobby on the statements made by the State Department officials could be seen.

The role of Tamil lobby on the US policy towards Sri Lanka was acknowledged by the Lankan Finance Minister Ronnie De Mel in a statement in Parliament saying that it was because of this lobby that the US aid was not coming in, *The Hindu*, 6 June 1986.

21. A brief discussion of the role of such expatriate groups appears in S.U. Kodikara, 'Internationalization of Sri Lanka's Ethnic Conflict', a seminar paper presented at the International Centre for Ethnic Studies, workshop in Colombo, 2–4 August 1989.

22. Public Opinion Trends (POT) on Pakistan, April 1985; also cited in *Lanka Guardian* (Colombo), 1 May 1985.

23. This was evident during the first SAARC Summit in Dhaka, in December 1985; texts of the speeches of South Asian leaders at this summit (mimeo). The author had covered this summit for an Indian weekly.

24. Mrs. Gandhi's statement in August 1984 cited in *Saturday Review*, Colombo, 3 November 1984.

25. *Lok Sabha Debates*, vol. 38, 1983, col. 418; also see Mrs. Gandhi's statement in Lok Sabha on 12 August 1983, *The Times of India*, 13 August 1983. Many such statements by her and other ministers were made during the period under discussion.

26. Dixit's USI address.

27. Wilson, *The Breakup of Sri Lanka*, p. 182.

28. See for instance reports in *Indian Express*, 17 January 1986; *Illustrated Weekly of India*, February 1986; *Sunday*, 31 July to 6 August 1988; and S.H. Venkataramani's reports in *India Today*, vol. 10, no. 6, pp. 76–80 and no. 18, p. 98; Tamil militant groups, particularly LTTE's connections with Tamil Nadu based smugglers and drug dealers have been hinted at by many press reports in Indian media. For instance see, *The Hindustan Times*, 12 August 1990.

29. For the details of this incident, see *The Hindu*, 3 and 4 August 1984. The Sri Lankan version of the incident is given in Ratantunga, *Politics of Terrorism*, pp. 100–2.

30. N.M.M. I. Hussain, 'The Role of Tamil Nadu in Indo-Sri Lanka Relations', BMICH Seminar Paper, January 1990; also Suryanarayana, *The Peace Trap*, p. 3.

31. *Ibid*.

32. A. Shivrajha, 'Indo-Sri Lanka Relations and Sri Lanka's Ethnic Crisis: The Ethnic Factor', A Seminar Paper submitted at the University of Colombo, 1987. Also see a Resolution adopted by the Tamil Nadu State Assembly on 25 October 1983.

33. Prof. K. Shivathamby of Jaffna University articulated this point at the BMICH seminar in Colombo, January 1990.

34. Gunaratna, *For A Sovereign State*, the paras cited here are on pp. 206 and 279 respectively.

35. Tom Mark, 'Counter-Insurgency in Sri Lanka; Asia's Dirty Little War' in *Soldiers of Fortune*, Febraury 1987, pp. 47 and 82; also Suryanarayana, *The Peace Trap*, p. 17. The LTTE leader Mahatya, in an interview published in *The Island* (Colombo) of 25 October 1987 disclosed that India never trained the LTTE.

36. For the Sri Lankan intelligence sources number, Ratantunga, *Politics of Terrorism*, pp. 243–57. The higher number was estimated by Tom Mark in his *Soldiers of Fortune*, February 1987, p. 41. These numbers, however, appear to be highly exaggerated.

37. Rajan Hoole and others, *The Broken Palmyra* (vol. I, Historical Background), Harvy Mudd College Press: California, 1988, Chapters 11 and 14; Dagmar Hellmann–Rajanayagam, 'The Tamil Tigers in Northern Sri Lanka: Origins, Factions, Programmes' in *Internationales Asien Forum*, vol. 17, no. 1/2, 1986, pp. 63–85; also her 'The Tamil Militants: Before the Accord and After', *Pacific Affairs*, vol. 61, no. 4, pp. 601–19; D.B.S.S Jayaraj, *An Overview of the Tamil Secessionist Movement of Sri Lanka 1976–1985*, International Centre of Ethnic Studies: Colombo, 1986.

38. RAW's task appeared to contain the Tamil militancy within Indian borders and thus make it amenable to India's overall policy towards Sri Lanka. Wilson, *The Breakup of Sri Lanka*, p. 204; also K. Manoharan in the Indian monthly *Seminar* (no. 324, August 1986) wrote that Mrs. Gandhi was inclined to use the militants 'to harass Colombo only to the extent of forcing it to reach an agreement acceptable to New Delhi'. Subsequently the DMK leader M. Karunanidhi in his Party Conference accused the Centre of being 'responsible at one stage for disunity among Tamil militant groups in Sri Lanka', *The Times of India*, 3 July 1989.

The other intelligence agencies—and it is difficult to say how many of them were involved besides Mossad and Shin Bet—penetrated the militant groups to subvert them in the interest of the Sri Lankan government. In this, groups having linkages with PLO, like PLOTE became main targets to serve Israel's own interests as well. Subsequently, as noted earlier, PLOTE established contacts with the Sri Lankan government.

39. See for instance, *Daily News* (Colombo), 8 March 1984; *Sun* (Colombo), 26 May 1984.

40. Wilson, *The Breakup of Sri Lanka*, p. 203.

41. Victor Gunewardena, 'Impact of Internal Ethnic Conflicts on the Region', a paper presented at the workshop on Indian Ocean as a Zone of Peace, in Dhaka, November 1985, published by International Peace Academy: New York, and also Ratantunga, *Politics of Terrorism*, p. 107.

42. Wilson, *The Breakup of Sri Lanka*, p. 203.

43. *The Times of India*, 9 and 10 August 1983; *The Hindustan Times*, 10 August 1983.

44. Amrithalingam disclosed this subsequently in an interview to N. Ram of *The Hindu*, *Frontline*, 23 March to 5 April 1985; Mrs. Gandhi met President Jayewardene in New Delhi twice when the latter had come to attend the

Commonwealth Heads Conference in November 1983. As a result of these talks, President Jayewardene agreed to hold talks with the TULF leadership without insisting on them to give up the demand of Eelam, *The Hindu*, 1 December 1983.

45. Text of Annexure 'C', is included as Appendix in this study.

46. A chronology of developments related to India's involvement in the Sri Lankan crisis is attached to this study as an Appendix. For some details of Indo-Sri Lanka interaction on evolving proposals for political solution of the crisis, see Vaidik, *Ethnic Crisis in Sri Lanka*; Stanley Jayaweera, 'The Ethnic Crisis and the Indo-Sri Lankan Peace Process, July 1983–July 1987', a seminar paper presented at Bandaranaike Centre for International Studies, Colombo, January 1990; (unsigned) 'The Sri Lankan Conflict: An Indian Perception', *Lanka Guardian*, vol. 10, no. 485, issues of 1 and 15 June 1987; Gurbachan Singh, 'The Ethnic Problem in Sri Lanka and the Indian Attempt at Mediation', in Satish Kumar (ed.), *Yearbook on India's Foreign Policy 1984–85*, Sage: New Delhi, 1987; P.S. Ghosh, *Cooperation and Conflict in South Asia*, Manohar: New Delhi, 1989, chapter VI.

47. Dissanayak, *The Agony of Sri Lanka*, p. 94. Contrast this with the supplies of military equipment sent from Pakistan around the same time in a chartered civilian aircraft through special intervention of President Zia; Ratantunga, *Politics of Terrorism*, p. 161.

48. Marshal Singer, 'Ethnic Crisis: Delhi's Changing Role' in *Lanka Guardian*, 15 November 1985. Elaborating this in an informal chat with me in Washington in 1987, he thought that Mrs. Gandhi's help to Tamil groups was meant to make the source of their support less radical. Perhaps she got indications to do so from the US. Help to Tamil militants was one of the issues she was believed to have posed to the Libyan leader Gaddafi when she met him during an offcial visit to Libya in 1984. Also see Singer's Testimony before the Congressional Sub-Committee on Asia and Pacific on 12 March 1987.

49. *India Today* was the first to report on the RAW's dealings with the Tamil militants and the training camps and military assistance provided to them in India. See report by Shekhar Gupta, 'Sri Lanka Rebels: An Ominous Presence in Tamil Nadu', *India Today*, 31 March 1984, pp. 84–94. Also see, *Sunday Times*, 4 April 1984; *The Island*, 25 May 1984; *South*, March 1985.

50. Wilson, *The Breakup of Sri Lanka*, p. 204.

51. The case of one RAW officer, K.V. Unnikrishnan assigned to the militant groups came to light later. This officer kept a liaison with the CIA and Sri Lankan agencies, and was later penalised for this. Story in *India Today*, as cited in *Forum* (Colombo), 15 October 1987.

52. K.M. de Silva, 'Indo-Sri Lanka Relations 1975–1989: A study in the Internationalization of Ethnic Conflict'; a paper submitted at an ICES International Workshop: Colombo (mimeo), August 1989, p. 25. Also Vaidik, *Ethnic Crisis in Sri Lanka*; Gurbachan Singh, 'Ethnic Problem in Sri Lanka'.

53. Wilson, *The Breakup of Sri Lanka*, cites examples of India dissuading Commonwealth and Canadian teams from visiting Sri Lanka for study of the situation there, p. 202.

54. De Silva, 'Indo-Sri Lanka Relations', p. 62; also Ratantunga. *Politics of Terrorism*, pp. 127–30.

55. Wilson, *The Breakup of Sri Lanka*, p. 178.
56. *Ibid.*
57. *The Times of India*, 18 November 1983; *The Hindu*, 18 and 24 November 1983.
58. Ratantunga, *Politics of Terrorism*, p. 124.
59. *The Times of India*, 10 May 1984.
60. Rupesinghe, 'Ethnic Violence'. Even those who were close to President Jaye-wardene admit that his was a very weak Presidency and government after 1983. De Silva, 'Indo-Sri Lanka Relations'. One Sri Lankan source went to the extent of saying that the President's telephones were being tapped and he could not do anything though he knew about this. Ratantunga, *Politics of Terrorism*, p. 135.
61. *The Hindu*, 27 June 1984.
62. Wilson, *The Breakup of Sri Lanka*, p. 177.
63. Gunaratna, *For a Sovereign State*, *op. cit.*
64. Marshal R. Singer's Congressional Testimony on 12 March 1987.
65. Wilson, *The Breakup of Sri Lanka*; De Silva, 'Indo-Sri Lanka Relations'; Jayawaeera, 'The Ethnic Crisis'.
66. *The Times of India*, and *The Hindu*, 17 November 1984.
67. It was reported that the Sri Lankan government openly expressed its displeasure with Rajiv Gandhi on the continuation of Parthasarathy as his chief negotiator on Sri Lanka and wanted him to be replaced, *Lanka Guardian*, 1 May 1985. Also Ratantunga, *Politics of Terrorism*, p. 141.
68. *Lanka Guardian*, 1 May 1985; *India Today*, 30 April 1985.
69. Official statement issued in Colombo at the conclusion of Bhandari's visit. Though the propriety of the statement was questioned in New Delhi, its con-tents were not disputed. The militants became very unhappy with the statement.
70. N. Satyendra, 'The Thimphu Negotiations: The Basic Documents', a paper presented at an International Conference on Tamil National Struggle and the Indo-Sri Lanka Peace Accord, London, 30 April–1 May 1988. The proceedings of this conference have been published. See N. Seevaratnam, *The Tamil National Question and Indo-Sri Lanka Accord*, Konark: New Delhi, 1989.
71. *The Times of India*, 16 July 1985; *Tamil Times*, 15 July 1985.
72. Text of these principles put forth by the Tamil organisations in Satyendra, 'The Thimphu Negotiations'. H.W. Jayawardene's proposals presented on behalf of the Sri Lankan government are found in *Sun*, 21 August 1985.
73. The LTTE leader Prabhakaran's initial displeasure for being forced to talk to the Sri Lankan government directly was clear. He even whispered to some of his colleagues that he would teach India a lesson for this whenever he got a chance. He indeed did so as the later developments showed. Interview with some of the Tamil representatives participating in Thimphu talks.
74. Satyendra, 'The Thimphu Negotiations'.
75. Balasingham's interview in *Financial Times* (London), as cited in *Lanka Guardian*, 1 May 1985, p. 5.
76. *Ibid.*, p. 1.
77. On this point, discussions with L. Ketheshwaran in Oslo (March 1990), the EPRLF ideologue, were useful.
78. *The Times of India*, 17 and 18 September 1985. Also *The Hindu* of these dates.
79. Ratantunga, *Politics of Terrorism*, pp. 166–67; Gunaratne, *For A Sovereign State*, p. 284; Wilson, *The Breakup of Sri Lanka*, p. 200.

80. Ratnatunga, *Politics of Terrorism*, p. 165.
81. *Ibid.*, p. 166. The question of American mercenaries fighting on the Sri Lankan army's side was brought to the notice of the State Department by India's Foreign Secretary, A.P. Venkateswaran in Washington in January 1987. The Americans did not deny it and promised to look into the matter, *Asian Recorder*, 5–11 March 1987. On US help for Sri Lanka to fight Tamil militants, also see *Indian Express*, 11 October 1986.
82. President Jayewardene asserted in September 1985 that the Tamil problem has to be tackled militarily. Again in December the same year, in interview to an Indian fortnightly, he confessed that his agreeing for cease-fire in June (which led to the Thimphu talks) was only an attempt to buy time. 'Now we are acquiring arms and getting our soldiers trained. We are getting ready for a decisive military action', he said. *India Today*, 15 December 1985; also of 31 August and 15 September 1985, on this point.
83. *The Hindu*, 22 and 23 March 1986.
84. For details see *Frontline*, 29 November–12 December 1986.
85. For details of the evolution of these proposals through discussions between the two sides, see Ratantunga, *Politics of Terrorism*; Wilson, *The Breakup of Sri Lanka*; Jayaweera, 'The Ethnic Crisis', also Gurbachan Singh, 'The Ethnic Problem'; Ghosh, *Cooperation and Conflict*, pp. 154–213; 'Sri Lankan Conflict: An Indian Perception', in *Lanka Guardian*, vol. 10, no. 485, 1 and 15 June 1987.
86. This was made clear to Jayewardene in a message by India, *Indian Express*, 7 and 8 February 1987; *The Times of India*, 7 and 8 February 1987.
    On 24 March 1987, Rajiv Gandhi in a Press Conference said that if the Tamil militants did not accept the 19 December 1986 proposals then India would have to take direct action.
87. Details of intervention have been widely discussed in the Indian, Sri Lankan and international press during those days. See for instance, *Frontline*, 30 May–12 June and 13–28 June 1987.
88. *The Times of India*, 28 March 1987 and the paper submitted at the International Conference in London in April/May by the LTTE mentioned that Prabhakaran had disapproved of the 19 December proposals in a letter written to M.G. Ramachandran for Rajiv Gandhi's notice.

4

The Indo-Sri Lanka Agreement of July 1987

Immediate Antecedents

India's intervention to deliver food and relief supplies to the beleaguered Tamils in the North and East, first through relief boats under Indian Red Cross Flag (Operation Poomalai) and then through air force planes (code-named 'Operation Eagle') was the most decisive factor in putting a halt to the intense conflict that had raged between the Sri Lankan armed forces and the Tamil militants since the end of 1986. This led to the creation of conditions that enabled the conclusion of the July 1987 Agreement between India and Sri Lanka, for resolving the Island's ethnic crisis.

As noted in the previous chapter, this intervention was motivated by India's sense of alienation from both the contending parties, neither of whom was taking India's mediatory role with deference or seriousness. The Sri Lankan Minister of National Security, Lalit Athulathmudali, termed India's intervention as an act of 'desperation'.[1] Through this act, India sought to re-enter the Sri Lankan situation from which it had withdrawn its good offices in February 1987. However, the circumstances of the intervention were such that now India was re-entering more as a major participant than as a mediator or an arbiter—a situation not seen either as an ideal one or the one which India would have preferred. That being so, it may be pertinent to ask if the direct intervention method was the only way to re-enter the Sri Lankan scene and shift the conflict away from a military approach to resolution through political negotiations.

In view of the military situation prevailing before the Indian move, it was clear that there could be one of the three outcomes:

(*a*) a military victory for Colombo, (*b*) a military victory for the militants, or (*c*) continuation of an indecisive conflict resulting into war fatigue and eventual stalemate that could then force the two sides or, to seek a non-military i.e. political solution. The first two outcomes would be unacceptable to India, being incompatible with India's perceived interests as discussed in the previous chapter. But by the end of May, and with the fall of Vadamarachhi from under the militants' control to the Sri Lankan army, the first outcome appeared within reach. There were, however, flaws in this assumption, as we shall see later. Now concretization of the first outcome could be militarily thwarted only by creating conditions for the third course to prevail, if India were to avoid direct intervention. The route for this lay through escalation of material support to the militant groups, particularly the LTTE. Let us look more closely at the feasibility of this scenario.

The militant groups, including the LTTE, were already being supported by India, more actively since the intensification of the conflict and the breakdown of the mediation process towards late 1986. Before the launching of the Vadamarachhi operations (Operation 'Liberation') by the Sri Lankan army, Tamil militants had also been given training in the use of anti-aircraft weapons (SAM-7), although the weapons were not provided to the militants as they already had some units with them procured from sources other than India.[2] These weapons were even used to down a Sri Lankan air force plane during the Vadamarachhi operations.[3] To thwart the advance of the Sri Lankan army, more such weapons would have to be provided to the militants; this, however, would have changed the nature of the conflict altogether, with India's deepening military involvement. The implications of introducing anti-aircraft weapons in the Afghanistan war by the USA were there for any one to see. The flow of such weapons through India to Tamil militants could also have implications for India's internal security in view of the raging insurgency in Punjab. It was therefore not an easy option for India to raise the level of sophistication of the militants' weaponry. Here we may recall that India always considered it in its interests to limit the level of Tamil militancy, rather than to expand and strengthen the same. Besides the weapons, India already had a commitment to assist the militants through other material means. Notable in this regard was the open grant of Rs. 4 crores (40 million rupees) to the two dominant militant groups, the LTTE and the EROS, by Tamil Nadu Chief Minister M.G. Ramachandran, on the day Colombo announced the launching of 'Operation Liberation'. Soon after announcing this grant, the Chief Minister met Prime Minister Rajiv Gandhi and declared that more such grants would be offered by him.[4] Subsequent developments suggest that these were signals meant to deter the Sri Lankan government from proceeding with its military operations, and also improve the political equation between India and the dominant militant group, rather than as steps to enhance India's back-up for the militants to escalate the conflict.

As already noted, it was indeed a problem for India to contain the militancy of the LTTE, which had acquired considerable autonomy vis-à-vis India on approaches to solving the ethnic problem. The LTTE even had direct, informal political talks with the Sri Lankan government delegation in December 1986; when these talks failed, the LTTE justified them in the name of 'impressing upon the Sri Lankan government' that the LTTE did not favour any attempt to 'undercut or circumvent India's role'.[5] And yet, as we noted in the previous chapter, in January 1987 the LTTE leader Prabhakaran had refused to accept the 19 December proposals that India had endorsed. Again, when the heat of military operations was strong on the LTTE and the Indian ministers approached them on 27 March 1987 for their response to political proposals, the LTTE refused to discuss the issue and pleaded instead that India ensure cessation of hostilities first. It was such tactics that had also considerably hampered Indian efforts, in pinning Colombo down to a specific package of political proposals. In order to contain the LTTE's militancy and goad it back on the political road, India found it necessary, even in the thick of the military conflict during early 1987, to resort to augmenting the strength of other militant groups.[6] A policy decision to escalate the conflict by raising the level of military support to the militant groups would have amounted to raising the militancy and autonomy of the LTTE, since it was the dominant and best organised fighting group. Such conflict escalation would also have meant conceding primacy to military means over the political approach. The LTTE also insisted on remaining the dominant force and was unwilling to coordinate its efforts with other militant groups, even when under increasing military pressure from the Sri Lankan forces.

What, however, if India had ignored or subordinated all these negative implications, in the interests of blunting the Sri Lankan military offensive through the militant groups? There was no certainty that even enhanced help to the militants would quickly have brought about a stalemate in the fighting between Sri Lankan forces and the Tamil militants, to enable the political process to be restarted. Obviously not, viewed against the background of the determined Sri Lankan moves and the success that they achieved in Vadamarachhi. And above all, time was of critical importance, because a lingering conflict with growing direct Indian military involvement would have brought into play various other complicating factors. One might argue that the battle of Jaffna would have proved far more expensive and bitter for the Sri Lankan forces, but there were sections in the Sri Lankan security establishment, both political and military, who wanted to proceed unhampered. This could be subsequently discerned from reports in late June 1987 quoting Sri Lankan Defence officials and Joint Operations Commander Cyril Ranatunga that 'Operation Liberation' had merely been suspended (following the Indian relief intervention) and that 'with the help of aerial cover, the army could take Jaffna within 36 hours'.[7] It is possible to say now, and on the basis of the evidence that surfaced afterwards (to be discussed below) that these claims were exaggerated and were only tactical ploys, meant either to secure a better political bargain with India and the militants, or to placate those sections of army's rank and file who were pressing for sustained assault. In fact Indian newspapers did report aerial bombings of Jaffna later in mid-July, when the final touches were being put on terms of the Agreement.[8]

Further, any open Indian military involvement on the side of the Tamil groups would have given greater legitimacy to Sri Lankan efforts to mobilize international support—which was in any case a significant factor behind the offensive of early 1987. We noted in the previous chapter that the UK had already allowed military supplies to Sri Lanka. Also from the USA supplies and mercenaries were coming to Sri Lanka to augment its military efforts, notwithstanding the official US position of non-involvement.[9] Chinese and Pakistani assistance was flowing uninterrupted. Pakistan, as we shall see below, was willing to help Sri Lanka strengthen its air defence capabilities, following the Indian intervention. It may be recalled here that India's Minister of State for External Affairs, Natwar Singh, reacted to the declaration of 'Operation Liberation'

by the Sri Lankan government and Jayewardene's call for 'fight to
the finish . . the fight will go on until they win or we win' by
saying that the new mood in Colombo 'signifies the increasing
influence of external elements inimical to security, stability and
peace in our region'.[10]

Thus the option of India escalating the intensity of war by
enhancing its open and material support to the LTTE and other
militant groups was not only fraught with adverse and undesirable
consequences for its immediate and long-term interests, it also
seemed uncertain whether it could blunt the Sri Lankan offensive
immediately. As against this, what appeared far more viable and
politically less expensive was a direct intervention in the name of
humanitarian assistance. This would come at a time when the
LTTE already stood demoralised, if not humiliated, and could
have decisive impact on the Sri Lankan offensive. Moreover, such
intervention would also convincingly demonstrate that there were
limits to the militants' capacity to confront the Sri Lankan state
militarily, and that only India had the will and the capability to
protect and promote legitimate Tamil interests.

One last point about the style and speed of India's intervention.
Some critics in India have argued that after the Sri Lankan navy
had stopped supply boats under the Indian Red Cross banner on 2 and
3 June, India should have waited to see the Sri Lankan response
towards their promised discussion of modalities for allowing the
relief supplies. As this procedure was not followed, the Indian
action was described as being unplanned and hasty.[11] This does not
seem a fair assessment, however. It appears that the Indian plans
were ready sometime in February or March 1987; in the course of
those two months, several messages were sent to the Sri Lankan
President, asking him to desist from the collision course. In March,
Sri Lankan opposition leader Mrs. Bandaranaike had also claimed
that she had averted a 'possible Indian invasion' of Sri Lanka by
her last-minute talk with Prime Minister Rajiv Gandhi.[12] Then in
mid-March, the Indian Prime Minister sent a special message
through a soft-spoken senior Congress leader, Dinesh Singh, who
in his talks with President Jayewardene even suggested the possibility of sending an Indian relief mission to Jaffna. To all this,
Colombo paid no heed.

Then, once the Indian decision had been taken to bring the
fighting to a halt through relief intervention, with what some

commentators described as 'bread bombs', it was not possible or advisable to delay its execution. In fact the relief boats should be seen as an essential part of air intrusion: the former was intended to justify the latter. If the Sri Lankan government had accepted the former mission and brought the fighting in Jaffna to a halt, the latter would not have been needed. But the chain of action could not have been broken except at the cost of defeating the very purpose of the mission. Time was indeed a crucial factor, and any delay would have only facilitated the military objectives of the Sri Lankan army.

Implications of the Intervention

India's relief-supplies intervention in Jaffna had four critical implications for all the principal actors involved. These implications in effect were to lead developments towards the conclusion of the July 1987 Agreement.

The *first* of these implications was that it decisively put the military solution as a non-option for both the Tamil militants and the Sri Lankan government. As mentioned, the LTTE being the strongest and the cleverest among the militant groups, wanted a political solution only on its terms and without any compromise. In order to achieve such a solution, short of a separate Eelam, it would bargain only from a position of strength acquired by military means. The Sri Lankan military offensive of the first four months of 1987, put tremendous pressure on the LTTE and other militant groups; at length they agreed, in their talks with the Indian ministers (Chidambaram and Natwar Singh) on 27 March 1987, to talk to the Sri Lankan government, but that was perhaps only a tactical ploy to gain time. The main condition was the cessation of Sri Lankan military operations. When the Sri Lankan government announced unilateral cease-fire, not in response to Rajiv Gandhi's message of 2 April 1987 on behalf of the militants but instead on 11 April 1987, after making a dent into the militants' stronghold, the militants refused to abide by it. Even the success of the Vada-marachhi Operations by the Sri Lankan forces, which had brought the militants to the verge of retreat to India so as to strengthen their resistance, did not really force them to foresake their reliance on military methods. What they wanted was greater military support from India to regroup and re-equip themselves, possibly with anti-aircraft guns—which, as we have discussed above, was not possible from India's point of view. The Indian intervention, which apparently was aimed to force moderation on the Sri Lankan side, was also clearly intended to convey to the Tamil militants that India was their only saviour, and that India preferred to get involved directly rather than further augment the militants' military capabilities.

We noted earlier that the Indian intervention was intended to put a halt to Sri Lanka's military approach to resolving the ethnic crisis by military means. True, there were inherent constraints in this approach and no easy victories were possible for the Sri Lankan side. The Indian government, through its various strong messages and public statements, had warned the Sri Lankan government to desist from a military course. In a strong statement, Rajiv Gandhi said on 28 May that 'the time to desist from a military occupation of Jaffna is now. Later may be too late.'[13] But this had little impact. The Indian High Commissioner in Colombo, J.N. Dixit, had also directly cautioned the Sri Lankan National Security Minister that India would not let them take Jaffna by military means.[14] In addition, there were tactical considerations as well. The Sri Lankan army camp in Jaffna Fort was heavily dependent upon supplies from the town, which was controlled by the militants. During the unilateral cease-fire announced by the Sri Lankan President on 11 April, the militants had mined the areas around Jaffna Fort heavily, thereby incapacitating movements of the troops stationed there. A direct attack on Jaffna was thus considered a risky proposition in military terms. That is why it was not attempted after February 1987 despite repeated directions to that effect by the President.[15] That was perhaps why it was decided to avoid Jaffna and take over Vadamarachhi instead, so as to demoralise the militants, since Vadamarachhi was the home-town of LTTE leader Prabhakaran.[16]

Yet another military limitation on the Sri Lankan forces was the hesitation to use the air force after one of the planes had been shot down in the Vadamarachhi operations. The air force had refused to undertake similar sorties unless provided with proper cover, since the militants had demonstrated the use of anti-aircraft missiles.[17] Thus it was quite natural for the Sri Lankan forces to assume that India might have totally committed itself to the militants' side. If so, it was militarily not advisable, in the absence of air superiority, to continue with operations for a 'fight to the finish' to which the President had committed himself in public. It was at this stage that there appeared differences between the assessment of senior commanders on the one hand, and lower officers and the rank and file on the other. While the latter wanted to proceed, the former had reservations and were cautious.[18] Thus the fate of military operations as the ultimate instrument for victory appeared doubtful in the objective calculations of the Sri Lankan armed forces themselves.

This being so, one may ask what was the rationale of India intervening to make the Sri Lankan armed forces desist from a military approach? Perhaps the Indian side did not have any proper assessment of the Sri Lankan strategy, another instance of the failure of intelligence on India's part. Otherwise, the Indian side would not have appeared so seriously disturbed about the prospects of Sri Lankan forces moving in to take over Jaffna. Further, the Sri Lankan government, after the Vadamarachhi operations, had taken steps to overcome the air-handicap by approaching friendly countries like Pakistan, as will be noted below. As such, even while knowing the constraints of the Sri Lankan armed forces on the air front, India could not ignore the thrust of their operations. The dropping of relief supplies under the escort of Indian air force fighter planes (Mirage 2000) was meant as a clear signal that the ethnic war in Sri Lanka would not be allowed to proceed unhindered and that no air cover or air defence for Sri Lankan forces from an adversary of India would be tolerated.

The *second* implication of the Indian intervention was that it exposed the limits of external support to Sri Lanka, particularly in the event of a determined Indian action. The most disturbing realization to the Sri Lankan government was the lack of support from the USA, to whom Colombo had consistently been presenting the possibility of Indian intervention. The USA had rejected such possibilities; indeed, even the simulated war game carried out by the National War College of the National Defense University in Washington DC had concluded that there was no likelihood of an Indian invasion of Sri Lanka on the ethnic question. In all fairness, such a US assessment was not so far off the mark, in view of the reasons we have presented earlier that India could not afford to take military action to create a separate Tamil Eelam. The Indian intervention, when it did come, was considered a small tactical move intended to moderate the ongoing conflict, and not as the first step towards a major offensive or a part of a bigger 'gameplan' aimed at military take-over of Sri Lanka. That is why the US reaction, while expressing mildest of 'regrets', almost endorsed the Indian action. The official US spokesman called for understanding between India and Sri Lanka to channel humanitarian assistance to the Jaffna Tamils. Rejecting the Sri Lankan claim of violation of sovereignty, the US statement said that such argument cuts both ways, as 'sending refugees was also a violation of sovereignty'.[19] Similarly, influential Congressman Stephen Solarz also defended the Indian action by saying that it was 'better to drop supplies than bombs', though he wished that Indian relief operation had been carried out in cooperation with the government of Sri Lanka.[20] It was, however, very hard for Sri Lanka to be confronted with such responses which made President Jayewardene feel that Sri Lanka had been abandoned by the US to the regional domination of India and that 'America will not lift a finger to help me without asking India.'[21]

Responses from other major Western powers were also moderate and more for the record rather than of any substantial help. This Sri Lanka realised when it tried to explore the possibility of raising the issue at the United Nations including in the Security Council. Sri Lanka was deterred because besides the lukewarm attitude of the great powers, there was also the possibility that India or some other country might raise the counter-questions of Colombo's treatment of the Tamil minority and its serious and continued violations of Human Rights, thereby diverting the focus of international debate from Indian intervention to the internal affairs of Sri Lanka. This could put the governmental conduct in the wrong light.

The most encouraging support for Colombo in the wake of Indian intervention came from Pakistan. We have earlier noted the substantial amount of military assistance, in terms of arms and training, provided by Pakistan to Sri Lanka. The visit of Sri Lankan Prime Minister Premadasa to Pakistan in March 1987 prior to launching 'Operation Liberation' had opened up prospects for expanding the scope of Pakistani assistance.[22] Pakistan strongly condemned the Indian action and offered all possible help in defence of Sri Lankan sovereignty. This led to the reports that Sri Lanka was considering a Pakistani offer to strengthen its air-defence system. This question was dealt with in detail when Sri Lankan Ministers of Education, Ranil Wikramsinghe, and of National Security, Lalit Athulathmudali, paid official visits to Pakistan in June (between 11 and 17) 1987. Their discussions with Pakistani authorities revealed the logistic and political constraints inherent in Pakistan coming out openly in support of Sri Lanka, particularly in the face of a determined Indian move to oppose Sri Lankan military action against Tamils. The idea of a Friendship Treaty between the two countries was explored to give greater legitimacy to Pakistani help, but it was subsequently dropped. However, General Zia assured the Sri Lankan ministers that 'Pakistan will welcome all opportunities for further consolidating the existing friendly relations'. When considered objectively, open Pakistani military involvement would have amounted to Sri Lanka joining the Pakistani effort of building up an anti-Indian strategic alliance in South Asia, and this Sri Lanka could not afford in the long run. Nor was Pakistan, located at such a distance geographically, in any position to sustain the inherent obligations of such an alliance in worst-case situations, and fight a war with India in Sri Lanka. There was also the domestic, political compulsion in Pakistan of not appearing to be a military ally of Sri Lanka who, in turn, was depending upon Israel for intelligence and military support. Accordingly, British reports of some 300 Pakistani troops helping the Sri Lankan army to fight Tamil militants were strongly denied. But Pakistan's help to Sri Lanka continued in various forms. Relief material and other goods were openly supplied to help Colombo meet its requirements.

Sri Lanka's South Asian neighbours stood by the Island republic on the question of the Indian intervention. They all disapproved of India's action—Pakistan, Bangladesh and Nepal more strongly than Bhutan and the Maldives. However, Sri Lanka was dissuaded from boycotting the SAARC Foreign Ministers' meeting scheduled for 17 June 1987 in New Delhi, not only by its South Asian colleagues but also by China.[34] Sri Lanka's efforts to get a SAARC resolution censuring India for intervention were blocked by India with reference to the SAARC Charter, which does not allow bilateral disputes to be raised in the regional forum.

Unlike Pakistan, China was correct but cautious in its reaction to the Indian intervention. Without naming India, China voiced strong disapproval of the bullying actions of big powers and 'interference in internal affairs' of nations.[25] Sri Lanka's Education Minister Ranil Wikramasinghe followed up the Chinese response with an official visit in the first half of June 1987, to explore the prospects of increased concrete help. In his report submitted to the government in Colombo after his return, Wikramasinghe describing the Chinese attitude as positive, said that China was to send a defence team to inquire into Sri Lanka's requirements of military equipment. He also disclosed that the Chinese favoured a political solution to the ethnic problem.[26] Notwithstanding this cautious advice from Beijing, Sri Lanka's Buddhist monks submitted petitions to the Sri Lankan government and the Chinese Embassy in Colombo, seeking China's military help in the fight against the Tamils as the latter were backed by India.[27] Therefore, though positive, the Chinese assistance was not adequate or effective in countering the immediate challenge posed by India. This limitation was reflected in Jayewardene's evaluation of China's support: 'They were good friends and gave us military equipments, guns etc. at very reasonable terms. But what could they do? I could not ask them to start a border war in the north to keep the Indians busy. Even if I had, I doubt if they would have done it.'[28]

Thus the Indian intervention brought to Sri Lanka the shocking realisation of how isolated it was in the international community on the ethnic issue. It seems that Indian diplomacy had done some spadework in this regard before the 'air-drop' [action] was actually undertaken. Without external political support and expeditious military aid, Sri Lanka could not carry on with its military campaign to resolve the Tamil question, notwithstanding various bold pronouncements, made by political leadership in Colombo and outside to keep face.

To the question of international support was linked the issue of economic resources. The Sri Lankan economy was surviving on a hand-to-mouth basis, and that too because of Western assistance. These Western donors had repeatedly stressed the need for a political and negotiated resolution of the ethnic crisis. Sri Lankan moves to impose a fuel and economic embargo on the Tamil areas and the launching of a military offensive did not fit into this framework. The heavy import of arms was also draining precious foreign exchange reserves, which prompted the World Bank to put pressure on Sri Lanka to devalue its rupee in order to improve the precarious balance of payments position. The 1987 budget projected a doubling of defence outlays from Rs. 991 million to Rs. 1,854 million, which meant an urgent need for additional resources.[29] Later, statistics disclosed by the World Bank and Sri Lanka's Peoples Bank Review clearly underlined that economic pressures were an important factor in forcing the Jayewardene government to decide in favour of bringing the Island's ethnic war to a close.[30]

The *third* implication of the Indian intervention was in terms of Sri Lanka's internal politics and the resulting pressures on the Jayewardene regime. Two aspects of this deserve notice here. One was that the internal weaknesses and contradictions of the regime were intensified as a consequence of the blow given to the regime's legitimacy by the act of intervention. The second was that it aroused Sinhalese national sensitivities by bringing their worst fears of an India–Tamil coalition nearer to reality. The myths thus became real life-size monsters. As a result, in some Sinhala chauvinist sections, anti-Indian feeling appeared to be replacing anti-Tamil sentiments. These aspects were politically exploited by Jayewardene's opponents, both within and outside the government. The positions taken by Prime Minister Premadasa on the one hand and the opposition parties like the SLFP and the JVP on the other may be recalled here. While the opposition parties led by the SLFP launched an anti-government stir, the JVP organised student strikes and armed attacks on government establishments, creating a situation of utter chaos in the country. It was under such circumstances that divisions within the armed forces became critical. Jayewardene subsequently admitted that he 'feared there might be a coup attempt with military assistance.'[31]

The *fourth* implication of the intervention concerned India itself. As mentioned earlier, the Indian action created compulsions for India to become a direct party in the Sri Lankan conflict. There is evidence to suggest that as early as on 10 August 1986, President Jayewardene proposed that India should sign an Agreement with his government, undertaking to help in establishing peace in the Island, curbing what he called 'terrorism', and also in holding elections for the proposed Provincial Councils for the Tamil areas. At that time, this was not acceptable to India as it was still hopeful that an Agreement could be reached between the Tamils and the Sri Lankan government. Jayewardene's objective behind that proposal then was also to secure India's support for resolving the ethnic conflict according to his judgement. After the intervention,

Sri Lanka's Foreign Minister made a statement on 12 June 1987 saying that by intervention, India had lost its credibility as a mediator, but now it had a moral obligation to solve the ethnic issue, through having involved itself directly.

India was still hesitant to enter into a bilateral deal with the government of Sri Lanka on behalf of the Tamils. This was indicated in its attempts to bring the Tamil militants around to some settlement; as late as 29 June, Prime Minister Gandhi expressed the opinion that the Indian 'air-drop' had not in any way impeded India's 'efforts to help the Lankan government and Tamils find a peaceful solution to the ethnic crisis'.[32] During July, India made serious attempts to bring the militants into the ambit of the proposed Agreement. The LTTE leadership was approached in Jaffna by an Indian delegation headed by Hardeep Puri of the Indian High Commission on 21 July 1987. He met with Prabhakaran again on 23 July. Earlier, talks with Tamil militant leaders had been conducted through the Tamil Nadu Chief Minister. Lastly, even as Rajiv Gandhi was leaving for Colombo to sign the Agreement, Prabhakaran was taken into confidence in New Delhi between 27 and 29 July 1987, and given reassurance on all his concerns. Admitting this, an LTTE document listed the assurances provided by the Indian Prime Minister as:

The problems and limitations of the proposed framework would be resolved to the satisfaction of the Tamil people. The LTTE would be given its due recognition. An interim government would be formed with LTTE playing a dominant role.

A Tamil regional police service would be set up under the interim government.

The Government of India would pay compensation to the LTTE for the maintenance of the organisation following the decision of the LTTE to withdraw the system of taxation in Jaffna. This relief fund would be paid on monthly basis until the formation of the interim government.

The Government of India also promised funds to the interim government for the rehabilitation and resettlement of Tamil refugees.

The Indian Peace Keeping Force would take over the responsibility of protecting the Tamils in the North and East until an adequate Tamil security system is created.[33]

These wide-ranging demands were conceded to get the LTTE's approval of the Agreement and, if possible, to get their participation in the signing of the Agreement. This, unfortunately, was not forthcoming.

This LTTE inflexibility and the Indian keenness for LTTE's endorsement made redundant the much softer and moderate position taken by the other militant groups and the TULF on the terms of the Agreement. One wonders if, on being approached by India, the other militant groups would have agreed to become a party to the Agreement without the LTTE and if they had done so, what would have been the fate of the Agreement? At any rate, the often-heard objections to the Agreement, that the Tamil militants were not consulted and that attempts to get them to endorse or become a party to the Agreement were not made, are not quite tenable in the light of these facts. What may be accepted here is that in the perceptions of the Tamil groups, particularly the LTTE, the level and the mode of consultations were not satisfactory. They viewed these Indian approaches to them as a process of *information*, not consultation. In their perception, consultations meant complete accommodation of their viewpoints—which, it seems, was practically impossible. Subsequent developments have also clearly underlined that the LTTE was not prepared to compromise whatsoever on their position on issues like their complete domination over Tamil areas and at least notional acceptence of the right to self-determination on the Eelam issue. No government in Colombo could accept that. Against this background, it appears that Prabhakaran's agreement with Rajiv Gandhi on 28–29 July 1987, was the LTTE's tactical ploy to wriggle out of a difficult situation.

While India's failure to secure participation of the Tamil militant organisation in the proposed Agreement was the most powerful factor in its decision to become a direct party itself, an equally important consideration behind this Indian decision was the influence of the USA. Officials made it very clear throughout the phase of intense fighting between Tamil militants and Sri Lankan armed forces (between December 1986 and June 1987) that they were in close touch with the Indian and Sri Lankan governments on the ethnic issue.[34] This close contact included US expectations that India would come to play a major role in the Sri Lankan peace process. The US Ambassador in Sri Lanka confided to an Indian journalist during these very tense months that he hoped India would 'accept a great part of the responsibility, not so much financial as politico-administrative, for the reconstruction of Sri Lanka when the time came for that after the ending of the civil strife.'[35] That the US President was the first to endorse the Agreement and compliment the Indian Prime Minister and the Sri Lankan President through a letter reaching them in Colombo within hours of the signing of the Agreement clearly indicated that the USA had had prior information about the Agreement and that it had been following the details closely. After the signing of the Agreement, a senior State Department official dealing with South Asian affairs stated in his Congressional testimony in August 1987: 'A key new factor in this Agreement has been the involvement of the Government of India in a very positive and complicated way in bringing this Agreement about.' Such US interest in the Indo-Sri Lanka Agreement led some of its critics to describe the Agreement as America's 'Camp David in South Asia'.[36]

Thus we find that the implications of Indian intervention were such that they created compulsions for both the Indian and the Sri Lankan governments not only to bring the ethnic conflict to an end through a bilateral agreement but also compromise so as to accommodate each other's concerns and sensitivities. In consequence, the intervention created compulsions for the Tamil militant groups also to see their interests protected within the parameters of the compromise entered into between New Delhi and Colombo.

The Agreement: A Sincere Compromise

As noted in the previous chapter, one of India's principal concerns in Sri Lanka was to ensure the protection and promotion of legitimate Tamil interests within the framework of a united Sri Lanka. This found adequate reflection in the Agreement of 29 July 1987. The Agreement began by reiterating the 'unity, sovereignty and territorial integrity of Sri Lanka', acknowledging it as a 'multi-ethnic and a multi-lingual plural society consisting, inter alia, of

Sinhalese, Tamils, Muslims (Moors) and Burgers.' (paras 1.1 and 1.2) A major Tamil demand was to be recognized as a separate nationality having a distinct cultural and linguistic identity, and a homeland with the right to self-determination. This demand could be met only partially and with qualifications, if it were to be adjusted with the conflicting thrust of Sri Lankan unity and territorial integrity.

Accordingly, the Tamil language was recognised as one of the official languages of Sri Lanka (para 2.18). This meant a shift in favour of the Tamils from the days of the 'Sinhala only' policy. However, the relevant provision in the Agreement was so formulated as to give a pride of place to the Sinhala language. It said: 'The official language of Sri Lanka shall be Sinhala. Tamil and English will also be official languages.' Such a formulation was obviously attempted to placate extremist Sinhala sentiments and must have been made on the insistence of the Jayewardene government.[37] The equal status of Tamil so defined can always be skewed, in implementation, to the disadvantage of Tamils depending upon the intentions of the regime in power in Colombo. Language has been a sensitive issue in the Tamil movement because of discriminatory educational policies thus far, so such formulations were bound to arouse Tamil suspicions.

The Agreement also conceded the idea of a Tamil homeland. It was recognised that: 'the Northern and the Eastern Provinces have been areas of historical habitation of Sri Lankan Tamil-speaking peoples, who have at all times hitherto lived together in this territory with other ethnic groups' (para 1.4). In this formulation, the insertion of 'other ethnic groups' meant that also the Sinhalese had a right to live there. This, by implication, not only justified the land settlement and colonization policies pursued by the Sri Lankan government in settling the Sinhalese in these areas since 1948 up to 1986, but also gave legitimacy to such policies in the future. The question of 'homeland' had additional provisions as well, relating to the merger of the Northern and the Eastern provinces into one administrative unit (para 2.1). But this merger was to be subjected to a referendum, the details of which were specified in the Agreement. One aspect of these details was that the President 'at his discretion' could postpone the referendum (para 2.3). Thus he could delay the holding of referendum for as long as possible to suit the political climate, either for the Tamils or for the Sinhalese, as he wished. However the Tamils had serious doubts whether that would be done to favour them since the President, even before the signing of the Agreement, had declared that this merger of the Northern and the Eastern provinces was a temporary measure, and that he himself would campaign against its being made permanent, at the time of holding the referendum. In his calculations, he cited a detailed logic of numbers, including the anti-merger Sinhalese and Tamils living outside the Eastern Province. Addressing the UNP's National Executive Committee on 25 July 1987 Jayewardene said:

> . . . only one thing has to be considered. That is a temporary merger of the North and East. A referendum will be held before the end of next year, on a date to be decided by the President to allow the people of the East to decide whether they are in favour or not of this merger. The decision will be by a simple majority vote . . . . In the Eastern Province with Amparai included, there are 33 per cent Muslims, 27 per cent Sinhalese and the balance 40 per cent Tamils. Of these Tamils there are two categories. More than half of them are Batticaloa Tamils and the rest are Jaffna Tamils. Then if the Jaffna Tamils form 20 per cent, then I think that 80 per cent are opposed to such a merger. Mr. Dewanayagam and Mr. Majeed have told me so. Then if the referendum is held by the central government and the approval of those who return to the East is sought, I think a majority will oppose it. Then the merger will be over. What do we gain by this temporary merger, the President asked and said that it would see the end of the terrorist movement.[38]

The numbers and percentages cited here were, however, not quite correct; it seems that Jayewardene was in a way trying to secure the UNP's endorsement of the question of merger by alleviating their fears. It is important to reiterate here that by adding the adjective 'temporary' and using the logic of ethnic numbers, Jayewardene wanted the provision of merger to be accepted by the Sinhalese. Further, by accepting the provision of the postponement, perhaps on India's suggestion, he wanted to make the provision of 'referendum' acceptable to the Tamils. An important aspect of the proposed referendum was that the Agreement provided that 'All

persons who have been displaced due to ethnic violence or other
reasons, will have the right to vote in such a referendum' (para
2.4). Such persons obviously included both Tamils as well as
Sinhalese.

What the Sri Lankan government was doing here was to take
with one hand what it had to give away with the other. The
question of merger was tackled differently in the 19 December
proposals, by slicing off the Sinhala-dominated Amparai district
and treating the remainder of the North-East as Tamil homeland.
This was not acceptable to hardliners in the Jayewardene regime—
maybe including himself. New Sinhalese settlements had been
brought about in Trincomalee district during 1984–86 in order to
break the demographic continuity of the claimed Tamil homeland.
We have mentioned this aspect in the previous chapter.[39] The Sri
Lankan position on this issue even with regard to the 19 December
proposals was that such reorganisation would have to be submitted
to a referendum before implementing it. Under the July Agreement, the referendum was to follow the merger, not precede it. As
such, this was an advance favouring the Tamils, and had been
secured by India's pleading with Jayewardene that the Sri Lankan
army's offensive, after the 19 December proposals were finalised,
had changed the situation and inflicted disadvantages on the Tamils.[40]
India had to press hard for this, because as late as 17–18 July,
Jayewardene held that a referendum would have to precede any
political solution.[41] Considerable efforts, including the unusual
exercise of the Indian High Commissioner explaining issues to the
Sri Lankan Cabinet, had to be made to bring Colombo round to
this point; that is how so many conditions and qualifications came
to be inserted to dilute the issue.[42] In fact, in Colombo's perception,
the idea of a Tamil nationality had never been accepted, as asserted
by Athulathmudali.[43] And seen from the Tamil viewpoint, the
Agreement's provisions on the 'homeland' aspect were unsatisfactory because of all the toning-down done by the Sri Lankan
government.[44]

There was of course, no acceptance of the right to self-determination, in conformity with the recognition of Sri Lanka's unity
and integrity. Nor was the right to self-determination in keeping
with the federal framework of polity adopted in India. India's
endorsement of this principle could open a Pandora's box in view

of the fragile Indian identity and potentially strong separatist forces, not only in Tamil Nadu but also in Kashmir, Punjab and the North-East.

Equally important to the question of recognition of the Tamil 'homeland' was the issue of devolution of power to Tamils within the Sri Lankan unitary constitution. As a minimum, Tamils were expecting to secure as much power as enjoyed by an Indian state in the federal polity. This emanated from Rajiv Gandhi's various assurances to the Tamil groups, as noted in the previous chapter. Thus, there was a conceptual difficulty in incorporating the idea of regional autonomy within a federal structure, into the devolution of power within the framework of a unitary polity. In addition came Tamil apprehensions, upon their recent historical experiences of the Sinhala-dominated Sri Lankan government. The devolution package had been worked out through India's mediation since the formulation of Annexure C in 1983. The latest stage of devolution package available as a basis for settlement at the time of signing the Agreement was the 19 December proposals.

There was, however, no finality about the 19 December proposals, which in turn had emerged out of the process initiated by the visit of Indian Minister of State, P. Chidambaram, to Colombo in May 1986. As noted in the previous chapter, both the Sri Lankan government and the Tamil groups, militants and moderates alike, had reservations on these proposals. The various Tamil groups, except the LTTE, were persuaded into endorsing the Agreement in the hopes that this devolution package would subsequently undergo further improvement. Accordingly, India accepted the obligation under the Agreement 'to underwrite and guarantee the resolutions, and cooperate in the implementation of these proposals' (para 2.14). But the details of the devolution package could not be finalised at the time of the signing of the Agreement. As a way out, the Agreement adopted this formulation concerning the contents of the devolution package:

> These proposals are conditional to an acceptance of the proposals negotiated from 4.5.1986 to 19.12.1986. Residual matters not finalised during the above negotiations shall be resolved between India and Sri Lanka within a period of six weeks of signing this Agreement. These proposals are also conditional to the Government of India co-operating directly with the government of Sri Lanka in their implementation (para 2.15).

This was in every respect a vague formulation. The language was confusing—note the mention of the word 'proposal' twice in the first sentence without any clarification as to which word was meant for whom or what. Moreover, nothing was said about the consequences of a disagreement between India and Sri Lanka on some of the aspects of the devolution package. This ambiguity was to assume serious dimensions when the Sri Lankan government moved to adopt the 13th Amendment to the Constitution on the question of powers for the Provincial Councils. This was done without taking India into confidence or without taking into account Tamil sensitivities on some of the devolution proposals worked out between 4 May and 19 December 1986. The Sri Lankan government took its own interpretation of these proposals and rushed through the legislation in November 1987.

This led to another round of talks between the Indian and the Sri Lankan governments. An additional agreement was signed between Rajiv Gandhi and President Jayewardene on 7 November 1987, promising that the devolution package would be further improved upon by the Sri Lankan government in consultation with the Government of India. This Agreement was not disclosed until mid-1989, in the wake of a controversy on linkages between the withdrawal of the Indian Peace Keeping Force from Sri Lanka and the devolution of power to the North-East Provincial Council.[45] Implementation of the 7 November 1987 Agreement remained unsatisfactory to India and, therefore, the question of devolution of power as a major grievance of the Tamils. The EPRLF-led North-East Provincial Government and the LTTE subsequently brought out the details of their respective views on the discrepancies between the 19 December proposals and the provisions of the 13th Amendment approved by the Sri Lankan government.[46] Constraints of time and space do not permit us to discuss such discrepancies in detail here, however. In view of these discrepancies, the LTTE has rightly (under the provisions of the Agreement) held India responsible for Sri Lanka's deviation from the letter and spirit of the Agreement in rushing through the 13th Amendment. It seems strange that on such sensitive issues, India accepted the sincerity of the Sri Lankan government at face value, without really providing in the Agreement a rectification mechanism for possible situations resulting from default on Colombo's part. The Rajiv–Jayewardene Agreement of 7 November 1987 was but a poor redressal of this lacuna.

Accommodating India's Security Concerns

Besides the interests and aspirations of Tamils, the other accommodation made by the Sri Lankan government related to India's
security concerns. Through an exchange of letters between the
Indian Prime Minister and the Sri Lankan President attached to
the Agreement, the latter agreed to 'reach an early understanding'
with the former that the presence of 'foreign military and intelligence
personnel' would not prejudice Indo-Sri Lanka relations (para
2.I). The Sri Lankan government also undertook to review its
Agreement with 'foreign broadcasting organisations' to ensure
India that they were to be used solely as 'public broadcasting
facilities and not for any military or intelligence purposes' (para
2.IV). On the question of Trincomalee port, Sri Lanka undertook
not to let any third country use it 'in a manner prejudicial to
India's interests' and accepted that the restoration of the oil-tank
farm on this port would be undertaken as a joint venture 'between
India and Sri Lanka' (paras 2.II and III).

   In the subsequent criticism of the Agreement in Sri Lanka, India
and elsewhere, these concessions on Sri Lanka's part were considered as unexpected, extensive and unilateral and thus a compromise on the sovereignty of the Island. Let us look at them a bit
closely. First, Sri Lankan accommodation on these issues was not
really sudden or unexpected. It was part of the ongoing discussions
between Sri Lanka and India on the overall question of ethnic
crisis and relations between the two countries since 1983 at least.
President Jayewardene admitted a year after surrendering his office
that he had offered to Mrs. Gandhi his willingness to meet India's
concerns on these security issues. And to do so, he was prepared
to sign a Friendship Treaty with India. As early as in 1984 a draft
of such a Treaty was sent for the consideration of the Government
of India. Excerpts of Jayewardene's interview in *The Sunday Times*
(Colombo, 11 February 1990) are relevant on these points:

   Q. Is it true that you sent her [Mrs. Gandhi] a draft of the
      Friendship Treaty in the early eighties?
   A. That is correct. In 1984. But it got stuck because of Indian
      officialdom. It was on the lines of the Indo-Soviet Treaty
      and she said she would look into it.
   Q. What are the issues that annoyed India about Sri Lanka?

A. There were four issues. The offer of Trincomalee oil tanks
to an American, Singapore, Pakistani firm, the Voice of
America transmitters, the presence of the Israelis and the
training of soldiers in Pakistan.
The foreign firms' offer of the Trinco oil farm did not
materialise and I offered India an opportunity to develop it
with us . . . . But it did not work out, though in the Accord,
a joint development was talked of. I understand they want
to do it now.

Q. And VOA?

A. I can't stop the VOA because it existed even before I came
to power. I told her. However, I said I have no objection to
her examining it.

Not only in 1984, but even in January 1987, long before India's
air intrusion into Sri Lanka, indications of Sri Lanka's willingness
to accommodate India's security concerns could be discerned.
After his visit to New Delhi to discuss the 19 December proposals,
the Land Development Minister, Gamini Dissanayake, stated in
Colombo on 22 January: ' . . . if India has certain geopolitical
perspectives about the region and feels that Sri Lanka should
support them, we should be willing to look at it and come to an
understanding with India on the vital perspectives of their concern.'[47]

Therefore, it seems clear that Sri Lanka's accommodation of
India's security concerns was not the direct result of the Indian
pressures that came with the 'air drop' intervention. In terms of
content, these concessions do not appear particularly extensive, in
the light of Jayewardene's interview cited above. The foreign
firms' contract for the oil tank farm in Trincomalee had fallen
through by 1984, and India had already been approached to join in
its restoration. The VOA deal, as per the 'exchange of letters', was
only to be reviewed to ensure that it was not made use of for
military intelligence purposes. It is doubtful if India or Sri Lanka
had any effective means of checking whether the station was to be
used for such purposes. From India's point of view, the ideal
would have been for Sri Lanka to abandon the project of expanding the VOA facility, but the July Agreement did not go that far.
We may also note here that though the Agreement mentioned
review of 'foreign broadcasting organisations', the focus remained
solely on the proposed expansion of the VOA facility. Neither the

VOA facility operating in Sri Lanka since 1952, nor an equally powerful facility of Deustchevile (German radio station) operating in Trincomalee, were treated as matters of controversy. On the question of foreign military and intelligence personnel, there is nothing to show that the two countries initiated the process of arriving at 'early understanding' on the presence of these personnel not being prejudicial to 'Indo-Sri Lanka relations'. It does seem that this provision helped in sending Pakistani military personnel back from Sri Lanka and reducing the strength of the Israeli Mossad and Shin Bet. This could however have been expected even otherwise, once there was an agreement for the resolution of the ethnic crisis and India had undertaken to control the operations of Tamil militants, as we shall see below. Such provisions, nevertheless, were to have long-term future assurances for India.

This leaves us with the question of possible military use of Trincomalee 'or any other ports in Sri Lanka' by a third country. In a way, Sri Lanka's position in the Agreement on this count was in line with its own policy of non-alignment which had a strong domestic political constituency in the Island. Further, in the context of improved strategic understanding between India and the USA, including calls of US ships at Indian ports, particularly since late 1984, India could scarcely consider the port calls of US ships in Sri Lanka as being prejudicial to its security interests. No wonder then that US naval ships have continued to visit Trincomalee and Colombo for refuelling and crew-rest, even after the signing of the Agreement. This is what the US interest presently seems confined to, regarding the use of Trincomalee and Colombo ports in Sri Lanka.[48] Had there been a major clash of interests between the USA and India on the use of ports in Sri Lanka, the USA would not have endorsed the Agreement of July 1987 as readily as it did. This concession on the part of Sri Lanka may, however, assume greater significance if and when US interest in the military uses of Sri Lankan ports should increase in future. And it is in this respect that there are reservations in some US circles, especially within the Pentagon, about the extent of Sri Lanka's accommodation to Indian sensitivities. As for the Sri Lankan accommodation of India's security interests being unilateral, this was more of an argument for technical reciprocity only. On substantive matters India did reciprocate by accommodating Sri Lanka's security concerns, as we shall see below.

In fact, the technical reciprocity of India assuring Sri Lanka that

it would not permit the use of its ports by a third co
manner prejudicial' to Sri Lanka's security interests
meaningless. Even in worst-case situations, India would n
to lend its ports to third countries to harm Sri Lanka milita.
India could wreak such harm on its own if it so decided. There.ore,
what was critical was to accommodate Sri Lanka's security concerns
vis-à-vis India; they related to the activities of Tamil militants
based in Indian territory and support to the Sri Lankan state in
dealing with internal threats. Here India's accommodation of Sri
Lankan concerns was explicit in the Agreement. Underlining the
reciprocity in this respect, the letters exchanged 'with the Agreement stated at the very outset: ' . . . it is imperative that both Sri
Lanka and India reaffirm the decision not to allow our respective
territories to be used for activities prejudicial to each other's unity,
territorial integrity and security'. (Para 1)

Accordingly, in the spirit in which Sri Lanka accommodated
India's concerns, India agreed to deport 'all Sri Lankan citizens
who are found to be engaging in terrorist activities or advocating
separatism or secessionism' (Letters, para 3.I). This was a highly
comprehensive guarantee, for it also included Indian obligations in
the case of advocacy of separatism or secessionism by Tamils even
within Indian territory. This was far wider than the scope of Sri
Lanka's Sixth Constitutional Amendment under which the TULF
members of parliament had to vacate their seats in 1983 because
they had underlined the goal of Tamil Eelam in their manifesto
and refused to take a fresh oath of allegiance to the Sri Lankan
Constitution, refuting this goal.

Against this background it may not appear as big a concession
on the part of India, but we have to look into the prevailing
political context of South Asia and the traditional Indian position
on the question of political opponents and dissenters of neighbouring countries seeking refuge in India and even carrying on their
activities from Indian soil. India has never given such blanket
guarantees to any of the neighbouring countries. This issue is
closely linked with the nature of neighbouring political regimes
and systems on the one hand, and that of values and ideological
coordinates of Indian polity on the other, as discussed in Chapter
1. It is because of this factor that India, even after 15 years of
diplomatic irritation, did not endorse Nepal's Zone of Peace proposal, which also, in one of its provisions, sought to obtain Indian
guarantees for curbing the 'hostile activities' of Nepali nationals in

Indian territory. Again, it was because of reservations on this count that India appeared cautious in joining the other South Asian countries while finalising the SAARC Convention on suppression of terrorism. Thus the significance of assurances given to Sri Lanka by India should be properly understood and appreciated. India's obligations to curb the activities of Sri Lankan Tamil militants were not confined solely to Indian territory but extended even to Sri Lankan territory with regard to implementation of the Agreement, if any of the militant groups did not accept the Agreement. The relevant provision (para 2.16) of the Agreement in this regard stated:

> These proposals are also conditional to the Government of India taking the following actions if any militant groups operating in Sri Lanka do not accept this framework of proposals for a settlement, namely, (A) India will take all necessary steps to ensure that Indian territory is not used for activities prejudicial to the unity, integrity and security of Sri Lanka. (B) The Indian Navy/Coast guard will co-operate with the Sri Lankan Navy in preventing Tamil militant activities from affecting Sri Lanka. (C) In the event that the government of Sri Lanka requests the Government of India to afford military assistance to implement these proposals, the Government of India will co-operate by giving to the government of Sri Lanka such military assistance as and when requested. (D) The Government of India will expedite repatriation from Sri Lanka of Indian citizens to India who are resident here, concurrently with the repatriation of Sri Lankan refugees from Tamil Nadu. (E) The governments of Sri Lanka and India will co-operate in ensuring the physical safety and security of all communities inhabiting the Northern and Eastern provinces.

To facilitate some of these tasks, the Agreement also laid down a provision for Indian military presence in Sri Lanka. The two parties agreed that: ' . . . in terms of paragraph 2.14 and paragraph 2.16(C) of the Agreement, an Indian Peace Keeping Contingent may be invited by the President of Sri Lanka to guarantee and enforce the cessation of hostilities, if so required' (Annexure, para 6).

Thus there existed a rather extended reciprocity on India's part not only to ensure Sri Lanka's perceived security concerns but also to help the Island over any difficulty encountered in relation to the Tamil militants, in implementing the Agreement. In addition to that, India agreed to its involvement not only in conducting a referendum for final decision on the merger of Northern and Eastern provinces (Annexure, para 1), but also in the surrender of arms by Tamil militants (Annexure, para 4) and in monitoring 'cessation of hostilities' (Annexure, para 5). Finally, India also agreed to 'provide training facilities and military supplies for Sri Lankan security forces' (Letters, para 3 (ii)). The Sri Lankan government had in turn agreed to lift emergency regulations, grant amnesty to the militants and help in their rehabilitation—where, again, India was to cooperate (para 2.11).

All these obligations taken together made direct Indian participation in the Agreement for resolving the ethnic crisis, critical and troublesome for India, as subsequent developments were to show. What proved even more risky was the involvement of Indian forces in the implementation process, soon after the signing of the Agreement. This, it seems, India had not anticipated while finalising the Agreement. The Indian idea was to let the Sri Lankan forces enforce the cessation of hostilities, while Indian forces were to be inducted into Jaffna only in the case of resistance from the LTTE, as could be expected. But this was not acceptable to the LTTE leadership which obtained an assurance from Indian Prime Minister that the security of the Tamils during the implementation of the Agreement was to be entrusted to the 'Indian Peace Keeping Force' (see note 33 in this chapter). Sri Lanka on its part was equally keen that India took charge of the security situation in the North-East so that Sri Lankan forces could be employed in Southern parts of the Island to meet the challenge posed by the JVP insurgency.[49] President Jayewardene later confirmed that he wanted immediate deployment of Indian troops in the North-East to relieve pressure on his security forces:

When Rajiv was in Sri Lanka to sign the accord in July 1987, there was an outbreak of violence. I asked the IGP [Inspector General of Police] why more police were not in Colombo and he said 2,400 policemen had been sent up to Kandy for the Esala Perehera.[50] He could not bring them down unless the Perehera was cancelled. I then turned to the Chiefs of the Security

Forces. They said they could spare some men but did not have
the planes to bring them from the North and East. Rajiv heard
of my difficulty and asked, 'Can I help?'

I told him of our difficulties and he said he will get some planes
to transport our troops. Then he asked whether I also needed
some manpower to assist in the North and East if some of the
troops were coming South. This was possible under the Accord.
I said, 'since the planes are coming empty, who not send some?'
That is how the Indian troops came to Sri Lanka.[51]

It was also on President Jayewardene's request that Indian frigates were anchored off Colombo port to deter the organisers of
the suspected coup.[52] It is difficult to know how credible were
President Jayewardene's fears of a coup in the offing, but the
signing of the Agreement was marked by attacks on the Indian
Prime Minister first (on 29 July while a guard of honour was
presented to him) and on the Sri Lankan President later (in early
August when he was addressing his Party's parliamentary group in
the Parliament House building). This would indicate that Jayewardene's fears were not totally unfounded.

However, the prompt response to Jayewardene's security needs
by the Indian Prime Minister underlined an element of ad-hocism
in deciding on matters so sensitive as deployment of troops in a
foreign country India's response was intended in sympathy for a
panic-stricken and beleaguered friendly regime, which appeared
willing to resolve the Tamil issue and also accommodate India's
security concerns. But then its consequence should have been
assessed thoroughly. Not doing so gave critics and opponents of
the Agreement a legitimate reason to dub it as a document of
regime collaboration and an Indian manifestation of helping a
power hungry ruling elite to perpetuate themselves in power.
However, we should also recall that the Agreement had been put
across not only to the Cabinet colleagues of Jayewardene and
those dealing with the relevant branches of administration, but
also to the parliamentary wing of the ruling party. Therefore, it
was an Agreement between the Indian and the Sri Lankan governments and not between Prime Minister Rajiv Gandhi and President
Jayewardene alone, as is sometimes mentioned. True, the value of
the Agreement would have been enhanced if it had enjoyed a
wider consensus of Sinhala opinion behind it, but anyone who

knew the dynamics of political forces then operating in the Island would accept that such consensus was far from the realm of possibility. President Jayewardene claimed subsequently that no one except one of his Cabinet colleagues really opposed the signing of the Agreement. He, at one stage, after the signing of the Agreement, had asked those who did not approve of the Agreement to resign from the government. No one did. In view of this, the stance adopted by some Cabinet colleagues—like the then Prime Minister and subsequent President, Premadasa—to show their opposition to the conclusions of the Agreement appeared to be politically inspired and tactical so as to absolve themselves of any responsibility should the Agreement run into difficulties, as it no doubt did later. This is, however, not to deny that there were differences on the details of provisions of the Agreement.

As to the Indian response on the issue of sending troops, or even of making a provision to that effect in the Agreement, a benign interpretation would suggest that having decided to become a party to the Agreement directly, India could not hesitate on specific details. After all, there was a clear understanding that there were forces opposed to the Agreement and that the possibility of sending Indian troops to Sri Lanka did exist. That being so, India could scarcely have backed out on Jayewardene's request. Concerning the difficulties in the interpretation and implementation of the Agreement, the then Indian Minister of State for External Affairs, Natwar Singh said: 'No government can go into an agreement of this nature without having tied up the obvious loose ends. We examined every possible option. There were no low cost options available. If anybody can suggest a better alternative, we will gladly examine it.'[53]

Appraisal

We have already noted that there was no consensus in Sri Lanka on the provisions of the Agreement or even on how to deal with the Tamil issue. Thus the Agreement was bound to invite opposition and protest from various political parties as well as from sections of the bureaucracy and the military. The opposition from the military was evident in the attack on the Indian Prime Minister. President Jayewardene later confirmed that the naval cadet who

had attempted to hit Rajiv Gandhi was given a hero's welcome
when sent to the barracks. In his court submission in August 1990,
the cadet himself disclosed that some of his officers and colleagues
had known of his intention to strike the Indian Prime Minister.
The JVP and the SLFP came to the forefront in opposing the
Agreement. Besides other factors, both these organisations saw in
this Agreement a tool for the consolidation of the Jayewardene
regime. To the JVP, it was particularly troublesome, since the Sri
Lankan forces were to be released from the North and East to
confront them in the South. The political climate created by this
opposition also made some members of the Jayewardene Cabinet
adopt tactical postures to distance themselves from the Agreement.[54] We should bear in mind that 1987 was the year before the
next Presidential election in Sri Lanka. The Left parties in the
Island, however, did support the Agreement.

In India as well, the Left parties went along with the Agreement. Their enthusiasm was far less evident than that of the ruling
party, the Congress, where Prime Minister Rajiv Gandhi had described it as a 'historic Agreement'. India's other opposition parties
endorsed it with obvious reservations, particularly on the questions
of ambiguity on the devolution package and the provision for
deployment of troops in Sri Lanka to implement the Agreement.
But generally, the Agreement was seen as the best possible under
the circumstances.

The Agreement also received a wide endorsement internationally.
Some of India's neighbours expressed reservations on the provision
of placing Indian troops in Sri Lanka, but this was accepted in view
of the fact that this was done in response to the request of the Sri
Lankan government. For Pakistan, however, it came as a setback
to its regional strategy of isolating India.[55] China's endorsement
was a guarded one, saying that the Agreement was bound to bring
at least a temporary peace, though its future was seen as uncertain.[56]
The most prompt and unqualified support, as noted earlier, came
from the Western countries, the USA and the UK in particular.

The Agreement did attempt to address all the relevant aspects
of the ethnic problem of Sri Lanka, and tried to find answers. It
sought to restore the multi-ethnic, multi-lingual and multi-racial
character of Sri Lankan society and reiterate its unity and territorial
integrity. It tried to meet the demands of Tamil aspirations; even
in areas where things were left vague, there existed hopes for the

Tamils that their legitimate expectations would be satisfied.[57] At the same time, the Agreement accommodated the security interests and susceptibilities of the Sri Lankan government. As for India, it secured accommodation of its perceived security concerns and opened up the prospects of Tamil refugees returning to Sri Lanka. Above all, the Agreement was compatible with India's ideological coordinates in the region. Accordingly, it served to reinforce India's credentials as an involved and indispensable actor striving to promote peace and stability in South Asia.[58] This was so, notwithstanding the lacunae and loopholes in terms of details discussed earlier. Much indeed depended upon implementation of the Agreement; this, again, depended, in view of the structure of the Agreement, on the sincerity of the Sri Lankan government as a whole and on the cooperation of the Tamil militant groups—also as a whole. Subsequent developments were to show that both these critical actors, the Sri Lankan government and the LTTE, were not forthcoming to extend the desired cooperation to India. And in that situation, the role of the Indian forces became one that had not been anticipated, thereby vitiating both the Agreement and its eventual outcome in terms of implementation.

Notes to Chapter 4

1. See his interview to Karan Thapar of *Indian Express* given on 24 July and published on 27 July 1987.
2. It was disclosed later by the LTTE that the Indian government, during a crackdown on their group in early November 1986 before the SAARC Summit in Bangalore, where they were taken for possible discussions with the Sri Lankan side, seized these weapons and then returned the same to them. So the Indian government knew that they had these weapons. It was also disclosed that India had provided them with training in the use of these weapons, *The Hindu*, 4 August 1988; *The Daily News*, 8 August 1988. On the question of the seizure and return of arms from LTTE in November 1986 and the overall relationship of MGR with Tamil militant group, new light has been thrown in a recent publication, Kondath Mohandas, *MGR: The Man And The Myth*, Panthar Publishers, Bangalore, 1992.
3. It was confirmed by President Jayewardene later that the downing of this plane had created a serious crisis in Sri Lankan air force operations during the Vadamarachhi assault. See his interview in *Sunday Times*, 11 February 1990. Earlier, on 21 January 1990, Jayewardene had explained this point to the author with the help of his private notes etc. in an informal interview at his Colombo Ward Place residence.

4. *The Hindu*, 25 and 29 May 1987.
5. The apparently informal talks between Colombo and the LTTE were held in the last week of December 1986. The Sri Lankan side was represented by a ruling party Member of Parliament Vincent Perera and a Tamil businessman Jayabalasingham. The failure of these talks led to the imposition of fuel embargo and then economic blockade on the North by the Sri Lankan government and the intensification of military operations. The LTTE explanation came after the failure of the talks when the LTTE knew that now it would need India's support. See *Frontline* (Madras), 10–23 January and 24 January–6 February 1987.

   This revealed the flexibility of the LTTE's tactics and their careful strategy of playing opposing forces against each other in order to pursue their own interests with single-mindedness. In this they had no qualms either of conscience or commitment.
6. This was a persisting concern in the strategy of India, as noted in the previous chapter; one unhappy implication of this strategy was to enhance the involvement and role of RAW in relation to the activities of the militant groups. *Indian Express*, 18 May 1987.
7. *The Times of India*, 29 June and 1 July 1987.
8. *The Times of India*, 13 and 14 July 1987.
9. The question of US mercenaries raised by the Indian Foreign Secretary in Washington in January 1987 has already been noted in the previous chapter. Also see *The Hindu*, 18 January 1987, on this point. Attention may also be drawn to reports, as early as October 1986, that the US State Department had written to the Congress on 29 September that Sri Lanka was to be helped under the US Foreign Assistance Act (Sections 571 and 572) for combating terrorism. *Indian Express*, 11 October 1986.

   In February 1987, the Sri Lankan Foreign Minister's pleas for starting the sale of military equipment were considered sympathetically by the US Secretary of State in Washington. Sinha Ratnatunga, *Politics of Terrorism: The Sri Lankan Experience*, International Fellowship for Social and Economic Development, Canberra/Melbourne, 1988, p. 166.
10. *Frontline*, 13–28 June 1987.
11. Pran Chopra, 'Fiasco in Palk Strait—"Good Offices" Crippled', *Indian Express*, 17 and 18 June 1987.
12. *The Statesman*, 28 March 1987.
13. *The Hindu*, 29 May 1987.
14. This was indicated in the Minister's interview to the *Indian Express* (27 July 1987) cited earlier. It was reconfirmed in President Jayewardene's interview after he had given up the Presidency. See *Sunday Times* (Colombo), 11 February 1990. He said in that interview: 'As for Dixit, he never made any threats to me. But he had told Lalith (Athulathmudali) that India would never allow Jaffna to be taken by the Sri Lankan Army'.
15. This was disclosed by Jayewardene in his *Sunday Times* interview of 11 February 1990.
16. This was explained by Lalith Athulathmudali in his interview to the *Indian Express*, 27 July 1987.

17. This was also disclosed by former President Jayewardene in his *Sunday Times* interview of 11 February 1990.
18. Jayewardene disclosed this to the present author in Colombo on 21 January 1990 at his residence in Ward Place.
19. See a report on the issue from Washington DC, by Shahnaz Anklesaria Aiyar, 'The US and Sri Lanka', *Indian Express*, 29 June 1987. It was, however, indicated in this report that US administration officials had privately deplored the Indian action.
20. *The Times of India*, 12 June 1987.
21. President Jayewardene said this in an interview to *New York Times*, as cited in *The Hindu*, 11 August 1987. Also reconfirmed in his interview to the *Sunday Times* cited earlier.
22. *Muslim* (Islamabad), 26 March 1987; *Nation* (Lahore), 26,27 and 29 March 1987; *Tribune* (Chandigarh), 28 March 1987.
23. *The Hindu*, 8 June 1987; *Indian Express*, 8 June 1987.
24. Ratantunga, *Politics of Terrorism*, p. 370.
25. *Sun* (Colombo), 4 June 1987. On the visits of Sri Lankan ministers to Pakistan see *Muslim* (Islamabad), 16 June 1987; *Pakistan Times*, 5 June 1987; *Frontier Post* (Lahore), 4 June 1987; *Public Opinion Trends (POT) on Pakistan* (New Delhi), Vol. 15, No. 112, 13 June 1987.
26. *The Hindustan Times* (New Delhi), 4 June 1987.
27. *Indian Express*, 20 and 24 June 1987.
28. *Sunday Times*, 11 February 1990.
29. *The Times of India*, 10 July 1987. For a contrary view of economic impact of ethnic crisis, see Lee Ann Ross and Tilak Samarnayake, 'The Economic Impact of the Recent Ethnic Disturbances in Sri Lanka', *Asian Survey*, vol. 26, no. 11, November 1986, pp. 1240–55.
30. *The Hindu*, 17 August 1987.
31. *Sunday Times*, 11 February 1990. Details of the possibility of such a coup are not known, but President Jayewardene learnt from the then Indian High Commissioner in Colombo that interested persons were informally probing what India's stand would be if such a coup were carried out successfully. India, however, seemed committed to President Jayewardene's regime and promised to help in thwarting the suspected coup attempt. Based on informal interviews of the author with highly placed persons in Colombo.
32. *The Times of India*, 30 June 1987.
33. Paper presented by the Political Committee of the LTTE at the International Tamil Conference on the Tamil National Struggle and the Indo-Sri Lanka Peace Accord, held in London in April/May 1988. Also included in the Conference proceedings: N. Seevaratnam (ed.), *The Tamil National Question and the Indo-Sri Lanka Accord*, Konark Publishers, New Delhi, 1989 (Chapter 19, pp. 203–23).

Subsequently in April 1988, the Indian High Commissioner in Colombo, J.N. Dixit, and the Minister of State for External Affairs, K. Natwar Singh, confirmed that Rs. 5 million per month was promised to Prabhakaran to help the LTTE change from 'military to peaceful democratic politics'. Only one payment was made under this promise since the LTTE, by the end of September

1987, went back on its promise to cooperate in implementing the Agreement. *The Hindu*, 26 April 1988; *India Today*, 30 April 1988.

34. For instance see statements of US State Department officials in the Congressional hearings on Sri Lanka during February and March 1987. The author was present at some of these hearings.

35. Chopra, 'Fiasco in Palk Strait'.

36. Nand Singh, 'One Year of the Indo-Lankan Accord', *Fourth International*, July-December 1988.

37. Athulathmudali admitted in his *Indian Express* (27 July 1987) interview that Rajiv Gandhi sent the package of Agreement to Jayewardene, who then 'worked on a few things, on this and that. Some of the things were toned down.' So this formulation on language could have been one of such things.

38. See his speech at the UNP National Executive Committee on 25 July 1987. *Daily News* (Colombo), 26 July 1987; also cited in N. Satyendra's paper, in Tamil Conference, *op. cit.* (n. 33).

39. Malinga H. Gunaratna, *For A Sovereign State*, Sarvodaya: Colombo, 1988.

40. This was reportedly stated by Rajiv Gandhi in his communication to President Jayewardene. *The Times of India*, 5 July 1987. Even earlier Rajiv said that the Sri Lankan army offensive had vitiated atmosphere and created difficulties in bringing the militants to the negotiating table. *The Times of India*, 30 June 1987.

41. *The Times of India*, 19 July 1987.

42. *Indian Express*, 14 and 23 July 1987.

43. See his interview in *Indian Express*, 27 July 1987.

44. N. Satyendra's paper in Tamil Conference, London, 1988. Also, *Indo-Sri Lanka Agreement 1989: An Emerging Consensus*, A Pro TEG Publication, Madras, 1988 (gives responses of all Tamil militant groups on the July Agreement.)

45. See correspondence between Prime Minister Gandhi and President Premadasa in June 1989. *Indian Express*, 9 July 1989. The text of this Agreement was put on the table of Sri Lankan Parliament on 11 August 1989. *The Hindustan Times*, 12 August 1989.

46. The North-East provincial government has brought out a document on the status of the actual implementation of the 13th Amendment and their own version of the desirable contents of the devolution package. For the LTTE's version of the discrepancies see, *Indo-Sri Lanka Agreement, 1987: An Emerging Consensus*.

47. *The Hindu*, 23 January 1987.

48. I have briefly discussed the question of narrowing divergences between India and the US on the strategic issues related to Sri Lanka in the previous chapter, as also in my 'Indo-Sri Lanka Agreement: Regional Implications', *Mainstream* (New Delhi), vol. 25, no. 48, 15 August 1987. Prafulla Bidwai's article on 'Bhandari Line on Sri Lanka' in two instalments in *The Times of India*, 18 and 19 May 1987, may also be recalled here.

49. See Indian High Commissioner J.N. Dixit's statement in Colombo at a Press Conference on 31 July 1987. *The Times of India*, 1 August 1987.

50. Perehara is a major cultural carnival paraded in the streets to mark the Buddhist religious rituals in Kandy.

51. *Sunday Times*, 11 February 1990.

52. *Ibid*

53. Interview in *India Today* as cited in N. Satyendra's paper in Tamil Conference.

54. For the analysis of political response to the Agreement in Sri Lanka see Ravinath P. Aryasinha, 'The Follies of a Small State: The Political Response to the Indo-Sri Lanka Accord in Sri Lanka' in Shelton U. Kodikara (ed.), *Indo-Sri Lanka Agreement of July 1987*, University of Colombo, Colombo, 1989, pp. 115–42.

55. Comments in Pakistani Press. Pakistan's unhappiness became evident when it strongly blocked the Sri Lankan and Indian attempt at the SAARC Summit in Kathmandu, December 1987, to get a regional endorsement for the Agreement. All other SAARC members had more or less agreed to endorse the Agreement.

56. *Beijing Review*, 8 September 1987. For the Bangladesh reaction where it was said that the presence of foreign troops in a sovereign country was not desirable except on the basis of a UN Resolution, see *The Hindustan Times*, 1 August 1987.

57. Kumar Rupesinghe, 'Indo-Sri Lanka Agreement 1987 and Conflict Resolution in Sri Lanka', *South Asia Journal*, vol. 2, no. 3, January-March 1989. pp. 271–94.

58. See S.D. Muni, in *Mainstream*, 15 August 1987, vol. 25, n. 48; and *The Hindustan Times*, 5 September 1987.

5

Role of the Indian Peace-Keeping Force: An Evaluation

Complex and Unprecedented Peace-Keeping Assignment

The provisions for placing an Indian Peace Keeping Force (IPKF) in Sri Lanka as made in the Indo-Sri Lanka Agreement of July 1987 have been discussed in the previous chapter. The political context and structural design of these provisions were such that they did not fit into the known parameters of a peace-keeping role. To begin with, this was not a peace-keeping operation either in a situation of inter-state conflict, or through an international organization like the United Nations, where preventive diplomacy had acquired considerable experience and effectiveness. It was intended as a peace-keeping exercise in a civil strife, a far more complex and difficult task.

A recent comparative study of peace-keeping operations in various situations makes even an optimistic prognosis of peace-keeping in the situation of civil strife sound extremely cautious. Paul Diehl in this study has observed:

Peacekeeping is not impossible in civil conflict but there are certain hurdles to its successful use under those conditions . . . . Peace means continued domination by the status quo elites in the eyes of rebel groups. Unless that perception can be changed, subnational groups will view the peacekeeping operations as hostile to their interests . . . . Before a peacekeeping force is sent to an area of civil internal unrest it must have at least the tacit acceptance of relevant subnational groups there.

To do this, its mandate should not include functions that give any advantage to the challenged government. This will be quite difficult without losing the approval of the central government. Agreement will also be complicated as the number of contending parties increases. Sometimes, it may be almost impossible to patrol areas where many different groups operate, much less balance competing interests among them . . . . Success is still possible but it must be much more difficult.[1]

All the risks and hazards anticipated in this prognosis were inherent in the Indian peace-keeping role in Sri Lanka. They were made further complicated by the manner in which India started approaching implementation of the Agreement by making com- promises outside the scope of the Agreement—recall the deal struck between Rajiv Gandhi and LTTE leader Prabhakaran in New Delhi on the eve of the signing of the Agreement. Under this deal, Prabhakaran was not only promised money and political dominance but also retention of substantial quantities of arms in the name of the personal security of the LTTE cadre. The Govern- ment of India had also promised the LTTE and other Tamil groups that they would have to surrender arms only to India, the guarantor of the Agreement, and not to the Sri Lankan authorities. The underlying assumption was that if the Sri Lankan government should break the Agreement, these arms would then be returned to the Tamil militant groups to let them carry on their fight. Tamil militant leaders were also assured that during the 'surrender of arms' their honour and dignity would be maintained. It was perhaps because of such a tacit understanding that India committed itself to the surrender of arms within 72 hours of the cessation of hostilities, and the procedure for the surrender of arms was not spelled out in the Agreement.[2] The question of arms surrender was so sensitive and the basis of understanding so fragile, that its implementation almost unavoidably ran into difficulties.

India's compromise with the Sri Lankan side lay in accepting that the Indian forces were to be called upon by the Sri Lankan President to help implement the Agreement. This made it appear a partisan provision in the eyes of the LTTE. In this respect, a good deal of avoidable confusion was created by the manner the Indian Forces were inducted into Sri Lanka, in an ad hoc way and almost explicitly for the benefit of President Jayewardene, as seen

in the previous chapter. We have, however, also noted that the
real objective of the IPKF was not to protect the Jayewardene
regime. It was also doubtful whether the IPKF, in the early stages,
was given any specific mandate. While the Ministry of External
Affairs kept on pressing the point that a confrontation with the
LTTE might become reality, the IPKF commanders and the military
leadership hoped that matters could be sorted out amicably. It was
in this hope that the IPKF officers and men continued to show
deference to the LTTE leadership, and even took lightly the
'operational instructions' from the Army Headquarters (in September 1987), to 'get tough' with the LTTE. Confusion on the
question of 'mandate' was confounded by the avoidable ambiguity
created with regard to the command structure of the Forces, which
was not defined in the Agreement. Soon after the induction,
President Jayewardene assumed that he was the Commander-in-
Chief of the Indian contingent in Sri Lanka. Then, one day after
the signing of the Agreement, Indian Prime Minister Rajiv Gandhi
stated in the Indian Parliament on 30 July that the Sri Lankan
Brigadier, Gerry De Silva, was to be the commander of the contingent. This was repeated by the Indian High Commissioner in
Colombo on 31 July and by the Prime Minister again on 22
October. This subsequently led to some controversy, and the
Foreign Minister of India explained that the Indian contingent was
under Indian charge. The local Indian Commander of the Forces
in Jaffna, Major General Harkirat Singh, reiterated on 3 December
that 'we take orders from the Government of India.' Accordingly,
the Prime Minister had also to rectify his position and state, in the
course of a press comment in Madras on 22 December, that 'IPKF
is not under Sri Lankan commanders; they are under our own
Commanders.' This confusion resulted essentially from the lack of
planning behind provisions for the IPKF.[3]

That a peace-keeper should be neutral or impartial is almost a
precondition for its smooth functioning and success. In this respect,
in addition to the confusion about the command structure, the
very provision of the IPKF in the Agreement was biased against
the Tamil militants as it was meant to help the Sri Lankan government in disarming the militants. Notwithstanding the Sri Lankan
government's preference on the subject, India had its own stakes
in the protection and successful implementation of the Agreement
to which it was a party itself. As such, it was unrealistic to expect

India to remain an impartial observer, interested simply in maintaining cease-fire and peace between the government of Sri Lanka and the Tamil militants.

Thus the IPKF mission was inherently complex and unusual. Added to this complexity was India's complete inexperience as peace-keeper in a civil strife in a neighbouring country. True, India had considerable experience of playing a peace-keeping role in situations of bilateral inter-state disputes or even civil strife—we may here recall India's role in Indo-China, Korea, the Suez Canal crisis and the Congo crisis. But in all these cases, the Indian contingent was part of a multinational force and derived its legitimacy from UN Resolutions or Multinational Agreements. In the case of Sri Lanka, however, India's peace-keeping role emerged essentially from a bilateral agreement. And there it had a host of mutually incompatible relations and linkages with the contending parties in the civil strife on the one hand, and a set of its own objectives on the other. Outlining this complexity, India's High Commissioner in Colombo until 1988 was later to say:

. . . I don't know, how many of us are conscious of the type of role which the IPKF is playing in Sri Lanka. Our armed forces in our history of post-independence India have been abroad several times. We have been to Congo and we have been to Gaza; we have been to Lebanon; we have been to Cyprus; we have been to Korea; we have been to Bangladesh. But what the IPKF is involved in Sri Lanka is much more multidimensional and complex. Our previous external projections of our armed forces were either a straightforward military projection or we were invited to project ourselves in classic terms of reference of a peace-keeping force. But this is the first time that, I think, the IPKF is several things in Sri Lanka.[4]

Notwithstanding all these complications, however, the IPKF initially tried to play its role as carefully and impartially as possible. The Indian forces, as expected, supervised the surrender of arms by militant groups in the presence of the Sri Lankan authorities, during most of August 1987. This became possible because India had secured assurances from the LTTE leader Prabhakaran that he would cooperate in the process of surrender of arms. On the strength of this, Rajiv Gandhi obtained President Jayewardene's

approval for Prabhakaran's return to Jaffna so that he could prepare
his cadres for the surrender of arms.[5] The arms actually surrendered,
however, covered little more than a fraction of what the LTTE and
other militants had. This was in keeping with India's assurances to
the LTTE and other Tamil groups that they would be allowed to
keep arms for their personal security. There was also the real
problem of precise knowledge and information about the quantity
of arms and ammunition and the locations of the weapon stores of
the LTTE. Neither the Government of India nor that of Sri Lanka
had any definite idea in this respect. But it was hoped that gradually,
with increased mutual confidence between the militants and the
Sri Lankan government resulting from the implementation of other
parts of the Agreement, the problem of militants' arms could be
resolved peacefully. The situation on the ground was also manageable for the IPKF. The remarks of a Sri Lankan observer (a
university teacher in Jaffna) on the situation prevailing in the
North and East of Sri Lanka towards the end of September 1987
may be recalled:

> One notices very quickly that the Indian forces are very much at
> home with the civilian population. At Manthikai we saw children
> playing with helmets belonging to Indian troops . . . . The peace-
> keeping force has so far maintained a low profile in Jaffna as the
> Sri Lankan forces were only too glad to get back to barracks and
> the problem of rival militant groups was minimal. The role in
> Jaffna has been mainly confined to mine clearing. The grief felt
> in Jaffna was both deep and universal at the deaths of Major
> Dilip Singh, Mohinder Rao and Lieutenant Vickram from the
> 8th Battalion (Engineers) in a mine clearing accident. These
> were men who gave their lives in a mission of peace for others.
>
> The situation in Batticaloa was different. Right up to the signing
> of the peace accord, the Special Task Force enjoyed a licence to
> kill which they used with total immunity. On the day the accord
> was signed (29 July) the STF was ordered to suspend operations.
> Crowd celebrated . . . while the STF watched sulkily . . . .
> Seeing this, some of the community leaders informed the Indian
> Embassy in Colombo that the situation in Batticaloa was ex-
> plosive . . . . Within two days the Indian forces were in Batticaloa.
> In Batticaloa, they have been strict with all parties. It is under-
> stood that the Indians have called for a closure of the dreaded

STF camps. In one incident, a militant group tried to prevent another from holding a public meeting. The Indian forces intervened and allowed the meeting to proceed in the name of democracy.[6]

Role Transformation

This situation was to change abruptly in the first week of October, when open and extensive fighting was resumed between the LTTE and the Sri Lankan forces. The responsibility for this must be shared both by the Sri Lankan government and the LTTE, for neither of the two refrained from indulging in a series of provocative actions against each other and the peace-keepers. LTTE provocations included propaganda against the Agreement, which started with Prabhakaran's speech at Suthamalai Temple in Jaffna on 4 August, within three days of his arrival from India.[7] Then there was the question of clashes between militant groups, where the LTTE started attacking other groups by the second half of August. When the other groups retaliated, the LTTE leadership blamed India for these clashes and threatened to launch agitation against the IPKF.[8] In fact the LTTE fired its first shot on the IPKF in Trincomalee on 7 September 1987. As a reaction to the LTTE's changing stance and non-cooperation with the IPKF, the Indian Navy put a blockade around the North and the East of the Island, but it failed to restrict LTTE's movements. This slowly changing situation also led to a stronger 'warning order' being issued by the Indian Army Headquarters to the IPKF, calling for the destruction of LTTE's communication network and raids to be conducted on LTTE strongholds to recover arms and ammunition. Such orders, however, remained unexecuted: even Indian High Commissioner Dixit had to complain about this.[9] There were also occasional exchanges of fire, particularly in the East, between the LTTE and the Sri Lankan security forces for which the latter were no less guilty.

Matters were, however, precipitated by the LTTE who started picketing government offices in early September to back up their demands. This brought the Jaffna and Batticaloa administrations to a halt. This was followed up by a 'fast unto death' by the LTTE leader A. Thileepan starting on 15 September. Among the demands were release of remaining Tamil militants held under the Prevention of Terrorism Act, stopping of Sinhala colonization in the East, and surrender of arms by the Sri Lanka home-guards to the IPKF. Unfortunately, this fast ended in his death, creating a highly volatile situation in Jaffna.[10] It was defused by the timely intervention of the Indian High Commissioner in Colombo who had extensive discussions with Prabhakaran from 23 to 28 September and finalized a written understanding for the continued cooperation of the LTTE in implementing the Agreement. In return of the establishment of an Interim Administration for the Northern and Eastern Provinces with a dominant role for the LTTE, the LTTE agreed on the following:

6. It was agreed that the establishment of an Interim Administration would facilitate the fulfilment of the five demands put forward by the LTTE in its resolution conveyed on 13 September 1987 to the High Commissioner.
7. Mr. Prabhakaran said that the LTTE would fully cooperate in the implementation of the Indo-Sri Lanka Agreement subject to assurances given to him by the Prime Minister of India in July 1987.
8. Mr. Prabhakaran said that the LTTE would surrender the remaining arms, i.e., other than the personal arms for the security of their leaders, once conditions of security for their leaders and cadres are created.
9. Mr. Prabhakaran agreed that the LTTE will cooperate fully and ensure smooth functioning of all aspects of the civil administration including the functioning of the police force.
10. Mr. Prabhakaran agreed that free and fair elections to the Provincial Council will be held and that the LTTE will cooperate fully in the process.
11. High Commissioner Sh.Dixit and Mr. Prabhakaran agreed that the LTTE and the Indian official media would desist from mutual criticism.
12. In view of agreement having been reached on paras 2 to 11 above, the Sri Lankan government will announce the establishment of the Interim Administrative Council within 48 hours of the signing of the agreed minutes.[11]

The success of this understanding in defusing the situation created by the death of Thileepan, however, proved extremely tenuous and fragile. This understanding between the Indian High Commissioner and LTTE leader Prabhakaran, finalized on 28 September had also laid down the composition of the Interim Administrative Council (n.10 above). Differences between the LTTE and the Indian High Commissioner came to the fore on the question of the appointment of Chief Administrator for this Interim Council. President Jayewardene had agreed to select the Interim Council from a list of 15 names (12 for Council, 3 for Chief Administrator) submitted by the LTTE. But the LTTE expressed dissatisfaction concerning the appointment of the Chief Administrator, and alleged that the President had passed over the candidate (Mr. N. Pathmanathan) whom the LTTE preferred.[12] In fact this was no breach of the understanding of 28 September, because the person actually appointed by President Jayewardene also came from the list submitted by Prabhakaran. It was nowhere mentioned in the 28 September understanding that President Jayewardene was to follow the order of preference in the list submitted. One can argue that it would have been prudent to follow such a preference, but Jayewardene had his own political calculations whereby he wanted to deny the LTTE a base in the ethnically volatile Eastern Province. It was also a part of internal political dynamics within the LTTE that Prabhakaran, while preferring a person from the East, had also proposed names from the North. One analyst has rightly questioned Prabhakaran's political intentions in this regard, noting that if Prabhakaran had wanted some one from the East only, then all the three names could have been from that region. This analyst's contention, based upon his long and informal interview with Prabhakaran on 7 September 1987, is that the LTTE leader was searching to create conditions for wrecking the July Agreement either by pitting India against Sri Lanka on questions related to implementation of the Agreement, or eventually having a showdown with India and the IPKF on pretext of protecting Tamil interests and security.[13] It may also be recalled that on 7 September, the LTTE had fired upon the IPKF in Trincomalee. While the LTTE's irritation on the question of the appointment of the Interim Council and the Chief Administrator was still fresh, another development was to vitiate the achievement of the Prabhakaran–Dixit agreement of 28 September.

This new development was caused by the Government of Sri Lanka. Before turning to the specific developments of early October, we must recall that some sections in the Sri Lankan administration, including the Cabinet Ministers and the military, were as unreconciled to the Agreement as the LTTE. This was evident in their continued intransigence towards the militants, which led to occasional exchange of fire. While the alleged settlement of Sinhalese in the East proceeded, the pronounced stance even of the President—to undo the merger of the North and the East in the proposed referendum—continued to arouse apprehensions and doubts among Tamils and foul the overall political atmosphere. Things were brought to a boil on 2 October, when the Sri Lankan navy arrested 17 LTTE men coming from the Tamil Nadu coast in a boat full of arms. These LTTE men included two of important commanders, Pullendran and Kumarappa. The Sri Lankan security forces insisted on taking these militants to Colombo. This was strongly opposed by the LTTE, as well as by the arrested persons, who threatened to commit suicide, if they were forced to go to Colombo. As the issue became tense, the Government of India tried to intervene in the matter and attempted to persuade the Sri Lankan President to leave the militants in Mannar where they were being kept. But President Jayewardene came under heavy pressure from security forces and possibly, National Security Minister Lalit Athulathmudali. Disclosing this later in Colombo, India's then Defence Minister Pant said that President Jayewardene realized subsequently that the suicide of the LTTE cadres in the process of shifting them to Colombo 'was a mistake'.[14] There was, however, no way in which India could prevent the arrest of these 17 LTTE militants by the Sri Lankan navy as they were carrying arms including machine-guns and radar. This was also an indication of the fact that while the IPKF was trying to maintain peace, the LTTE was not only not surrendering, but collecting more arms.

President Jayewardene also subsequently accepted the importance of this event in triggering a conflict between the LTTE and the IPKF, as also his inability in stopping their transfer to Colombo because of pressure from security forces. While answering questions from a Colombo-based Sunday paper on the subject, he said:

Q. Why did the LTTE break the promise?

A. They said it was because some of their people were to be brought to Colombo, after they had been apprehended by the security forces and detained for questioning. They took cyanide pills and several died.

Q. Who wanted them brought to Colombo?
A. The Security Services.
Q. What did Dixit say?
A. To listen to the LTTE. How could I? The service chiefs had said they must be brought to Colombo. I had agreed and I had to stand by them.
Q. But were you not splitting hairs?
A. They had violated the law. If not this, they would have found some other excuse to go back on their word.[15]

This development, which resulted in the death of 12 of the 17 LTTE detainees, proved to be a crucial point for change in the course of the Agreement's implementation. At least that is how the LTTE projected this development. Prabhakaran himself told this to an Indian M.P. (from the DMK party) Mr. Gopalswamy, when the latter called on him in the jungles of North-East Sri Lanka after undertaking a long and secret journey in March 1989. According to Gopalswamy:

I was told that the death of 12 Tigers after consuming cyanide pills while they were in the custody of the Sri Lankan army and **the helplessness of the Indian army and government in securing** their release, was the turning point. Mr. Prabhakaran told me that when he took back his pistol and gun at the funeral of those 12 Tigers, all his colleagues picked up arms once more, after having laid them down with the signing of the Indo-Sri Lanka Agreement.[16]

There were other explanations of this development as well. One was that when these LTTE cadres were taken to the Jaffna camp of the Sri Lankan army, they appeared relaxed. But then they were visited by the LTTE leaders Yogi and Mahattya, who handed over a note from Prabhakaran to Pullendran and Kumarappa— perhaps instructing them to take cyanide. A few hours later they were dead. There could be two possible objectives behind the LTTE's decision to sacrifice these cadres. One could be to precipitate a crisis which could justify their open resort to arms against the Sri Lankan government as well as Indian forces, enabling the LTTE to wriggle out of their commitments on implementation of the July Agreement. The second could be an LTTE rebuff to the attempt of the Sri Lankan army and the National Security Minister,

Athulathmudali, to use the arrest of these LTTE cadres for securing
the release of Sri Lankan soldiers taken as prisoners by the LTTE.
That is why the resistance to Dixit's efforts to get these LTTE
cadres released through President Jayewardene's intervention came
from the Sri Lankan Service Chiefs, as admitted by Jayewardene.[17]

Whatever the reasons, the suicide of the LTTE cadres resulted
in the LTTE restarting armed hostilities. In a sweeping action,
they killed Sri Lankan army prisoners in their custody in addition
to nearly 300 Sinhalese peasants settled in the East. The ethnic
violence between the Tamils and the Sinhalese spread rapidly in
Trincomalee, and Indian and Sri Lankan forces had to be rushed to
the area. These two armies set up a Joint Operations Centre to
monitor the situation. There were also incidents of the Sri Lankan
police or army firing on IPKF soldiers who had been instructed to
return fire only in self-defence.

Pressure mounted on the IPKF to put an end to this violence in
the East, since under the Agreement the Sri Lankan security
forces were to remain confined to barracks. The LTTE announced
in Madras that they had worked out a five-point plan with the
IPKF to stop violence but this was neither authenticated nor
actually put in practice.[18] After a meeting with the Chief of the
IPKF in Sri Lanka, Lt. General Dipender Singh, the Sri Lankan
President announced that either the IPKF should act quickly, or
should quit Sri Lanka. India could not have decided to pull back
the IPKF, because that would have meant an end to the Agreement
and all that it promised towards peace and stability in Sri Lanka, as
well as towards the preservation of India's security and ideological
interests. This forced the Indian High Commissioner in Colombo
to warn the LTTE that by backing out from the Agreement of 28
September it was sabotaging the Indo-Sri Lanka Agreement.[19]
Thus began the new role of the IPKF: to confront the LTTE. The
details of this new role were worked out during a visit of Indian
Defence Minister Pant and Army Chief K. Sunderji to Colombo
on 9 October 1987.[20]

It is clear that those sections of the Sri Lankan security forces
that were keen on pitting the IPKF against the LTTE, succeeded.
A key contribution in their success was made by the LTTE—who,
if it could have shown tolerance and maturity and avoided precipitating ethnic violence, might have had the IPKF on its side. After
all, the IPKF had already been fired upon by Sri Lankan forces

(whether police or army could not be established) on 2 October. The IPKF had come to Sri Lanka with considerable sympathy and goodwill for the LTTE. But then, perhaps, as we noted earlier, the LTTE on its own was also looking for a showdown and direct clash with the IPKF.

These developments led to the transformation of the IPKF from a peace-keeping to a fighting force. It was fighting not on behalf of the Sri Lankan government, as was alleged and propagated by the LTTE, but in order to help in preserving and implementing the Agreement, which was seen as being conducive to India's perceived interests in Sri Lanka. The idea of the IPKF being placed in Sri Lanka to implement the July Agreement was very clear in the Indian mind. Prime Minister Rajiv Gandhi had mentioned this in his first statement to the Indian Parliament on the Agreement on 30 July.[21] It was reiterated by Defence Minister Pant on his visit to Colombo on 9 October, when he said that the IPKF would take action against all elements who obstructed the implementation of the Agreement.[22] This was perhaps the time when Indian Army Chief, Gen. Sunderji, reportedly asked for a change in the nomenclature of the IPKF from a peace-keeping to an 'Accord Implementation Force'. It was the army's brief to ensure the full implementation of the Agreement; accordingly, 'pulling out before that would be political and military suicide'.[23]

In creating conditions for the implementation of the July Agreement, the IPKF had to ensure cessation of ethnic hostilities in Sri Lanka and surrender of arms by Tamil militants. Once confrontation with the LTTE started, the IPKF also had to ensure that this organisation was militarily weakened, thus forcing the LTTE to collaborate in implementation of the July Agreement. The provisions regarding the IPKF as spelled out in the Agreement were such that its presence and operations in Sri Lanka were a part of Indian pressure on the Sri Lankan government to ensure safety, security and legitimate aspirations of the Sri Lankan Tamils as recognised under the July Agreement. Neither of the two contending parties in Sri Lanka—the government and the LTTE—ever accepted or appreciated these varied dimensions of the IPKF role. While the LTTE grumbled about the first aspect, cessation of hostilities and process of disarming them, the Sri Lankan government disapproved of the IPKF's relevance and India's say on matters related to security of the Tamils and devolution of power to them.

This disapproval, which became pronounced and a major political issue after Premadasa's coming to power, was clearly evident even during Jayewardene's rule, particularly in his Defence and National Security Ministries as well as higher echelons of other bureaucracy. Many a senior Defence and National Security Ministry's higher official not only failed to cooperate smoothly with the IPKF, but also taunted its commanders as to why they were not delivering 'Prabhakaran's head' to Colombo. Precisely this common opposition to the IPKF within the LTTE as well as the Sri Lankan government eventually brought them closer, to sabotage IPKF operations and finally sending it back, as we shall see later. Any evaluation of the IPKF, therefore, should be based not upon the criteria set by either of these parties (the LTTE and the Sri Lankan government) or applicable to a conventional peace-keeper, but on how far the IPKF managed to create conditions for the implementation of the July Agreement.

It may be pertinent to recall here that the mandate for the IPKF came from paras 2.14 and 2.16(C) of the July 1987 Agreement. Para 2.14 had a very broad canvas of covering the Government of India's obligations to 'underwrite and guarantee the resolutions and cooperate in the implementation of these proposals'. It is true that the IPKF was placed in Sri Lanka on the invitation of the President of Sri Lanka (Annexure para 6) but then, while concluding the Agreement, no one could have envisaged that having invited the IPKF, the President would ask it to withdraw even before completing the purpose for which it was invited. The change in Sri Lanka's political situation with the coming to power of a new President meant that these aspects were overlooked when President Premadasa publicly demanded in June 1988 that the IPKF withdraw from Sri Lanka in a matter of a few weeks.

IPKF Operations

The outbreak of ethnic violence that transformed the role of the IPKF also defined its immediate task, which was to ensure cessation of hostilities and to force the Tamil militant groups to surrender arms. This meant mainly the LTTE, as the other Tamil militant groups neither had many arms, nor resisted the IPKF's attempts to make them surrender whatever they had. The LTTE, having decided to have a military showdown with the IPKF, resisted the IPKF in this task and thus a direct conflict between the two ensued. Two things were implied in this situation. First, that the earlier claims of the LTTE about the surrender of arms,[24] duly endorsed by the IPKF and the Indian High Commissioner, were merely an eyewash, arranged largely in order to initiate the process of implementing the Agreement. Subsequently, after the outbreak of violence in the first week of October in which the LTTE killed large numbers of Sinhalese, the Indian High Commissioner conceded that the 'Tigers gave up only 60 per cent of their heavier arms which they were unable to hide. They retained their infantry arms, including the AK-47s, 82mm mortars and grenades'.[25]

The second implication of the new situation was that once the IPKF decided to force the LTTE to surrender its arms and the LTTE decided to resist such surrender, open conflict between the two became inevitable. In this conflict, there was no scope for the IPKF to appear neutral between the Sri Lankan government and the LTTE, nor could it remain only a restraining force and avoid fighting. This was inherent in the terms of reference as defined in the July Agreement and also the assurances given by the Indian Prime Minister to President Jayewardene in his cable of 1 August 1987, while asking for the return of Prabhakaran to Sri Lanka. In view of President Jayewardene's declared position that IPKF should either act 'fast or quit', the IPKF's refusal to confront the LTTE would have meant its withdrawal from Sri Lanka and the consequent collapse of the Agreement. This was seen to be contrary to India's interests. Further, in India's perception, the LTTE had gone back on its words, both as enshrined in the understanding of 28 September between Prabhakaran and Dixit and also between Prabhakaran and Rajiv Gandhi finalised in the last week of July 1987. How then could the IPKF remain neutral towards the LTTE? Dixit, reacting sharply to Prabhakaran's accusing India of not fulfilling assurances given to him, rebutted this claim and made it clear that India remained determined to implement the Agreement and would not be deterred by the Tigers' 'attempts to subvert its implementation'.[26]

There is no doubt that the burden of disarming the LTTE fell on the IPKF rather suddenly and at a time when it was not quite prepared for this. This task had been envisaged in the Agreement, but that was seen more as a contingency; and the placing of the

Indian contingent in Sri Lanka almost simultaneously with the
signing of the Agreement had nothing to do with it, as we have
already discussed. Neither the manpower nor the equipment
available with the IPKF indicated that it had come to the Island to
wage a determined war.[27] However, once the battle lines had been
drawn up and conflict set in, a massive induction of troops and
equipment had to take place.

The IPKF's fight against the LTTE was carried out in three
major operations, code-named 'Operation Pawan', 'Operation
Checkmate' and 'Operation Toofan'. Between 'Pawan' and 'Checkmate', two other comparatively smaller but tactically significant
operations, 'Vajra' and 'Virat–Trishul', were also undertaken. All
these operations were aimed at neutralizing the LTTE in the
Northern areas. For the same purpose in the East, particularly in
Batticaloa, operations 'Tulip Bloom' and 'Sword Edge' were carried
out. It is not possible to identify exact dates and specific objectives
of the operations, as these remain closely guarded military secrets.
On the basis of published accounts available, we can, however,
gain a rough idea.

'Operation Pawan' was the first assault launched to dislodge the
LTTE from Jaffna. Starting on 10 October, it was concluded by
the end of the month, or mid-November 1987 at the latest. This
was one of the most difficult and costly campaigns in terms of time
taken and casualties suffered by the IPKF, for reasons to be
discussed below. Constraints of minimizing civilian Tamil casualties
meant the IPKF was not able to use air power. Hinting at the
restraints imposed on the IPKF in the first phase of its operations
(the Pawan Phase), India's Prime Minister Rajiv Gandhi said in
Lok Sabha on 9 November 1987:

> The IPKF were given strict instructions not to use tactics or
> weapons that could cause major casualties among the civilian
> population of Jaffna, who were hostages to the LTTE. The
> Indian Army have carried out these instructions with outstand-
> ing discipline and courage, accepting in the process a high level
> of sacrifices for protecting the Tamil civilians.

There were allegations that this was not true, but subsequent
enquiries discovered that 'over-enthusiastic Sri Lankan air force
pilots' had taken a couple of sorties on the first two days of the

IPKF assault without informing the Indians or even clearing it with Sri Lankan high command.[28] Even the use of mechanised infantry became possible at later stages, around 20 October, mainly due to logistic constraints.[29] This operation, however, witnessed an effective coordination of army and navy in a manner not experienced by the Indian forces earlier. Naval commandos not only fought along with the army for the assault from the Northern sea side, but also destroyed underwater ammunition dumps of the LTTE. Since the navy was not equipped with smaller boats for shallow waters, the services of Coast Guards were also summoned. Besides fighting a war, the Indian navy also transported more than 3,000 Sri Lankan Tamil civilians from the captivity of the Sri Lankan army to their respective hometowns during this operation.[30] 'Operation Pawan' was a five-pronged attack on Jaffna to drive out the LTTE. It took about two weeks, far longer than originally expected.[31]

'Operation Vajra', carried out between early February and mid-March 1988, was confined to the Mullaithivu and Vavuniya districts of the North. It involved a total strength of four brigades, i.e., about 6,000 men, and was aimed at combing the areas to get LTTE leader Prabhakaran 'dead or alive'. Though this operation succeeded in destroying important LTTE headquarters and camps in the area, the leadership, including Prabhakaran, succeeded in dodging the IPKF. The other operation, 'Virat Trishul' which was launched sometime in March 1988, covered a vast area comprising the whole of North from Mannar to Mullaithivu and going up to Killinochchi. Its objective was to neutralise any remaining hideouts of the LTTE and push them from urban areas to the jungles.

It was the culmination of the 'Vajra' and 'Virat Trishul' that led to the launching of the 'Operation Checkmate', which started around May 1988 and concluded towards the end of August. It was planned in three stages and its aim was to hole up the LTTE in the jungles of Vavuniya and Mullaithivu. This strategy could help the IPKF to use firepower on the LTTE without fear of hurting the civilian population. It also insulated the intense fighting from the public gaze as the areas were inaccessible to the press, unless press visits were organised by the IPKF or the LTTE at considerable risk. Pushing the militants and their leadership away from populated areas, as a result of 'Checkmate', was seen as a necessary condition for holding elections, first for the Provincial Assembly in November, then for the Presidency in December 1988, and for the Sri Lankan Parliament in March 1989.

The last major IPKF operation undertaken was 'Toofan', i.e.
storm. It started around mid-June 1989, against the political backdrop of the demands of new Sri Lankan President Premadasa for
the withdrawal of the IPKF by the end of July 1989, and opening
of negotiations between the Sri Lankan government and the LTTE.
The main point on the agenda for these negotiations was to secure
the expeditious withdrawal of the IPKF before any accommodation
on substantive issues could be worked out mutually.[32] 'Operation
Toofan' was perhaps meant to set the stage for the IPKF's eventual
withdrawal by the end of the year, as promised by India. It aimed
at storming remaining strongholds of the LTTE so as to weaken it
as much as possible, in order to blunt its expected challenge to the
EPRLF-led Provincial Council when the IPKF would no longer be
there to provide the necessary security cover. The operation covered
an extended area from Pulmoddai in the north of Trincomalee
district to Paranthan in Killinochchi, taking Vavuniya and Mullaithivu in its fold in-between.[33] New battalions of jungle-trained
commandos were called in from India for this operation. The
LTTE claimed that the IPKF had threatened to use napalm bombs,
which was, however, strongly refuted by the Indian side·in Colombo.
The use of helicopter gunships in 'Toofan' was admitted.[34] As the
operation advanced, political pressure from Colombo to stop it
also increased. The LTTE and the Sri Lankan government then
declared a formal cessation of hostilities, which removed the
rationale of IPKF operations provided in the Agreement of July
1987. It is, therefore, doubtful if 'Operation Toofan' could have
been brought to its culmination.

The main thrust of IPKF operations was in the Northern region,
since the LTTE's mainstay and strength lay primarily in the North.
The Eastern region had a less homogeneous demographic composition, due to the presence of Sinhalese and Muslims in considerable
strength. Of the three districts of the Eastern Province, one—
Amparai—was completely dominated by the Sinhalese; it remained
largely under the protection of the Sri Lankan security forces.
Even among the Tamils of the East, the LTTE lacked solid social
support as a result of caste hierarchy and traditional linkages.
Other groups, particularly the EPRLF and TELO, enjoyed a
better standing in the East. That is why the IPKF found it comparatively easy to dislodge the LTTE from the East after a few
serious encounters in the early months of the engagements.

Constraints on Operations

The military operations of the IPKF were conducted under various constraints. Of them, three important ones deserve further mention. The first was the ambiguity surrounding precise objectives and targets. Military purposes require that such targets should be clearly defined. Creating conditions for the implementation of the July 1987 Agreement was the overall objective of the IPKF, but that was not precise enough for an ordinary soldier or an officer in the field. A team of Indian defence analysts, commenting on this aspect, said:

> The confused political thinking which bogged down military operations stemmed from one basic flaw—the failure of the Indian state to define its national aim and permanent interests in the Island of Sri Lanka. Selection and maintenance of 'aim' is a cardinal principle of war. Lack of a clear-cut politico-military aim leads to ad-hocism, dithering and pure confusion. A peace accord cannot be an end in itself.[35]

Along similar lines, the then Indian High Commissioner in Sri Lanka, Dixit, also admitted later that there was confusion in the minds of IPKF soldiers as to why were they fighting in Sri Lanka. He said:

> I begin by saying that one undercurrent, which I noticed among my colleagues in armed forces, specially in the middle and younger levels, there was no question of loyalty to the task assigned and the discipline and efficiency with which they have functioned and on which they are functioning. But in moments of introspection, they were always wondering. This is not China, this not Pakistan, why are we in Sri Lanka? We were originally supposed to come and protect the Tamils. Why is it that the situation has arisen, when they are shooting at some of the Tamils? Legitimate questions![36]

This is where the sudden transformation of the peace-keeping role of the IPKF discussed earlier, and its unexpected plunge into conflict with the LTTE, were responsible for creating considerable confusion and ambiguity about the real IPKF mission in the minds of its rank and file. Critical was the question of what was to be done to the LTTE—to decimate it as a military force, or only to put military pressure on it, to force it to come to the negotiating table and agree to cooperate in implementing the Agreement. The confusion in the minds of the IPKF, save the few top-ranking officers, was very real and almost inevitable under the circumstances. But this confusion became further confounded, as various and sometimes diverse statements were made by political and military superiors on how to deal with the LTTE. For instance, while Indian diplomats in Colombo strongly criticized the LTTE for its betrayal and brutal treatment of the Indian soldiers taken by them as prisoners, Defence Minister Pant said in Parliament on 28 November that India had 'no desire to hurt the LTTE' and announced a 48-hour cease-fire in response to the release of Indian soldiers by the LTTE.[37] In December 1987, Lt.Gen. Dipender Singh, who was commanding the IPKF in Sri Lanka when operations against the LTTE were initiated, said in a press interview that the IPKF would get Prabhakaran one day and was not interested in fighting his myth, but that the ultimate solution lay in political settlement.[38] Then, as we noted above, 'Operation Vajra' was launched to get the LTTE leadership, including Prabhakaran, 'dead or alive'—but an Indian official in Colombo was quoted by the *Daily News* (10 August 1988) as saying: 'We certainly do not want a dead leader. We want him alive. We want him at the conference table'.

It is understandable that, with IPKF operations being a part of an overall strategy to make the LTTE accept the Agreement, the IPKF was not intended to physically eliminate the militant group, even if this might be militarily possible (which in itself was doubtful, as was conceded from the very beginning). There were also powerful political pressures in Tamil Nadu against any harm being done to Prabhakaran.[39] The decimation of the LTTE as an objective was also seen to be counter-productive, since that would merely strengthen hardliners in the Sri Lankan administration against conceding any more effective devolution of power to the Tamils. However, such constraints seemed fairly complex for the straightforward approach of the IPKF's men in uniform.

The slow advance of the IPKF and the lingering instability caused by the LTTE insurgency gave rise to apprehensions that the IPKF was deliberately slow in order to perpetuate its presence in Sri Lanka and remain in physical control of the strategic port of

Trincomalee. This was obviously not part of the IPKF mandate. India could easily monitor military movements in and around Trincomalee from its own coasts and presence in the Indian Ocean. Nor did it need the use of Trincomalee for its Indian Ocean movements or operations in times of emergency. Furthermore, such allegations completely ignored the fact that ever since the British naval presence from Trincomalee was withdrawan in the late 1950s, India had hardly bothered about this natural port. Discounting such apprehensions, General Pande, General Officer Commanding-in-Chief, said: 'We have better places in India from where we can protect our strategic interests'.[40]

Besides the confusion on clear goals and targets, yet another important constraint concerned terrain and logistics. The IPKF was not familiar at all with the terrain, particularly the long stretches of dense forests and the strategic lagoons. Intimate knowledge of the topography of the region gave a clear advantage to the LTTE militants. On the top of this was the urban cover of houses and streets which offered formidable fortification to the militants. They dug up long trenches and bunkers (as much as 40 to 45 feet) even in the foreground of the houses to give tough resistance to their attackers. Some of the jungle camps of the LTTE were found to be linked through underground tunnels, such as in Alampil camp in the Mullaithivu area, providing the guerrillas and their leaders with perfect protection and easy exit.[41] This was one of the factors that helped the LTTE leaders to dodge the IPKF. Knowledge of the terrain also enabled the LTTE to plant their landmines with considerable advantage. The landmines, as is well-known now, proved the most effective and devastating weapon in the militants' armoury, inflicting a large number of casualties on the IPKF. Many of these were from the engineering corps, who had to locate and destroy the landmines before troops could move in. The terrain advantage of the militants also enabled them to obtain continuous supplies of weapons and explosives, even despite Sri Lankan and Indian naval patrolling. By contrast, personnel and supplies for the IPKF had to travel thousands of kilometres before reaching air and sea ports in Jaffna and Trincomalee, respectively. From there, they would be distributed to various locations. In an eye-witness account, Col.C.L. Proudfoot wrote:

Long convoys of heavily laden trucks crawl slowly along dusty roads with infantry escorts, while engineers out front tread carefully, prodding for concealed explosives, which have to be diffused when discovered. Hence a journey of nearly 50 km which would normally take about an hour, takes six hours at walking pace.

Fresh rations are flown in every day and distributed to outlying locations by IAF helicopters while command and liaison visits to distant locations are carried out by Army Aviation helicopters of the Air OP Flight. This continuous cooperation and inter-dependence between the Army, Navy and Air Force as perhaps never before, has built up a close working relationship that will be of lasting value to all three services.[42]

In a difficult and unfamiliar terrain, the problem of logistics became harder in the absence of adequate and reliable advance intelligence. This is where the performance of RAW became a subject of deep resentment and criticism in the IPKF and in the media as well. For one thing, the RAW's estimates concerning the LTTE strength and arms stores were an important factor behind the military's calculation of the 72-hour time period needed to secure the surrender of arms. These estimates proved totally un-realistic as the IPKF started discovering newer and bigger LTTE ammunition dumps in the course of 'Operation Pawn'. The IPKF even unearthed an LTTE arms factory.[43] These incorrect estimates forced the IPKF advances during 'Operation Pawan' to be very slow, and costly in terms of casualties.[44] Yet more serious damage done by the faulty intelligence concerned the 30 Indian paratroopers who were air-dropped to capture the LTTE headquarters in Jaffna University in the initial phase of 'Operation Pawan', on the assumption that resistance would not be greater than commando strength. This turned out to be otherwise and the paratroopers had to suffer heavy casualties. In operations like this, the lack of accurate military intelligence was a very unfortunate factor. The IPKF stayed in Jaffna from the end of July, so it does seem surprising that for a full two months and more, they did so little to gather intelligence about the area of their responsibility, even when they were not expecting any immediate confrontation. This was particu-larly regrettable because in this Operation, the newly created 54 Air Assault Division of the army was inducted for the first time.[45]

The biggest constraints on IPKF operations involved the human factor: the tremendous social support enjoyed by the LTTE, par-ticularly in the North. This gave the LTTE militants a real 'fish in water' advantage and made the IPKF task correspondingly more difficult. The situation in Sri Lanka was quite the opposite of what the Indian army had experienced in Bangladesh where the Pakistani army, against which the Indian forces were fighting along with the Mukti Bahini, had no popular support or sympathy. The LTTE boys belonged to the area, they looked like everyone else and had their homes and families there. They could, therefore, employ hit-and-run tactics most effectively. They also very successfully projected the view that India had sided with the Sri Lankan government in order to serving its own strategic interests and as such had taken up arms against the Tamils. This meant that none of the local population could or would offer any assistance to the IPKF, which made fighting an urban insurgency in built-up areas all the more difficult and costly. Newspaper accounts have gone into the details of the LTTE's advantages in this respect. The sole exception was the information provided to the IPKF about the LTTE movement by anti-LTTE Tamil militant groups. Such information was more effective in the East where the EPRLF and TELO had a wider base. To overcome this disadvantage, the LTTE even threatened all those found to be 'collaborating with the occupation army', and they demonstrably carried out such threats. Extensive popular support for the LTTE in the area also gave it a significant propaganda advantage, enabling the LTTE to level exaggerated allegations and spread them fast and far regarding the so-called excesses of the IPKF. The extensive social support enjoyed by the LTTE was also used in building public and political pressure for ceasefire, on its terms, through posters, public appeals, petitions and fasts unto death.

Because it was easy to mix up the LTTE guerrillas with the local civilian population, the IPKF could scarcely avoid civilian casualties, despite their best efforts and repeated claims to the contrary. Such casualties grew in numbers also as a result of the deliberate LTTE tactics of covering themselves with human shields of women and children while attacking IPKF positions. A closer look at the nature of IPKF encounters gives the impression that the LTTE in fact sought to ensure greater civilian casualties at the hands of the IPKF so as to discredit it and make it unpopular with Tamil masses. Accordingly, in the market places and in residential localities, the LTTE would fire upon the IPKF patrols from inside the houses and shops. Any retaliation from the IPKF would necessarily damage civilian life and property. To avoid such encounters, the public in

Jaffna repeatedly pleaded with the LTTE to vacate populated areas and desist from provoking armed encounters in such areas. The IPKF's search and seizure operations further alienated the local population and brought in strong public criticism. In the early phase of the conflict, the IPKF had neither female para-military personnel to help in frisking women suspects nor interpreters to communicate with the local people during searches, roadblocks, etc. The movements of troops and armour also resulted in the destruction of fields and farms, causing serious economic hardships to ordinary people which made them turn against the IPKF.[46]

After the first phase of operations, the IPKF tried to overcome the constraints of the human factor by appealing directly to the common people through pamphlets, posters and intermediaries. A Central Reserve Police Force (CRPF) *mahila* battalion was inducted into Sri Lanka to deal with the female population to avoid charges of sexual misbehavour against the IPKF. The IPKF also received help from other militant groups who had agreed to cooperate in the implementation of the Agreement and who were also against the LTTE, having been its victims in one form or the other in the past.[47] The IPKF's welfare measures and rehabilitation work in various areas after these had been cleared of LTTE control also helped to improve its public image somewhat. But all this was too little and too late. Above all, it was almost impossible to convince the parents and relations of the LTTE cadres that their kith and kin deserved to be killed. In such a situation, no amount of effort could fully succeed.

Achievements, Costs and Failures

The aims and objectives of the IPKF being complex, there cannot be any easy answers as to what it managed to achieve and what it could not do. Further, as stated earlier, the IPKF performance should be assessed not within the classical framework of a peace-keeping assignment but as a force that was assigned the task of helping in implementing the Agreement. In that sense, techni-cally at least, the IPKF did prove to be a decisive factor in bringing about a cessation of hostilities between the Sri Lankan government and the LTTE. True, this cessation of hostilities was

announced by the Sri Lankan government to facilitate their negotiations with the LTTE and create pressures for the withdrawal of
the IPKF. It is also true that India and the IPKF were still not
quite satisfied with the nature of cessation of hostilities so announced,
since the LTTE meant it as cessation of hostilities only against the
Sri Lankan army and not against either the IPKF or other Tamil
militant groups. In India's perception, this move on Colombo's
part was motivated by short-term political considerations of the
new Premadasa regime. The basis for this was provided by the
LTTE's and Sri Lankan establishment's common dislike of the
role of the IPKF, as mentioned earlier in this chapter. Such considerations included joining an anti-India bandwagon of Sinhala
nationalism to take the wind out of the JVP insurgency's sails. All
this had nothing to do with the performance of the IPKF as such.
This was indirectly conceded by President Premadasa when in a
letter to the Indian Prime Minister asking for an early withdrawal
of the IPKF, he said:

> The complete withdrawal of the IPKF will hopefully contribute
> to stabilising the situation in Sri Lanka, where the presence of
> the IPKF has become a deeply divisive and resentful issue . . . .
> I am confident that a complete withdrawal of the IPKF will
> enable me to secure the trust and confidence of my people.[48]

We may return to the relevant aspects of the IPKF withdrawal
issue and that of the JVP insurgency later. Suffice it to say here
that manner and motives of the announcement of cessation of
hostilities showed that the LTTE had started open negotiations
with the government of Sri Lanka only because they had no
capability left to sustain a fight against the IPKF. This fact was
quite candidly admitted in Sri Lanka even by the President and his
Minister of Defence.[49]

Related to the question of cessation of hostilities was the surrender of arms by Tamil militant groups. The IPKF could not
secure any formal agreement with the LTTE for the surrender of
arms due to political intervention and short-cutting of its operations
after mid-1989. But the General Officer commanding the IPKF in
Sri Lanka, General A.S. Kalkat, disclosed that huge quantities of
LTTE arms had been captured by the IPKF, who had also destroyed

a number of arms, ammunition and explosive dumps during their operations. In an interview to an Indian daily, he said towards the end of the IPKF operations:

> In the process of application of military force, we have captured nearly 2,500 weapons from the LTTE. When the IPKF first came to Sri Lanka, even by the Sri Lankan government's estimate, the number of weapons with the LTTE was between 700 and 800. Therefore, in essence, we have disarmed the LTTE thrice! The fact that they have been continuing to get weapons and assistance from vested interests and interested parties inimical to India is outside my purview.[50]

This indicates that like the Indian intelligence (whose failures have been mentioned above), Sri Lankan intelligence was also misinformed on the size of LTTE's weapon-stores. There were a number of factors behind this. First, the LTTE kept its stores scattered, and except for a select few of the top leadership, the general rank and file in the LTTE had no idea of the actual quantities of arms they possessed as an organisation. This was indicated in one of the rounds of talks between the LTTE and the IPKF when, even after an agreement on the number of arms to be surrendered, the LTTE wanted a long cease-fire period to surrender them because they were located in various dumps scattered throughout the North and East regions, and thus time would be needed to collect them.[51] More important than the location of stores was the continuous supply of arms to the LTTE from diverse sources. General Kalkat's statement cited above hinted at this. Earlier, Lt.Gen. Dipender Singh and Gen. Pande had also mentioned LTTE's continued supply of arms from outside sources.[52] There were frequent media reports of LTTE arms-carrying boats dodging the Indian and Sri Lankan naval patrols, as well as seizure of LTTE arms of Chinese, Pakistani and many other Western origins.[53] Many observers following developments in Sri Lanka also suspected that a section of the Sri Lankan security forces was conniving with the LTTE's drive to secure arms from various sources to carry on its fight against the IPKF.[54] Recently (8 August 1990) allegations were made by the EPRLF, Member of Parliament Secretary General Suresh K. Premachandran that in order to sabotage IPKF operations, the Sri Lankan armed forces themselves supplied large quantities of arms to the LTTE.[55] It was, however, public knowledge that ever since the beginning of secret talks between the LTTE and a section of the Sri Lankan security establishment in February 1988, there had existed effective linkages and liaison between the two.[56] We should also bear in mind that even during IPKF operations, the LTTE continued to obtain plastic explosives and other warlike material from India, through its political and underworld supports in Tamil Nadu. This spoke volumes about the laxity of the Tamil Nadu state apparatus on the one hand and the softness of the Indian state as a whole. The LTTE had its own munition factories, in Sri Lanka and also in some hidden locations in Tamil Nadu.[57]

A minor public controversy was raised with regard to the foreign sources of arms to the LTTE when the Indian High Commissioner in Colombo drew attention to the discovery of surface-to-air missiles (SAM-7) in the LTTE arsenal, as these could come only from Western sources. We have discussed this aspect briefly in the earlier chapter, mentioning the LTTE's claims that had had these missiles as early as in 1986 and India had known about this. At no stage, however, did the LTTE disclose the source of these missiles.[58] It seems that these missiles, after having been seized from the LTTE in Madras, were returned by India to the LTTE again during the final stages of 'Operation Liberation' launched by Sri Lankan security forces in May 1987. The missiles were again surrendered during the token surrender of arms by the LTTE in the first few days of August 1987.[59] At that time either the LTTE did not surrender all their SAM-7s, or they managed to obtain more subsequently. One cannot even be certain that when Tamil Nadu police raided LTTE locations in November 1986, all the SAM-7s that the LTTE had, were located there only. Some of these missile units may well have been hidden in LTTE stores and camps in Sri Lanka as well. The continuous foreign supply of arms to the LTTE led the Indian navy to chase arms-carrying ships from Singapore even up to Bangladesh ports in mid-1988.

It is clear from the foregoing discussion that the IPKF could not disarm the LTTE. However, the IPKF could manage to ensure the almost complete disarming of the other militant groups. Of them, the PLOTE had a close relationship with the Sri Lankan security establishment, as we have noted in Chapter 3.[60] However, a controversy developed during the final phase of IPKF operations (after

mid-1989) regarding the rearming of non-LTTE, militant groups
and raising a new force to be called the Tamil National Army. The
IPKF and the Indian official sources have continued to deny this.
But this rearming of other militant groups was resorted to for the
post-IPKF withdrawal situation, where the LTTE, not having
abandoned arms and still desiring to dominate the Tamil scene,
could become a threat to the other militant groups, particularly the
elected Provincial Council headed by the EPRLF. The Sri Lankan
government had in principle approved of this rearming, in the
name of equipping the Citizens Volunteer Force (CVF) which was
to take charge of the security of Tamils after the IPKF withdrawal.
A meeting of the Security Co-ordination Group, attended, among
others, by the Sri Lankan Defence Minister and Defence Secretary,
decided on 19 October 1989:

> The requirement of automatic weapons for the CVF and Police
> Reservists was discussed. Due to non-availability of weapons
> with the Sri Lanka Police, the Sri Lanka government made a
> request to the GOC IPKF for the IPKF to provide weapons on
> loan to enable the Chief Minister to meet the situation. The
> GOC IPKF said that he would refer the request to his govern-
> ment and advise the Group shortly. Meanwhile, the Chief
> Minister and the Inspector General of Police would work out
> the requirement of weapons and inform the GOP IPKF.[61]

It was clear that the Sri Lanka government made an issue of
such IPKF arming once the LTTE raised it with them. It was also
possible that, under these provisions, the IPKF armed more of the
militants than the supposed CVF. However, once the IPKF realised
that the CVF recruits and other militants armed in the name of
Tamil National Army would not be able to withstand an LTTE
onslaught and would surrender arms to the LTTE or sell these on
the black market, to buy tickets for travel abroad, these militant
groups were again disarmed.[62]

No less important than these achievements in the field of cessation
of hostilities and surrender of arms was the fact that the IPKF
managed to restore a large measure of law and order and at least a
semblance of normalcy in the area of its responsibility, the North-
East Province of Sri Lanka. At a time when the entire Island was
caught up in a cycle of murders and mayhem by the JVP insurgency

and the counter-terror unleashed by the Sri Lankan state, the North-East Province appeared relatively stable and orderly with hospitals, schools and administration working.[63] One of the notable features of IPKF's achievements was the creation of conditions in Sri Lanka enabling the Tamil refugees within Sri Lanka as well as in India's Tamil Nadu state to start returning to their homes. By the time the IPKF completely withdrew from Sri Lanka in March 1990, some 50,000 Sri Lankan Tamils had returned to their country, out of a total of nearly 1,50,000; and about 25,000 displaced Tamils within Sri Lanka had also returned to their homes. The slow pace of the return of Tamil refugees from India to Sri Lanka was due to such factors as continued LTTE insurgency and lack of adequate facilities for the security and rehabilitation of these refugees within Sri Lanka. The North-East provincial government could not be of much help, since the devolution of power to them had not been effected. Even assistance granted by friendly countries to Sri Lanka for the rehabilitation of Tamil areas remained withheld and unutilized by the Premadasa administration. One important consideration behind such tactics was to build up an equation with the LTTE against the IPKF and the EPRLF government of the North-East province which was considered pro-India. These refugees were also helped by the IPKF in their rehabilitation and resettlement.[64]

Closely connected with the restoration of law and order in the North-East Province was the reactivization of democratic political process throughout the Island. This began with the averting of the suspected coup that President Jayewardene had talked about. The highmark in reactivizing the democratic process came with the successful holding of three elections, beginning with that of the Provincial Council for the North-East region in November 1988, followed by the Presidential and Parliamentary elections in December 1988 and March 1989 respectively. The LTTE questioned the legitimacy of the Provincial Council elections, since the Northern region's seats in those elections were claimed uncontested by their rival militant groups—the EPRLF, TELO and ENDLF. But that happened because the LTTE and its ally, the EROS, boycotted these elections. The TULF did not participate in them, for fear of violence and intimidation of their candidates and their families.[65] Any other allegations on the IPKF's impartiality and manipulations were politically motivated.[66]

Further, it was the same IPKF protection that helped the Presidential and Parliamentary candidates to canvass and mobilise support for themselves. Free and fair voting at these elections, particularly in areas under IPKF responsibility, was endorsed by international and independent observers. Thus if the IPKF presence could be used to cast doubts on the legitimacy of the North-East Provincial Council elections, then the same must be said about the legitimacy of other elections, including the Presidential one which brought Premadasa to power.[67] It may also be mentioned here that the IPKF had in fact begun its withdrawal process as early as June 1988 when the then Indian Defence Minister, Pant, was in Sri Lanka. That was, however, only a token withdrawal. A firm decision for phased withdrawal of the IPKF was taken by the Indian Prime Minister and Sri Lankan President Jayewardene in December 1988 during the SAARC Summit in Islamabad. On President Premadasa's election, the IPKF withdrew a second batch, on 9 January 1989. But then, both the new President as well as Sri Lanka's army chief General Hamilton Wanasinghe asked the IPKF to slow down its phased withdrawal in view of the scheduled Parliamentary elections in March and the pressure on Sri Lankan security forces from the JVP insurgency. This underlines the significance of the IPKF presence in Sri Lanka as a source of support for reactivizing its democratic processes. It also exposes the opportunistic and unethical approach taken by the Premadasa administration on the question of IPKF withdrawal. In March 1989, Sri Lanka's Parliamentary Elections were held peacefully; in April/May, the LTTE and the Premadasa administration started coming closer and by June President Premadasa summarily demanded withdrawal of IPKF by the end of July 1989. And then—as a most effective demonstration of the positive role of the IPKF in Sri Lanka—about 10 weeks after its complete withdrawal, the Tamil areas were once again plunged into conflict, chaos and complete disorder. There now seems to be no viable way out from this confrontation.

Thus the IPKF back-up for Sri Lanka's internal security by means of containing the Tamil militant challenge and providing support for the Sri Lankan armed forces under the provisions of the Agreement (Exchange of Letters, para 3.II), proved crucial for Sri Lanka. This indirectly gave an important cushion to Sri Lanka's military manpower and its war-torn economy. And of course, it preserved the unity and territorial integrity of the Island by fighting the separatist challenge, in the terms stipulated by the Agreement. We may note a *Daily News* editorial written on the first anniversary of Indo-Sri Lanka Agreement, 27 July 1988:

> . . . there has been increasing acceptance of the bitter truth, that far from being a sell-out, the Accord almost certainly saved the Island from dismemberment. The strength and capacity of the LTTE alone have been amply manifested in the contest against as many as 50,000 Indian troops.
>
> It must be recognized that at the time of the Peace Accord, the Lankan victory at Vadamarachchi notwithstanding, a whole garrison was under siege in the fort of Jaffna. It must be recognized that the LTTE had not begun their attacks from the rear. The war had already claimed a large number of Lankan lives. Even the IPKF, now engaged in a campaign of going out to round-up and disarm the militants, have already lost over 500 of their men.
>
> Thus their intervention is now recognised as beneficial to Lankan interests. Already the war in the North had begun to cost the government of Sri Lanka over Rs. 13,000 million by 1987. It was thus economically crippling. It slowed down our development programmes and brought our tourist business to a standstill. The war up to July last year, had set Sri Lanka on a collision course with India herself which could have imperilled our very survival.

These IPKF achievements involved heavy costs—the IPKF alone suffered about 1,200 dead and nearly 2,500 injured. Among the dead were a considerable number of officers, since they led out from the front. In consequence, the Force came to adopt a new practice of hiding officers' ranks so that the LTTE, which consciously went for the officers, could not identify them. One estimate as to officer casualties put the figure at 13 battalion commanders, one officer for every 18 of other ranks dead or wounded.[68] Such a high casualty figure cast a demoralizing spell on the Force and was considered unacceptable. Thus the IPKF itself was keen that an early political solution should be found so it might withdraw—a point which many in Sri Lanka overlook in their assessment. The

financial costs of IPKF operations were officially estimated at
more than Rs. 299.12 crores (approximately US $180 million) in
addition to salaries and allowances of the soldiers. Other estimates,
taking everything into account, compute a figure ten times higher
than this.

No less important than the human and financial costs of the
IPKF was the damage and destruction caused by IPKF operations
in Sri Lanka. Besides more than 3,500 casualties (nearly 1,500 dead
and 2,000 wounded) suffered by the LTTE, many innocent civilians
also had to die or suffer injuries, despite the caution and care
observed by the IPKF. In addition to the unavoidable compulsions
of war, fought in urban residential areas with deliberate LTTE
tactics of using innocent people as cover, there were civilian casualties resulting from retaliatory strikes by the IPKF. One such
widely reported example concerned the IPKF reprisals in Valvetti-
turai on 2 August 1989.[69] There were other sporadic instances,
such as of a soldier going berserk as a result of the death of a
close associate or a relative who had been fighting with him, and
then shooting indiscriminately in a fit of rage. The IPKF treated
such cases as murder, and tried and punished the guilty person.

More than the death and injuries, the IPKF was charged for
violation of human rights, of rape, torture, detention under in-
human conditions and disappearances. Amnesty International and
various other international groups and media sources, including
the Sri Lankan and Indian media, published innumerable tales of
such violations both by the IPKF and the LTTE.[70] It may, however,
be mentioned that powerful social support for the LTTE particularly
in the North did sometimes lead to exaggerations. For instance,
the Amnesty International Report on Human Rights Violations in
Sri Lanka before and after the July Agreement, which cited several
instances of violations by the IPKF, also said:

> After its forces had entered Sri Lanka, the IPKF faced increas-
> ing charges of human rights violations, notably after it started
> its military offensive to disarm the LTTE. Many of these allega-
> tions were made by the LTTE itself and most could not be
> substantiated, being hard to have corroborated by independent
> observers.[71]

In another instance, Rajan Hoole, one of the authors of *The
Broken Palmyra*, narrating his experience said:

We heard an allegation from a lady at Manthikai, who seemed to believe it, that an Indian solider had raped a woman at Thondamanaru, who had been admitted to the hospital and had just been discharged. On checking with the hospital we were told that a 45-year old woman from Thondamanaru was admitted to ward 2 with abdominal pains on 3rd August. She had alleged rape and had made a police report. But the party against whom the allegation was made had no connection with the Indian army.[72]

Notwithstanding such cases of false propaganda and exaggerations, there is no denying the fact that the IPKF was guilty of some such charges, and even the officers were aware of them. That is why they, from the very beginning of their operations, constituted local citizens' committees and encouraged them to bring to their notice any instances of excesses on the part of soldiers. All such cases were tried and duly punished, which is mentioned in the Amnesty reports as well.[73] This could not be said about the LTTE, because there was no system of internal accountability within the organization. Moreover, fear of the LTTE also led to the suppression of many instances of the LTTE's high-handedness.[74]

In addition to human rights violations by the IPKF, the damage to agriculture and the economy of the region caused by the IPKF operations was significant. Perhaps, India will help in rehabilitation and rebuilding of the economy of the region, but the scars and the experience will remain as a part of historical memory. The brutalization of Tamil society which has continued ever since the early 1980s was exacerbated by the IPKF, although it had no intentions of contributing to this sad development.

The IPKF also had to pay a heavy price in terms of an increasingly tarnished image in the course of its operations in Sri Lanka. The interest of ordinary soldiers and junior officers in carrying cheap electronic goods—VCRs, stereos and TV sets—made them objects of ridicule in the media.[75] The length of the operations and the appearance of invincibility of the LTTE, however unrealistically projected by the interested sections, allowed people to cast aspersions on the 'fourth largest army of the world'. It even prompted some Sri Lankan observers to suggest that the Sri Lankan army should take lessons from Prabhakaran and his LTTE, and not fear India's military might in future.[76] In the informal circles of diplomats from Western countries, it was a matter of additional amusement that this army was known to be equipped with Soviet weapons.

After all this, it remains on record that the IPKF did not manage to get the LTTE to agree to a surrender of arms and acceptance of the July Agreement. We have noted here that the IPKF was aware of its limitations, realizing from the start that its role was supplementary, as an instrument in creating conditions for political resolution of the ethnic crisis in Sri Lanka. Whatever success that was achieved by the IPKF in this respect was marred by the compulsions of political dynamics in Sri Lanka. For instance, if the Premadasa regime had facilitated real devolution of power to the elected Provincial Council in the North-East—as he had promised to the Chief Minister in early April 1989 in the presence of senior administrators of his government—the credibility of the LTTE claim as the sole representative of the Tamils would have suffered serious erosion. Further, if he had not been persuaded by his narrow political calculations to interfere with IPKF operations, particularly in order to woo the LTTE, then also the eventual outcome could be different. However, notwithstanding appearances and political expediencies, when the present Colombo regime succeeds in finding a final answer to the Tamil question, the role played by the IPKF may be objectively recorded as positive and substantial in the overall analysis.

This leaves us with one final question. Did the IPKF presence in Sri Lanka create new conflicts or exacerbate prevailing ones? This question has been raised elsewhere also.[77] The answer depends on how you look at the situation. One way was indicated in President Premadasa's letter to Rajiv Gandhi cited earlier, saying that the IPKF presence had become a 'deeply divisive and resentful issue'. This was in reference to the intensification of the JVP insurgency and the widening of political cleavages between the ruling party and the opposition. Both the JVP and the opposition had focused attention on the continued IPKF presence in the Island in their attacks on the government. Therefore, on the face of things, the IPKF appeared to have intensified the prevailing internal conflicts in Sri Lanka.

However, if we scrutinize various aspects of this question more closely, we find a different answer. There is no denying the fact that the JVP insurgency and the conflict between the ruling party and the opposition were not due to the IPKF presence in Sri

Lanka. They were the products of Sri Lanka's internal social and political disorientation, resulting from past policies towards broader social, economic and political issues. When the IPKF came to Sri Lanka, the UNP had clung to power without general elections for ten years, creating what some analysts described as a 'New Gaullist–Bonapartist' state.[78] Under such circumstances, the opposition was already up in arms against the government. The JVP, which remained an ally of the ruling party until 1982, was driven to a collision course after being proscribed on false charges in July 1983. Until 1985, the JVP tried to secure a reprieve from the government, but in vain.[79] Thus JVP violence had systematically started in 1986, even before the July Agreement between India and Sri Lanka was concluded. We have noted earlier that JVP pressures were an important factor behind the Jayewardene regime's decision to conclude this Agreement with India.

It is true that the violence in Southern Provinces witnessed a spurt after the IPKF presence in Sri Lanka. But a close study of the JVP campaign would suggest that the IPKF was merely one of the issues on their agenda, and more often than not, a secondary and consequential one. That too because the presence of the IPKF in the Island, having resulted into greater capabilities and manoeuvrability of the Sri Lankan security forces, appeared to be a cause of frustration in the JVP's perceived advance towards its objective of capturing the Sri Lankan state. The JVP accordingly, had to fight hard because the Sri Lankan state too was fighting hard against them. The demanded withdrawal of the IPKF could otherwise facilitate their task. Evidently it was Premadasa's June 1989 ultimatum on IPKF withdrawal that brought about a spurt in the JVP attacks, rather than the reverse. That became clear when Sri Lanka's army chief General Hamilton Wanasinghe and Defence Minister Ranjan Wijeratne publicly stated in December 1988 that they wanted the IPKF to remain in Sri Lanka 'until the Sinhalese rebels were under control, then leave the Sri Lankan army to "demolish" the Tamil Tigers . . . .'[79]

Now that the Sri Lankan security forces have demolished the military challenge posed by the JVP during the IPKF presence in the Island, we can see how the IPKF did in fact contribute to bringing one of the major sources of violence to an end. The ultimate resolution of the insurgency problem, in the South as well as North-East, lies in the political and socio-economic approach of the Sri Lankan government. If the IPKF had not done what it did in sharing Sri Lanka's security burden, one may wonder whether the threatened dismemberment and internal collapse of Sri Lanka could have been averted.

Notes to Chapter 5

1. Paul F. Diehl, 'Peacekeeping Operations and the Quest for Peace', *Political Science Quarterly*, vol. 103, no. 3, Fall 1988, p. 505.
2. Interview with Tamil militant leaders in Colombo, Madras and New Delhi.
3. A senior Indian decision-maker confided to the author that this confusion was created 'partly deliberately', so as to help Jayewardene make the IPKF more acceptable in Sri Lanka, without really submitting the Indian forces to the Sri Lankan command. The question of command structure and the weaknesses of this structure have been commented upon in a study of IPKF operations by Indian Army officers, Major Shankar Bhaduri, Major General Afsir Karim and Lt. General Mathew Thomas, *The Sri Lanka Crisis*, Lancer Paper 1, Lancer International, New Delhi, 1990, pp. 46–47.
4. His address at the United Services Institute of India in New Delhi in March, published in the *USI Journal* and reproduced in *Lanka Guardian* (Colombo), vol. 12, no. 18, 15 January 1990, p. 9.
5. Disclosing this, President Jayewardene said later:

    On August 1, Rajiv sent me a message. He said in it: 'Prabhakaran has agreed to participate in the implementation of the Agreement and the surrender of arms. He would like to be in Jaffna personally to organise the surrender of arms. In the interests of peaceful implementation of the Accord, Prabhakaran will be flown to Jaffna by the evening of August 2. I would like to assure you that if Prabhakaran goes back on his word in any manner or fails to organise the surrender of arms, the Indian army will move to disarm the LTTE by force.' *Sunday Times*, 11 February 1990.

6. Rajan Hoole, 'Point Pedro Revisited', *Christian Worker*, (Special Supplement), 2nd and 3rd Quarter, 1987, p. 6.
7. This speech was a clever mixture of acceptance of the Agreement and also its criticism. Its thrust was that the Agreement fell far short of Tamil expectations and yet the LTTE had to accept it because it was being forced on it by India and there was no other option. For the text of the speech see *The Hindu*, 7 August 1987; *India Today*, 15 August 1987.
8. Such a threat came from LTTE leader Thileepan as early as on 6 September 1987 following the killing of three important LTTE militants of Vavuniya. *Sun* (Colombo), 7 September 1987.
9. Bhaduri, Karim and Thomas, *The Sri Lanka Crisis*, pp. 61–63.
10. There was considerable mystery as to Thileepan being chosen for the fast unto death and allowed to die, even when talks were in progress between Prabhakaran and Dixit on the demands for which Thileepan started his fast. Leadership

rivalries and Prabhakaran's personal preferences within the LTTE were alleged to be important factors behind this. It is also true that Thileepan was not removed from the fast by the LTTE, in order to make political capital for the organisation in a situation where it was becoming increasingly isolated. See Rajan Hoole et al., *The Broken Palmyra* (Volume I. Historical Background), Harvey Mudd College Press, Claremont, California, 1988, pp. 95–102.

11. In the Interim Administration it was agreed to allot six places to the LTTE and in addition appoint the Chief Administrator from among the list of three proposed by the LTTE. Two seats each were to be given to Muslims and Sinhalese and another two were meant for the nominees of the TULF. It is important to note that the other militant groups found no place in the proposed Interim Administrative Council. This gives a lie to alegations that the IPKF or India was siding with these other militant groups to balance the LTTE. This situation, however, was to change once the LTTE decided to break this agreement and the overall understanding with India.

   As for the delegation of executive powers to this Interim Administration, President Jayewardene had agreed to go by the Bangalore proposals (paras 10.1 and 10.2), i.e., the 19 December proposals. Such powers included law and order besides other responsibilities. For the full text of this understanding, see Appendices.

12. For details see Rajan Hoole et al., *The Broken Palmyra*, p. 102.

13. P.S. Suryanarayana, *The Peace Trap: An Indo-Sri Lankan Political Crisis*, Affiliated East-West Press, New Delhi, 1988, pp. 16–17, 24–25.

14. As cited in *The Times of India*, 29 November 1987.

15. *Sunday Times* (Colombo), 11 February 1990.

16. As cited in *Tamil Voice International* (London), 15 March 1989, p. 10. A detailed account of Gopalswamy's journey also appeared in *Illustrated Weekly of India* (Bombay), written by K.P. Sunil in the 21 May 1989 issue.

17. Personal interview with Tamil militants and Indian and Sri Lankan highly-placed persons.

18. For these details, see *The Times of India* and *The Hindu* of 4 October 1987. Possibly this was a local arrangement.

19. *The Times of India*, 5 October 1987.

20. *Indian Express, The Times of India* and *The Hindu* of 10 and 11 October 1987.

21. *The Times of India*, 31 July 1987.

22. *Indian Express*, 10 October 1987.

23. As reported by Dilip Dobb in *India Today* in December 1987, cited in *Island* (Colombo), 20 December 1987.

24. It may be useful to recall Prabhakaran's address to Tamil masses at Suthumalai Convention in early August where he said:

   The weapons that we took up and deployed for your safety and protection, for your liberation, for your emancipation, we now entrust to the Indian government. In taking from us our weapons—the only means of protection for Eelam Tamils—the Indian government takes over from us the great responsibility of protecting our people. The handing over of arms only signifies the transfer of this responsibility. I wish to emphasize very firmly here that by the virtue of our handing over our weapons to it, the Indian government should assume full responsibility for the life and security of every one of the Eelam Tamils . . . .

as cited in a paper presented by the Political Committee of the LTTE, at the International Tamil Conference on the Tamil National Struggle and the Indo-Sri Lanka Peace Accord, London, 30 April to 1 May 1988. Available in published form: N. Seevaratnam, *The Tamil National Question and the Indo-Sri Lankan Accord*, Konark, New Delhi, 1989.

25. *The Telegraph* (Calcutta), 18 October 1987. Many in Sri Lanka believed that the LTTE surrendered much less than 60 per cent of their heavy arms (only about 20 to 25 per cent).

26. *The Times of India*, 5 October 1987.

27. According to both Indian and foreign observers, in the beginning of the conflict the Indian infantry was equipped with old self-loading rifles which were no match for the speed and power of the AK-47 used by the LTTE. The Indian soldiers thus preferred to fight with weapons captured from the militants, a very unusual phenomenon in low intensity/insurgency warfare. See comments by the Indian officer Lt.Gen. P.C. Katoch cited in *Tamil Voice International*, 1 June 1989; also see an article by Rohan Gunasekara in *International Defence Review*, January 1990, pp. 41–42; also *India Today*, 31 January 1990. Details of several operational lapses on the part of the IPKF in not preparing itself for the eventual confrontation with the LTTE despite warning signals sent by Army Headquarters and the Ministry of External Affairs, through its High Commission in Colombo may be found in Bhaduri, Karim and Thomas, *The Sri Lanka Crisis*, pp. 31–35.

28. *Telegraph* (Calcutta), 18 October 1987. Earlier, the IPKF's claims that air power was not used to avoid civilian casualties were confirmed by the Sri Lankan minister saying that though the commanders had demanded air cover for operations of such a vast magnitude, the Chief of the army staff had turned it down in the interests of civilian population. *The Times of India*, 15 October 1987.

This denial had left some of the junior officers grumbling, saying that Delhi politicians were preventing the generals from fighting in the way they knew best and wanted to do. (*Telegraph*, 18 October 1987).

Political interference in operational tactics has been resented by the defence analysts of IPKF operations. See Brigadier H.S. Sodhi (Retd.), 'Army at the Crossroads' in *Indian Defence Review*, January 1990, pp. 143–44; also *India Today*, 31 January 1988. The absence of proper use of air power in IPKF operations has surprised many defence analysts. See, IDR Research Team, 'Afghanistan and Sri Lanka: A Comparison of Operational Styles', *Indian Defence Review*, January 1990, pp. 82–86.

29. *The Times of India*, 20 October 1987. Also, *Indian Defence Review*, January 1990, p. 82.

30. For an account of the Navy's role in the IPKF operations during 'Operation Pawan' and later, see reports by Mahendra Ved in *The Hindustan Times* of 10 November 1987, 27 December 1987 and 31 May 1989.

31. For a discussion of the operation details of 'Operation Pawan', see Bhaduri, Karim and Thomas, 1990, *The Sri Lanka Crisis*, pp. 66–79; also, Edgar

O'Ballance, *The Cyanide War (Tamil Insurrection in Sri Lanka, 1973–88)*, Brassey's London, 1989, pp. 88–110.

For an insider's view of 'Operation Pawan', see a letter by a battalion commander involved in the operation, in *Indian Defence Review*, January 1990, pp. 192–94.

32. See my piece in *The Times of India*, 'Premadasa and the LTTE: Strange Bedfellows' on 21 April 1989; also my 'Sri Lanka Crisis and the IPKF' in *Patriot*, 10 July 1989.

33. *The Times of India*, 3 July 1989.

34. *Ibid.* Also see *Telegraph* (Calcutta), 4 July 1989.

35. *Indian Defence Review*, January 1990, p. 85. Also Bhaduri, Karim and Thomas, *The Sri Lanka Crisis*, pp. 31–35, 60–62.

36. Dixit's USI Journal speech.

37. *The Times of India*, 29 November 1987, for Pant's statement. For the statements of the Indian diplomats see *The Times of India*, 5 October 1987, and *Telegraph*, 18 October 1987. The latter paper reported that Prabhakaran was described as a psychopathic killer.

38. *Tribune* (Chandigarh), 31 December 1987.

39. See *Tamil Times* (London), April 1988, p. 10; P. Nedumaran, 'The Role of Tamil Nadu in the Tamil Eelam Liberation Struggle' in *Tamil Voice International*, 1 May 1989, pp. 19–22.

40. *The Hindu*, 2 April 1988. Control of Trincomalee did not figure in what may be considered as the most outspoken articulation of IPKF's mission by High Commissioner Dixit. In his USI speech he conceded that the IPKF operations amounted to

> . . . an external projection of our influence to tell our neighbours that if, because of your compulsions, of your aberrations, you pose a threat to us, we are capable of, or we have a political will to project ourselves within your territorial jurisdiction for the limited purpose of bringing you back . . . to the path of detachment and non-alignment where you don't endanger our security.

41. *The Hindu*, 27 and 30 May 1988.

42. *The Hindu*, 13 February 1988.

43. *Indian Express*, 11 October 1987.

44. Surayanarayan, *Peace Trap*, pp. 17–18; also *Indian Defence Review*, January 1990, pp. 85, 143; and Bhaduri, Karim and Thomas, *The Sri Lankan Crisis*.

45. *The Times of India*, 14 and 16 October 1987. First it was feared that all the 30 paratroopers dropped were killed. These estimates were revised when it was found out that only 8 had been killed and the rest wounded. See *Indian Defence Review*, January 1990, p. 83; also Bhaduri, Karim and Thomas, *The Sri Lankan Crisis*.

46. N. Shanmugaratnam, 'Seven Days in Jaffna: Life Under Indian Occupation', *Race and Class*, vol. 31, no. 2, 1989, pp. 1–15.

47. See Gen. Pande's statement in *The Hindu*, 2 April 1988, where he admitted that the IPKF was making use of the hatred between the LTTE and other militant groups to its advantage. Also Lt. Gen. Dipender Singh's interview in *Tribune*, 31 December 1987.

48. Text of the Exchange of Letters in *Indian Express*, 9 July 1989; the letter was dated 2 June 1989 (text included in Appendices).

49. President Premadasa said so to me in a long interview in Colombo on 4 August 1989 at his ancestral home. He repeated this on 20 January 1990 in a similar interview at the Presidential Secretariat in Colombo. Defence Minister Ranjan Wijeratne admitted this in New Delhi in December 1989 while talking informally to a select group of Indian intellectuals, where I was present.

50. *National Herald*, 2 November 1989.

51. *The Hindu*, 27 June 1988. These talks broke down because of disagreement on the period of cease-fire and other issues.

52. *Tribune*, 31 December 1987 for Lt. Gen. Dipender Singh's statement, and *The Hindu*, 2 April 1988 for Lt. General Pande's statement.

53. See for instance *The Hindu*, 21 October 1987, *The Hindustan Times*, 10 November 1987, *The Times of India*, 21 December 1987, *Indian Express*, 13 January 1988, *Daily News* (Colombo) 31 August 1988. Also see, Edgar O'Ballance, *The Cyanide War*, pp. 68, 113.

54. Interviews in Colombo during 1988–89 with foreign and Sri Lankan journalists, diplomats and other observers.

55. These allegations were denied by Sri Lankan Minister of State for Defence Ranjan Wijeratne, but the authenticity of such arms transfers have been supported by many others in Sri Lanka in personal interviews with the author. The quantities of the arms given by the Sri Lankan army to the LTTE reportedly included 7 tonnes of plastic explosives, 18 0.50 calibre guns capable of being used against low-flying aircraft and helicopters, two truckloads of light machine guns with 20,000 rounds of ammunition per piece of gun supplied. Some highly-placed Sri Lankans now resent that these weapons, explosives and ammunitions are being used by the LTTE against the Sri Lankan forces themselves in hostilities and confrontation renewed between them after 11 June 1990.

56. For these talks see *The Hindu*, 28 February 1989; *Tribune*, 29 February 1988; *Tamil Times* (London), April 1988, p. 3. It was reported that the LTTE leader Yogi was taken for talks in a Sri Lankan air force helicopter and dressed like a Sinhala soldier. It seems that President Jayewardene was not aware of these talks or of the liasion that existed between the LTTE and the Sri Lankan security forces, the objective of which, as commented by Indian High Commissioner Dixit, was to isolate India and embarrass the IPKF operations.

57. Robert McDonald, 'Fighting with the Tamil Tigers', *Janes Defence Weekly*, 1 August 1987, pp. 191–93; Edgar O' Ballance, *The Cyanide War*, pp. 60–72, 102, 106.

58. See reports in *The Hindu*, 4 August 1988, and *Daily News*, 4, 8 and 31 August 1988.

59. *Telegraph* (Calcutta), 18 October 1987, referring to Dixit's remarks on LTTE's partial surrender of arms.

60. For some evidence to this effect see *Sri Lanka News*, 16 September 1987, and *Sunday Times*, 25 October 1987 (Report by Simon Freeman) as cited in N. Satyendra's paper presented in International Tamil Conference (London, 30 April to 1 May 1988).

61. Para 4. 'Minutes of the Security Co-ordination Groups Meeting Held on 19th

October 1989 at OP HQ Mod'. At this meeting others present included GOC-IPKF Gen. Kalkat and the Chief Minister of N–E Province A. Varatharaja-perumal (for text of minutes, see Appendices).

62. For some reports of the arms being given to the LTTE or sold on the black market, see article by J. Stissanayagam in *Island* (Colombo), 21 May 1989.

63. Dixit's USI talk. Also General Kalkat's interview in *National Herald* (New Delhi), 2 November 1989.

64. *The Hindustan Times*, 31 May 1989, also of 10 November and 27 December 1987.

65. The TULF President told this to the author in an interview in Colombo in November 1988 before the elections.

66. I observed the Provincial Council Elections in Trincomalee and Batticaloa along with a group of Indian, Sri Lankan and foreign journalists. After the elections, the media reports endorsed that they had been free and fair. An unexpectedly large number of Muslims, Tamils and Sinhalese (in Amparai) voted in these elections.

67. A court case is pending against President Premadasa's election. For a detailed argument, based on statistical support, to show how fraudulent President Premadasa's election was particularly in the South, see Janaki Perera, *Subversion of the Electoral Process in Sri Lanka*, n.d.

68. Col. Prithvi Nath (Retd.), 'Overview of the IPKF Mission', *The Statesman*, 6 December 1989.

69. *Financial Times* (London), 18 August 1989; for another account of reprisal killings, see *Tamil Voice International* (London), 15 May 1989.

70. Besides Amnesty International Reports see for instance, *International Alert* report by Eduardo Marino in December 1987; *Sunday Observer* (Bombay), 18–24 December 1988; A report by Tavleen Singh in *Indian Express*, 1 June 1989; *Tamil Times*, March and April 1988; *Tamil Voice International*, 1 May 1989; and Rajan Hoole *et al.*, *The Broken Palmyra*.

71. *Tamil Times* (London), June 1988, p. 6.

72. Rajan Hoole in *Christian Worker* (Special Supplement), 2nd and 3rd Quarter 1987.

73. Gen. Dipender Singh's interview, *Tribune*, 31 December 1987.

74. Shanmugaratnem, in *Race and Class*, 'Seven Days in Jaffna', 1989. Also Rajan Hoole et al., *The Broken Palmyra*.

75. *Indian Express*, 2 March 1988; the LTTE leader Mahattya commenting on the IPKF in a press interview after two weeks of operations said, 'We are cyanide capsule guerrillas. How can these people who were buying electrical goods and TV sets in Jaffna have the same courage as we have. They have never tasted urban guerrilla warfare before'. *Island* (Colombo), 25 October 1987.

76. Malinga H. Gunaratna's study, *For A Sovereign State*, Sarvodaya, Colombo, 1988.

77. Kumar Rupesinghe, 'Peace-Keeping and Peace Building', in *Bulletin of Peace Proposals*, vol. 20, no. 3, September 1989, pp. 335–50.

78. See M.P. Moor's contribution in James Manor (ed.), *Sri Lanka in Change and Crisis*, Croom Helm, London, 1984.

79. This was disclosed by Ronnie de Mel, Finance Minister in Jayewardene's

government until early 1988, to the author in an informal conversation in New Delhi, in 1990.

80. See my 'JVP and the IPKF', *The Hindustan Times*, 24 August 1989. This point was also clearly emphasised in a Sinhala paper, *Raviya*.

81. Rohan Gunasekera, 'Sri Lanka's Security Nightmare', *International Defence Review*, January 1990, pp. 41–42.

6

Appraisal: Reflections on Theoretical Aspects and Policy Prospects

India's peace-keeping role in Sri Lanka has come under considerable public and press criticism both within and outside India. It eventually ended without resolving the Island's ethnic conflict. India had to terminate the mission in the midst of this process and withdraw its peace-keeping forces under intense political controversy raised by the Sri Lankan President. This exposed India to unnecessary political embarrassment and humiliation. We have discussed some of these aspects in the preceding chapter, while evaluating the IPKF's role by weighing objective factors against stated criticism and popular perceptions.

When we look at the totality of the Indian involvement in Sri Lanka's ethnic crisis since 1983, the peace-keeping role should be seen as a continuation and logical culmination of India's peace-making role i.e. one of third-party mediation. There has been a clear shift from mediation to peace-keeping, the latter being an inevitable part of the obligation to enforce the Indo-Sri Lanka Agreement of 1987, arrived at following a long-drawn and difficult mediation process. This implementation part, including the question of deployment and use of Indian forces, was provided for in the Agreement and was undertaken, not only with approval and support but also at the intiative and on the insistence, of the legitimately constituted government of Sri Lanka, as already discussed.

Leverage Mediation

India's mediatory role in Sri Lanka does not fall into the categories of such a role played either under UN auspices or by private, unofficial groups of individuals or organizations. There exists a sizeable literature on case studies and theoretical aspects of these categories of third-party mediation,[1] but with less emphasis on mediation in a conflict between domestic guerrillas and the established government. Particularly so, when such guerrillas are waging a war of ethnic separation like as in Sri Lanka. There is a striking parallel between the Sri Lankan case and that of Sudanese civil war, yet the character of Indian mediation in Sri Lanka was different. In the Sudanese case mediation was carried out mainly by non-governmental organizations, although occasional involvement of third-party official agencies was not completely absent. In Sri Lanka, the principal mediating agent was the Government of India, which at times did use some private individuals like press people for information and communication with either of the conflicting sides.[2]

While undertaking the role of mediation in Sri Lanka, India was not an uninterested or unaffected party, a condition that many third-party mediators are expected to fulfil. India's stakes were very clearly defined and articulated. In fact, however, no mediator is totally uninterested in a conflict resolution process, as is sometimes claimed or even projected as a desirable condition. All third-party mediators have their specific motives and seek specific material or other rewards.[3] India's objectives and interests underlying its mediatory role in Sri Lanka were several and varied. They ranged from the sublime to the obtuse, involving the narrow objectives of the ruling Congress Party to consolidate its alliance with the regional All India Anna DMK Party of M.G. Ramachandran to perpetuate its influence in Tamil Nadu; the stalling of Tamil separatism in Sri Lanka and its undesirable consequences in India; as well as keeping Western and other inimical external influences away from Sri Lanka and the Indian subcontinent as a whole. No less important for India was the objective of ensuring and strengthening peace and stability in its neighbourhood because the conflicts like the one in Sri Lanka, had serious spillover implications for India itself. The order of priorities and the nature of these objectives were continually reformulated as the dimensions of the conflict and India's mediatory role evolved through various stages.

India, as an interested and affected party in the Sri Lankan ethnic conflict, did not have to wait for any invitation from the combatants in Sri Lanka to initiate the mediation process. It invited itself to do so. The Tamil militant groups welcomed India's involvement in the conflict, hoping that this would be supportive of their broader as well as specific goals—notwithstanding divergent perceptions among militant groups about what exactly the Indian role should be and precisely how it should be carried out.

The attitude of the Sri Lankan government towards Indian mediation was not positive. It was initially seen as an unwanted imposition, and was accepted subsequently with considerable reservations as an unavoidable compulsion, until the signing of the July 1987 Agreement. We have already discussed the factors behind the Sri Lankan attitude towards Indian mediation. They included the Island's apprehensions and sensitivities towards a big and powerful neighbour, India's known identification and sympathy with the Tamils, and political and psychological incompatibilities between the Indian and the Sri Lankan leaders, particularly between Mrs. Gandhi and J.R. Jayewardene. We have also mentioned earlier that a good deal of Sri Lankan resistance to the Indian mediation stemmed from expectations of support from Western and anti-Indian sources like China and Pakistan. When these eventually proved ineffective, the result was the setting aside of resistance, as President Jayewardene explained after signing the 1987 Agreement.

The driving force behind India's third-party mediation in Sri Lanka was the *leverage* that India's capabilities, its geo-strategic location and its ethnic (Tamil) identity gave it in relation to the nature and area of the conflict. Here it is important to note that the leverage basis of the mediatory role has not been analysed in the available literature. Accordingly, there are no theoretical insights or analytical framework to fall back upon. But it is obvious that leverage, of whatever nature and extent, constitutes an asset for the peacemaker, the mediator. This was decisively demonstrated in the case of the US mediation in Middle East where the Camp David Argreement would not have been possible without the leverage enjoyed and acquired by the USA in relation to Egypt and Israel. The USA has also made use of its leverage in its peace-making role elsewhere in the world, most recently between India and Pakistan. The special focus of this US peace-making role concerns confidence building between the two traditional South Asian adversaries in the areas of nuclear and conventional conflict.[4] In South Asia, the Soviet Union also exercised its leverage to bring

about peace between India and Pakistan after the 1965 war over
Kashmir. The outcome of the Soviet peace-making was the Tashkent
Agreement signed between India and Pakistan in January 1966.
India played a leverage-based mediation role in its neighbourhood
even earlier. The resolution of internal conflict in Nepal between
the Rana rulers on the one hand and King Tribhuwan and the
democratic forces on the other during 1950–51 may be recalled
here.

Leverage-based mediation is therefore, a viable subject for serious
and systematic theoretical exploration. A working hypothesis may
be that a mediator exercises leverage through a complex and
evolving process of incentives and punishments to each of the
combatants who cannot afford to ignore or defy the mediator, who
in turn has his specific stakes in resolution of the conflict in a
desired manner. In order to be effective, the mediator has, to
begin with, to transform his potential leverage into an active and
functional instrument of policy by creating channels and linkages
with the combatants through which leverage can be exercised. The
leverage to be exercised can be of various forms—economic, political, military, cultural, personal, psychological and so on.

With regard to India's peace-making role in Sri Lanka, the
potential of Indian leverage vis-à-vis the Tamil militant groups lay
in the fact that they were based in India and enjoyed political and
material support for their struggle there. The Government of India
could, therefore, offer them further support, but it could also
obstruct their operations. India could likewise put pressure on the
Sri Lankan government to come to terms with the Tamil militants
and accommodate their genuine and legitimate grievances. Accordingly, from the militants' point of view, there was a strong possibility
that the Government of India would act as their ally in the ethnic
conflict. To translate this potential leverage into an active instrument of policy, the Government of India established linkages and
channels of interaction with the Tamil militant groups at various
levels. This involved clandestine contacts through its intelligence
outfit, the Research and Analysis Wing (RAW), and open political
contacts at the political level through bureaucratic and party channels of the state of Tamil Nadu and the central government in
New Delhi. The much-criticized strategy of providing arms and
allowing training and operational bases to the Tamil militants was
a calculated move by the Indian government to enhance its leverage

and establish channels. This also helped India to bring the militant groups under close watch and control, so that it could not only counter other influences operating on the Tamil groups, including those of the Sri Lankan and extra-regional intelligence agencies, but also use them to further its own desired form of conflict resolution accommodating India's perceived interests. India's moves through its political, bureaucratic and intelligence agencies to multiply the numbers of the militant groups and create and exploit their mutual internecine contradictions were also aimed at enhancing and activating the leverage.

We should note that proliferation of channels and autonomy of action granted or acquired by a given agency of the Government of India in the long run, sought to undermine the leverage by making the policy process complex and uncontrollable. This also tended to vitiate the image of Indian government among the Tamil groups, making it into a partisan and dishonest broker. The LTTE remained the most disenchanted militant group vis-à-vis the Government of India in this regard, which was to prove a crucial factor in the later stages of mediation and the final outcome of India's overall role. The LTTE's refusal to fully endorse India's leverage was also partly due to the fact that it could rely on other channels and sources of support, both within and outside India, which were not quite conducive to the Indian role. Recent revelations by a former Israeli intelligence (Mossad) agent have graphically described his agency's contacts with and support to the LTTE.[5]

The factors that provided for Indian leverage vis-à-vis Tamil militant groups also in turn gave leverage to India vis-à-vis the Sri Lankan government. India's geographical proximity to the scene of conflict, its tremendous military and other capabilities, its political influence on opposition parties in Sri Lanka and its willingness to exercise its influence on the outcome of the ethnic conflict added to the Indian government's leverage in relation to Colombo. As noted earlier, the pro-Tamil bias in India's position on the Sri Lankan conflict and poor political rapport between the top leadership of the two countries led to strong resistance from Colombo to India's mediatory role. To break, or at least weaken, this resistance so as to turn the potential leverage into an effective instrument of policy, Indian Prime Minister, Mrs. Gandhi, delivered a strong statement saying that India would not remain silent or inactive in view of the ethnic conflict in Sri Lanka. Following this, she literally forced Colombo to accept the visit of her then foreign minister, Narasimha Rao. The final assertion of leverage to get the Indian mediation accepted by the Sri Lankan government took place during President Jayewardene's visit to India towards the end of 1983, in connection with the Commonwealth Summit Conference in New Delhi.

All these attempts led to the facilitation of the mediation process begun by India's senior diplomat and Mrs. Gandhi's special envoy, G. Parthasarathy, who succeeded in drafting the much-debated document called Annexure C. This document provided the basis for evolving the final package for settlement of the Tamil issue. The induction of Parthasarathy in the medition process was important since, in addition to being a suave diplomat, he also had a close rapport with the Tamil groups, being himself a Tamil from Tamil Nadu. His association with some of the Tamil groups (the moderate TULF) was close and of long standing.

In order to enhance their leverage with the Sri Lankan government, Indian leaders and policy-makers at all levels repeatedly asserted that they had no support for the separatist Eelam objective of the Tamil militants. Emphasis that India sought a solution to the Tamil problem within the framework of a united, independent and sovereign Sri Lanka was, besides being in India's perceived interests, also a necessary precondition to facilitate the mediation.

India's leverage and peace-making efforts were subsequently enhanced by two other developments. First was the removal of Mrs. Gandhi from the scene in October 1984 and the shift in the US position on the Sri Lankan question, wherein contrary to the initial expectations of the Sri Lankan government, the USA endorsed India's mediation efforts and persuaded Sri Lanka to cooperate with these efforts to find a viable and mutually acceptable solution. Despite these developments, however, the mediation process broke down and the Sri Lankan government resorted to seeking a military solution to the problem in early 1987. Then India even directly intervened in May–June 1987, by the dropping of 'bread bombs', to restore the mediation and assert its leverage.

Driven by its own perceived interests and confidence of leverage, the Indian third-party mediation in the Sri Lankan conflict did not follow the expected stages of the mediation process.[6] India's mediation relied mostly upon communication and exchange of information between the two contending parties. This was, however, not a simple case of passing on messages from one side to the other, or of clarifying issues of mutual confusion and misunderstanding. Instead, India's role was marked by its own initiative in formulating proposals and pursuing them assertively. In the process, many of these proposals were reformulated to accommodate specific suggestions of the concerned parties.

A close scrutiny of this process would suggest that India often found it difficult to get Colombo to accept its proposals. Even when it secured the endorsement of the top leadership in the government, difficulties arose at other political and bureaucratic levels, and the conversion of these proposals into decisions and agreements could not be achieved smoothly. This was due to internal dynamics of Sinhala politics, which generated pressures so powerful at times that the Sri Lankan government had to retreat from arrived at positions, which in turn vitiated the endorsement secured by India from the Tamil militant groups on given proposals. The fate of Annexure C, the All Party Conference move, the 19 December 1986 proposals, the pre-Agreement negotiations and the execution of the 1987 Agreement on the Sri Lankan government's part, may be recalled here to illustrate the point. The complexity of Sinhala politics and the depth of the Indian leverage can be guessed from the fact that at one stage in June 1987, during the final round of negotiations on the 1987 Agreement, President Jayewardene thought it proper to let the Indian High Commissioner in Colombo address his cabinet colleagues to explain various aspects of the proposed Agreement. It is important to recall here that by then, India had almost decided to deviate from its mediatory role in favour of becoming a party to the Agreement, and President Jayewardene had decided to accept India as such.

India's interaction with the Tamil groups in formulating the proposals had a greater degree of confidence, but also more arbitrariness. Consultations with militant groups mostly took place in informal and unstructured forms. Only seldom were serious attempts made to coordinate systematically the positions of all the militant groups and evolve a consensus among them on key issues. There were tactical advantages in this procedure, since it gave greater manoeuvrability to the mediator, India. Accordingly, on many sensitive proposals like the question of autonomy and devolution of power to the Tamil areas, India generally went by its own perception of Tamil interests and what it thought could be feasible in terms of securing Colombo's endorsement. This style did not go very well with some of the Tamil groups, particularly the LTTE, whose uncompromising stance created many practical difficulties. It appears that the Indian mediation had an underlying assumption that it had more leverage over the Tamils than over the Sri Lankan government. Lack of strong and viable consensus among Tamil militants further strengthened this assumption, and made India's stance of 'taking Tamil groups for granted' possible as well as unavoidable.

An important aspect of India's leverage mediation was that no real attempt was made to bring the combatants face to face with each other and make them resolve the issues involved in their conflict. This was due to several factors. In terms of India's own specific interests, this mode of mediation was not considered appropriate. But no less important in this respect was the mutual antipathy of the two combatants towards negotiating with each other. The attitude of the Sri Lankan government was quite rigid on this issue since, in view of the pressures of Sinhala politics, they did not want to yield any legitimacy or respect to Tamil militant groups. The Tamil militant groups were also equally strongly convinced that the Sri Lankan government was not serious in wishing to accommodate the legitimate demands of the Tamils: therefore, there was no use sitting with them to negotiate a solution of the ethnic conflict. Both these attitudes emerged clearly at the only attempt made to bring the two parties face to face in two rounds at the Bhutanese capital of Thimphu in mid-1985. The choice of Thimphu was interesting, as it underlined India's concern to not let the mediation stray from its area of influence. India was present in full diplomatic strength at Thimphu and was assertive—so much so that it ran into acrimonious exchanges with some of the Tamil militants. Thimphu also reflected the Sri Lankan desire to refuse to sit with the militants for talks while on Indian territory. Each of the Sri Lankan combatants, however, used the Thimphu round to make a tactical point that the other party was not sincere in seeking to resolve the conflict. It was hoped by each of the parties that by doing so it would bring India's position nearer to its own. The reluctance of the two parties to face each other also frustrated India's second attempt to get them face to face in November 1986 during the SAARC Summit in Bangalore. This reluctance, in a way, contributed to India's decision to become a party to the July 1987 Agreement, since there seemed to be no other alternative. Both the Sri Lankan government as well as the Tamil militants must share the blame, or credit, for this.

The Peace-keeping Adventure

India's decision to become a party to the 1987 Agreement ensured that its peace-making role was to be transformed into a peace-keeping role. Analysing this role is difficult, since we lack a reliable theoretical framework. Commenting on this difficulty, the well-known analyst of peace-keeping operations, Allen James, observed that 'peace-keeping is an international activity but there are no, or very few, internationally agreed procedures." There is also the difficulty of defining the peace-keeping role both in terms of the 'host(s)' and the peace-keepers. Most peace-keeping experiences so far have been classified into two categories: those under UN auspices, and those resulting from individual initiatives bordering on or constituting outright intervention, such as the US action in Grenada. There is a vast body of literature on UN peace-keeping,[8] whereas interventionist peace-keeping has been analysed more as a form of intervention than peace-keeping, for theoretical purposes.

The Indian peace-keeping in Sri Lanka does not fall into either of these categories. It had nothing to do with the United Nations, as neither the Agreement nor the deployment of the peace-keeping force was done with any reference to, let alone approval of, the UN. Nonetheless it had many features in common with experiences, particularly those related to the execution or enforcement of the Agreements, and those undertaken in situations of civil war. The significance of the execution and enforcement aspects is expected to grow in view of the emerging challenges to UN peace-keeping. And in the face of these challenges, it has been argued that analysts must 'eschew any general theory of peace-keeping' and depend more upon the concept of 'pragmatic flexibility'.[9]

India's role in Sri Lanka cannot be put in the category of interventionist peace-keeping either. At times reference is made to this category, for two reasons: one that India intervened in May–June 1987 under the pretext of dropping relief supplies to Jaffna, which was under attack from the Sri Lankan forces. But, as noted earlier, this was intended to restore India's mediatory role and was not in pursuance of peace-keeping. This intervention, it may be reiterated, was carried out to seek a political and peaceful resolution to the Sri Lankan conflict. Morever, the May–June 1987 intervention proved totally non-violent, without any use of force.

The second reason for not characterising the Indian peace-keeping force as interventionist was because the IPKF was a part of the July 1987 Agreement and was provided for in that. The unfortunate controversy raised by the new Sri Lankan President, Premadasa, on the operations and presence of the IPKF has been dealt with earlier. We have also noted that it was the political change in India that provided legitimacy to Premadasa's approach to the IPKF, but in no way can the Indian peace-keeping be seen as a case of intervention.

The controversy, however, did focus attention on a vital lacuna in the July 1987 Agreement: there was neither a clear definition nor any detailed guidelines for the use of force by India in Sri Lanka. The mutual obligations and responsibilities of the 'host' country and the 'visiting' force ought to have been spelled out in the Agreement or in some other document appended to it. This could be done even subsequent to the beginning of IPKF operations, which presumably started under the strain of unexpected developments. It was the absence of these provisions and guidelines that enabled President Premadasa to interpret the obligations of the 'host' country in a manner suitable to his narrow political interests. Similarly, the Janata Dal government of V.P. Singh in India also felt itself free of any responsibilities to ensure the precise relationship between the execution of the July 1987 Agreement and the continuation or withdrawal of the IPKF.

Lessons for the Future

While India's peace-making role produced the July 1987 Agreement, its peace-keeping role ended on an unhappy note. This was so, notwithstanding a number of positive achievements secured by the IPKF in restoring peace and order in Sri Lanka's Tamil areas. In India, the sore national experience resulting from the IPKF role gave rise to the instant emotional and normative reaction that such a responsibility should not be undertaken in a neighbouring country, particularly not in a situation where deployment and use of force is envisaged to deal with a civil war. Expressing this mood, India's new Foreign Minister, I.K. Gujral, stated in a press conference on his return from the Maldives in March 1990, that India 'would never send its forces to a neighbouring country.'[10] This was in reaction to a question on the IPKF withdrawal from Sri Lanka, though it may be of interest to note here that the Maldives had also invited Indian forces to help it crush a coup attempt; and those Indian forces were still in the Maldives when Gujral made this statement. In addition to reflecting the emotional and normative mood of the country on the IPKF question, Gujral's statement also had a political undertone: to highlight what was considered as a faulty policy of the Rajiv Gandhi regime towards India's neighbours.

Gujral's statement did not go down well with many in India's foreign and defence policy establishments, nor with the strategic community (experts, commentators and analysts). Though the underlying sentiment was endorsed in the light of the experience in Sri Lanka, it was seen as a hasty and somewhat polemical evaluation of a complex foreign policy endeavour on India's part. It was also seen as an indirect attempt to undermine the sacrifices made by the Indian armed forces and the achievements secured by them under harsh operational conditions. Above all, the statement was seen as an attempt to foreclose India's foreign policy options in unforeseen contingencies in the strategically vital neighbouring region. This was undesirable, particularly so when done at the level of a foreign minister, and that too of a minority government like the Janata Dal government.[11]

In looking at the lessons of India's role in Sri Lanka for future policy perspective, we need to make an objective evaluation of this role in the comparative context of past experiences in similar situations and possible future scenarios. In Chapter 1 we mentioned past situations where India got involved in dealing with or resolving internal conflicts in neighbouring countries—Burma (1948–49), Nepal (1950–51 and 1951–52), Sri Lanka (1971 and 1983–89), Bangladesh (1971) and the Maldives (1987–90), may be recalled here. (For details, refer to Chapter 1, Table 1.) In these South Asian internal conflicts, Indian armed personnel were despatched and force was used except on two occasions, namely Burma (1948–49) and Nepal (1950–51). This was done at the explicit request from the concerned neighbouring governments. The case of the Bangladesh crisis (1971) may be taken as an exception in this regard, though not quite so. Technically, in the final stages of the Bangladesh struggle, a government in exile formed under Tajuddin Ahmed, a close associate of Mujibur Rahman, had made a unilateral declaration of independence and asked the Government of India to help the Bangladesh nationalist forces led by Mukti-Bahini to rid the new country of Pakistani domination. Open and declared entry of Indian armed forces into what was then East Pakistan, could seek legitimacy on the basis of the request of the Tajuddin government. Prior to that, however, India's military involvement on the side of the Bangladesh struggle was of a clandestine nature, but it did amount to interference in the internal affairs of Pakistan in the legal as well as political sense of the term.

Out of all the experiences of India's involvement in the internal conflicts of neighbouring countries in response to requests from friendly governments, it was only in Sri Lanka (1987–89) that political and military embarrassment occurred. In all other cases, India completed the roles assigned to its various missions to the satisfaction of the respective host governments. In none of these cases were the questions of mutual obligations of the 'host' and the 'visitors' specifically defined, nor did they come under any controversy or dispute. This was perhaps one reason why it did not occur to India to make such definitions and lay down proper guidelines in its Agreement with Sri Lanka. In the past, India had relied upon mutual good faith and political understanding with the regimes and leaders of the neighbouring country where it took responsibility to deploy and use force. India's broad objectives of ensuring peace and stability in the neighbourhood had generally converged with those of the country affected, so the possibility of conflict—even in the absence of a clear definition of mutual obligations of the 'host' and the peace-keeping 'visitors'—did not arise.

This was the underlying assumption of the Indian decision-makers in the Sri Lankan case as well. There indeed existed the desired political understanding and good faith between the Indian and the Sri Lankan regimes at the time of concluding the July 1987 Agreement and the obligations to enforce that Agreement even with the use of force, if required. We may recall here that during the first week of October 1987, Sri Lankan President Jayewardene went to the extent of threatening a breakdown of the Agreement if the Indian forces present in Sri Lanka did not use force against the LTTE.

The political understanding and good faith prevailing between the Indian and Sri Lankan regimes ran into difficulties subsequently with the change of political leadership in Sri Lanka. This could not have been anticipated because not only was the ruling party, the UNP, returned to power after the 1988–89 elections, but Premadasa's candidature for Presidentship had been announced by the outgoing President Jayewardane, who had concluded the July 1987 Agreement with India. Under these conditions, no one in India would have predicted the breakdown of political rapport with the new Sri Lankan leadership—except perhaps someone blessed with astrological foresight.

Another critical distinguishing factor between the Sri Lanka experience (1987–89) and other cases of Indian involvement was that in the latter cases the challenge to internal stability and peace had come mostly from rebel/insurgent groups neither so deeply entrenched nor so determined and skilled as were the LTTE in Sri Lanka. The strength and diversity of internal and international sources of support enjoyed by the LTTE made all the difference to the IPKF experiences in Sri Lanka. Indian forces did fight a larger and more ferocious war with the Pakistani military in securing the liberation of Bangladesh. But that was a full-fledged conventional war, with no constraints on the Indian forces imposed for political reasons. The Bangladesh mission of the Indian forces was clear and it enjoyed the great strategic advantage of support from the local people. The IPKF operations against the LTTE were of a very different nature. Towards the latter stages of these operations in 1989, the LTTE was supported not only by the Tamils in the North and East of Sri Lanka but also by the Sri Lankan government and armed forces, though clandestinely with the insidious purpose of humiliating the IPKF and India.

The foregoing discussion suggests that the critical lessons from the Indian experience in Sri Lanka are in the realm of the dynamics of political relationship between the 'host' and the peace-keeping country on the one hand, and the military and operational aspects of the peace-keeping obligations on the other—taking into account the nature of internal conflict and the forces to be confronted with in the given neighbouring country. Before we discuss these lessons in terms of future policy projections, it may not be out of place to look at the situation in Sri Lanka after the withdrawal of IPKF.

The withdrawal of the IPKF did not cause political and military embarrassment to the Government of India alone. Its Sri Lankan counterpart was also to suffer in this regard soon after, if not earlier. During the controversy on the question of IPKF withdrawal, President Premadasa's impetuous style of diplomacy and inept handling of sensitive foreign policy issues had come in for a good deal of criticism in Sri Lankan media and political and diplomatic circles. The Premadasa government's political image was to suffer a greater setback after the withdrawal, when in less than three months, war between the LTTE and the Sri Lankan forces broke out on 11 June 1990. Conflict between the two since then has become as deep and intense as ever—contrary to the promises of the Premadasa government that it would be in a position to resolve the ethnic issue peacefully and through negotiations, once the IPKF had left the scene. Paradoxical though it was, soon after the revival of the ethnic conflict, Colombo approached New Delhi for support and understanding. A senior delegation from Sri Lanka even brought photographic evidence to show to the Indian authorities how brutal and barbaric the LTTE insurgents were. The Indian authorities could not help looking at such evidence with a certain amount of amusement and disdain, for they had learnt about the LTTE's brutalities at an enormous cost to their country, while it was the Premadasa government that had sought to befriend the LTTE, ignoring the sacrifices made by India. However, India did decide to respond to Sri Lankan concerns as far as possible and help by curbing possible sanctuaries of the LTTE in India, and providing training and assistance to the Sri Lankan military forces as well as economic and cultural cooperation.

After the revival of conflict in Sri Lanka, not only the Sri Lankan government but the LTTE has also been seeking support and understanding from India. First, the LTTE used its happy relations with the Karunanidhi government (DMK) in Tamil Nadu to circumvent the implications of the Janata Dal's promise of support to Colombo. This was necessary to keep LTTE sanctuaries and sources of supplies in Tamil Nadu intact. The soft attitude of the Karunanidhi government towards the LTTE not only became a sore point in Indo–Sri Lanka relations but also acquired political significance in local Tamil Nadu politics and Centre–State relations. Eventually, this became the main factor behind the dismissal of the DMK government by the Centre in early 1991. The changing dynamics of Indian politics further forced the LTTE to approach the Congress Party and its leader Rajiv Gandhi in February–March 1991, because by then, the prospects of the Congress Party's return to power had brightened. If recent allegations of the LTTE's hand in the assassination of Rajiv Gandhi in May 1991 prove correct, that will show the extent to which the LTTE's military campaign depends on the nature of the political forces in power in India. The Sri Lankan government also cannot afford to have an unsympathetic or uncooperative government in New Delhi and in Tamil Nadu in view of the raging ethnic conflict. This, in principle at least, brings the situation back to the 1983–87 period which underlined India's critical location in relation to the Sri Lankan conflict. An additional complicating dimension introduced in the present situation by the assassination of Rajiv Gandhi is that the Sri Lankan ethnic conflict and Tamil politics as a whole have clearly emerged as an important factor in India's national politics.

While the Sri Lankan ethnic politics is exerting pressure on India, there are other possibilities that internal conflicts, though of somewhat different magnitude, in the neighbouring countries may spill over to India, thereby calling for definitive policy responses from India. Reference to the tribal insurgency of the Chakmas in Bangladesh and the democratic struggle against military junta in Burma may be made here. Then there is serious turmoil and instability in the Sindh province of Pakistan, adjoining the states of Rajasthan and Gujarat in India. A serious politico-ethnic conflict is also brewing in the hitherto quiet kingdom of Bhutan, between the dominant and ruling Drukpas living in the mountainous region and the Nepalis concentrated in the southern flat land of the kingdom. The Nepalese concentration, which has become a region of conflict and instability in the wake of recent developments, borders on India's politically volatile states of West Bengal and Assam. These Indian states also have a sizeable Nepali population (including Indian citizens and those emigrating from Nepal) with ethnic and political support for the struggle of the Bhutan–Nepalis. As the conflict intensifies, so will the challenge for Indian policy to deal with its consequences; more so since the newly installed democratic government in Nepal has already expressed its support

for and solidarity with the Nepalis' movement in Bhutan.[12] Yet
another place of potential conflict is Nepal, whose recently established democratic system is still fragile. The monarchy, with the
vested interests around it, and the remnants of the discarded
Panchayat system put together are still quite powerful. To make
the situation worse for the democratic forces, the Communists
emerged as a powerful challenge to them in the parliamentary
elections of May 1991. The fact that some of the Communists have
taken an extremist position on the question of constitutional
monarchy and others boycotted the May 1991 elections deserves
attention. Those Communists who have emerged as a powerful
force in the elections view the popular Nepali Congress government headed by Girija Prasad Koirala as pro-Palace, pro-West
and pro-India: a combination they would not like to see stabilized.[13]
All these conflicts, if and when they erupt into violence and
disruption, will activate India's security interests and ideological/
cultural coordinates discussed in the first chapter, and demand
appropriate Indian response. Indeed, this is already so in the case
of Bhutan and the renewed conflict in Sri Lanka.

In any future conflict in India's neighbourhood, when India is
either asked by the concerned friendly government to respond or
is compelled to do so by the force of circumstances impinging on
its vital national interests, the lessons of the Sri Lankan experience
and the changing context of global and regional politics will have
to be taken into account. The most important thing for India to
bear in mind is that induction and use of military forces must be
the rarest of rare exceptions. The costs and complexities of using
force in peace-keeping operations are becoming both materially
prohibitive and morally repugnant. Above all, there are growing
doubts about the effectiveness and success of such operations.[14]
Recent moves on the part of some Western nations to intervene
militarily in Iraq's Kurdish conflict and create a 'safe haven' for the
Kurds may be seen as an exception in the emerging context of the
post-Cold War world order. The outcome of such intervention is
uncertain at best. Above all, this seems an option for only the big
and the mighty, which a country like India cannot and must not
emulate.

Besides the heavy costs of military operations and the changing
global context being against them, recent developments in the
regional political context in South Asia also call upon India to

desist from resorting to the Sri Lanka type role in a neighbouring country's internal conflict. India is now also on the receiving side of the involvement of its neighbours in its own internal conflicts, including those related to extremist and separatist forces. Pakistan's involvement with the Kashmiri Muslims and the Sikh insurgents has been internationally acknowledged and disapproved. Nepal's potential sympathies for the Gorkha movement that erupted in West Bengal a couple of years back was known widely in India. The reported links between Sri Lankan militants (the LTTE particularly) and Andhra extremists (Naxalities) and Punjab and Assam insurgents, as also Bangladesh's alleged involvement with the extremists in Tripura during recent years, may be recalled here. Thus there exists now a regional compulsion for India to evolve a framework of responding to the problems of internal turmoil and conflicts in South Asia. For this purpose, the SAARC (South Asian Association for Regional Cooperation) Convention on suppression of terrorism adopted in 1987 and subsequently ratified by the member countries may serve as a useful, though a limited, guide. On the other hand, this regional approach can only supplement the bilateral approaches, since objective reality in the region is essentially bilateral.

The most desirable way for India to approach the question of internal conflicts in the neighbouring countries is to work politically to pre-empt them, and then deal with them if necessary. In this approach, the temptation to get militarily involved must be resisted, notwithstanding the nature of pressures and compulsions. There is tremendous scope for India to assert its political and peaceful role in moderating and resolving internal conflicts in the neighbouring countries. In the neighbouring countries there are powerful ethnic, ideological and political constituencies that India can prudently and constructively activize. It can also use its economic and adminis-trative resources to give effect to its policy responses and avoid the pitfalls that it suffered in Sri Lanka.

All the same, the question of the contingency of India using military force in a neighbouring domestic conflict must be addressed, albeit as a hypothetical proposition. In any such situation, India will have to take care of all the political and military implications of deployment and use of forces. Politically, India may have to rush its forces to the help of a neighbouring country at short notice. This may not allow much time for finalizing, precisely and sufficiently, the framework of mutual obligations of the 'host' and the 'visitors' but this aspect cannot be allowed to continue un-attended. Indian policy-makers will have to apply their minds to such contigencies and even prepare a blueprint for India's expected obligations. In future, India should not take the good faith and political understanding of the neighbouring regime for granted on such sensitive issues as deployment and use of external forces. It may be recalled that in 1967, even the UN peace-keeping force ran into difficulties because Egypt as a 'host' had refused to permit them on its territory. India itself decided in 1971 after the Indo-Pak war on Bangladesh and the conclusion of Simla Agreement (1972) to withdraw cooperation from the UN Military Observer Group stationed on the India–Pakistan border. Therefore, the possibility that a 'host' country may change its decision on the continuation of alien peace-keepers is real and serious.

In any situation of the deployment and use of force, India as well as the concerned 'host' country will be well advised to set up a coordinating mechanism to monitor and supervise day-to-day developments. A mechanism of this type can have various tiers of operational and policy levels; each vested with the requisite poli-tical authority and administrative back-up, to deal with all the relevant aspects of the situation and even unanticipated emergencies. Such a mechanism was in fact provided for in the Indo–Sri Lanka Agreement of July 1987, but was not properly made use of, for reasons still not discovered. Even Sri Lanka did not seem parti-cularly interested in activising the coordination mechanism, although it is difficult to see why. When this mechanism was briefly put into effect towards the end of IPKF operations, in the form of the Security Coordination Group, its decisions were not carried out sincerely and effectively. It is possible to envisage that a 'host' country might not be either capable of/or interested in putting together a well-defined arrangement that calls for prompt responses and allocates sensitive responsibilities. The political consequences of the workings of such a mechanism can create domestic political difficulties for the 'host', but India would be ill-advised to ignore this aspect.

As regards the military aspect of the deployment and use of force by India in a neighbouring country, recent experience indicates scant room for complacency or overconfidence. The Indian military needs to do a great deal of homework to prepare itself—in terms of doctrines, command structure, equipment, training and intelligence—before agreeing to undertake military adventures. The Indian military has gained considerable experience in undertaking counter-insurgency operations within India, but to translate this experience into unfamiliar environment and in relation to unknown forces and people is in itself a major task. The role of intelligence agencies will also have to be regulated to restrict their unhindered interaction with the insurgent and militant groups of the neighbouring countries, to avoid unnecessary complications and undesirable restraints on the basic policy of India. On the whole, in our assessment, the option of military involvement is not the best way for India to respond to internal conflicts in its neighbourhood.

Notes to Chapter 6

1. There is a vast body of literature on the third-party mediation role by the UN and other states or unofficial agencies. See for instance C.R. Mitchell and K. Webb (eds.), *New Approaches to International Mediation*, Greenwood Press, New York, London 1988. Oran R. Young, *The Intermediaries: Third Parties in International Crises*, Princeton N.J., Princeton University Press, 1967. The project on peace-making, completed under the grants from the United States Institute of Peace, Washington, may be found in the bibliographical note prepared by the Institute, December 1990.

2. For a study of mediation in the Sudanese civil war, see Christopher R. Mitchell, *Conflict Resolution and Civil War: Reflections on The Sudanese Settlement of 1972*, Working Paper 3, Centre for Conflict Analysis and Resolution, George Mason University, 1989.

3. In a study on mediation, C.R. Mitchell has listed five categories of rewards for the mediators in a given conflict situation, namely (a) material rewards, (b) influence rewards, (c) support rewards, (d) security rewards, and (e) status or reputational rewards. C.R. Mitchell in Mitchell and Webb (eds.), 1988, *New Approaches to International Mediation*, pp. 29–51. In an earlier study, Oran Young (1967) also held that in the Arab-Israeli conflict the so-called uninterested intermediaries got involved.

4. A separate study on this subject has been initiated by the author.

5. Memoirs of the Mossad agents were widely published in Sri Lankan and the international press.

6. The mediation stages of (a) initiation, (b) bilateral contacts, (c) face to face discussions, (d) negotiations and (e) implementation have been discussed by Mitchell in his study of mediation in the Sudanese civil war, *Conflict Resolution and Civil War*, p. 21.

7. Alan James, 'International Peace-keeping: The Disputants' View', *Political Studies*, Vol. 38, June 1990, pp. 215–30.

8. For an interesting debate on UN peace-keeping see *Survival*, vol. 32, no. 3,

May/June 1990. Also Robert C. Johansen, 'UN Peace-keeping: The changing utility of military force' in *Third World Quarterly*, vol. 12, no. 2, April 1990, pp. 53–70. John Q. Blodgett, 'The Future of UN Peace-keeping', *The Washington Quarterly*, Winter 1991, vol. 14, no. 1.

9. Johan Jorgan Holst, 'Enhancing Peace-keeping Operations', *Survival*, vol. 32, no. 3, May/June 1990.
10. *The Times of India*, March 1990.
11. Such views were articulated in a number of editorials in national dailies as well as in foreign policy discussions held in New Delhi during those days.
12. See my article 'Bhutan in the throes of ethnic crisis', *India International Centre Quarterly*, May 1991, New Delhi.
13. See my article in *The Hindustan Times* (New Delhi), 29 May 1991.
14. Johansen, 'UN Peace-keeping'; and Blodgett, 'The Future of UN Peace-keeping'.

Appendix I

Indo–Sri Lanka Interaction on the Ethnic Crisis
(Chronology of important developments, July 1983—July 1987)

24 July 1983

Rioting breaks out in several parts of Colombo.

25 July 1983

India conveys its distress at the happenings and seeks assurances from Sri Lanka that the lives and properties of Indians there will be protected.

26 July 1983

The Sri Lankan government resents India expressing its concern and describes this as interference in its internal affairs.

27 July 1983

Expressing 'anxiety' over 'the cycle of violence in Sri Lanka,' the Indian Minister for External Affairs P.V. Narasimha Rao, hopes in the Lok Sabha that in dealing with the problem, Sri Lanka 'will bear in mind the sentiments of the Indian people'.

DMK President Karunanidhi asks for India's armed intervention, to stop bloodshed in Sri Lanka.

28 July 1983

The External Affairs Minister of India, P.V. Narasimha Rao, flies to Colombo to make an on-the-spot assessment of the situation and to discuss with President Jayewardene urgent measures to protect the lives and property of Indians.

30 July 1983

Karunanidhi calls for a Cyprus-type solution in Sri Lanka, 'in order to prevent the extermination of the Tamil race.'

India offers relief supplies for the victims of ethnic holocaust and plans to send a passenger ship to Colombo to evacuate displaced Tamils to Jaffna.

Sri Lankan Foreign Minister A.C.S. Hameed arrives in Delhi for the SAARC ministerial meeting.

2 August 1983

Following a report that Colombo has asked for assistance from the
United States, Britain, Pakistan and Bangladesh, the External Affairs
Minister reportedly warns all powers to keep out of the current turmoil
in Sri Lanka.

4 August 1983

India tries, at high level, to persuade President Jayewardene to say at
least a few reassuring words to restore the confidence of the Tamils,
but he chooses to remain inexplicably silent.

9 August 1983

H.W. Jayewardene, special emissary of the Sri Lankan President, has
discussions with Mrs. Gandhi on the situation in Sri Lanka.

12 August 1983

Mrs. Gandhi reassures Jayewardene that India stands for the independence, unity and integrity of Sri Lanka. India has not interfered in
the internal affairs of other countries. However, because of the historical,
cultural and such other close ties between the peoples of the two
countries, India cannot remain unaffected by such events there.

Mrs. Gandhi sets up a Sri Lanka Relief Fund Committee under her
chairpersonship with a contribution of Rs. 1 crore (10 million) from the
Prime Minister's Relief Fund.

17 August 1983

In a speech in Parliament, Mrs. Gandhi announces that India has
offered to send its emissary G. Parthasarathy to Sri Lanka to facilitate
the process of negotiations between the Sri Lankan Government and
its Tamil minority.

18 August 1983

Jayewardene says that he does not need any good offices for talks
'which is my own problem'. Of course, the offer of India's good offices
was there, 'but we have not decided about availing ourselves of this. At
the moment I want India to keep quiet, rather Tamil Nadu to keep
quiet, and I have no idea of calling for any help from India.'

25 August 1983

G. Parthasarathy, special envoy of the Indian Prime Minister, Indira
Gandhi arrives in Sri Lanka. President Jayewardene reportedly tells
the Indian envoy that neither the Government nor the people of Sri
Lanka will agree to a division of the country. He, however, proposes to
implement fully the scheme of District Development Councils.

21 September 1983

Mrs. Gandhi reiterates that while India abhors interference of any kind and firmly believes that it is in India's interest to have strong, stable and peaceful neighbours, it cannot remain a silent spectator to any injustice done to the Tamil minority.

23 October 1983

President of the Ceylon Workers' Congress and Sri Lankan Minister for Rural Industries Development, S. Thondaman, affirms that Indian mediation is the best way to find a solution to the ethnic crisis in Sri Lanka. He says the ball is now in the Sri Lankan government's court since the TULF and the Tamil militants are prepared to accept a viable alternative to 'Eelam'

27 October 1983

President Jayewardene invites G. Parthasarathy to resume mediation efforts to find a lasting solution to the Tamil problem, reversing the earlier decision of the cabinet not to invite Mrs. Gandhi's special envoy.

5 November 1983

Hector Jayewardene, special envoy of the Sri Lankan President, says, 'Mrs. Gandhi had offered her good offices to assist in bringing about a settlement. It was not "mediation" as asserted in certain quarters but more correctly an offer to assist in breaking the deadlock'.

10 November 1983

G. Parthasarathy arrives in Colombo; meets President, Prime Minister and others.

In a major achievement of silent diplomacy, a broad framework for political settlement within a united Sri Lanka emerges under India's good offices. The proposals necessitate that the TULF give up its demand for a separate Eelam in exchange for a new set-up of Regional Council after merging the District Development Councils within a Province, with the consent of the Council's members and referendum in the districts.

11 November 1983

The Tamil groups reject as 'too little and too late' the offer made by the Sri Lankan Government to form Regional Councils. They say that what is being offered is 'not even federalism and not even regional autonomy' and nothing short of total regional autonomy in the absence of an Eelam can be acceptable.

17 November 1983

The Sri Lankan President says he will do all he can to get the people to accept the proposals the government has finalized to end the ethnic crisis. 'I do not propose to impose upon the people of this country a Jayewardene–Mrs. Gandhi or Jayewardene–Amrithalingam pact', he adds, pointing out the unfortunate ends of earlier pacts.

23–30 November 1983

President Jayewardene arrives in India to participate in the Commonwealth Summit. Holds talks with Mrs. Gandhi and G. Parthasarathy. These talks give final shape to the draft proposals which subsequently became Annexure 'C' for the All Party Conference.

10 December 1983

Jayewardene says that he will not enter into any pact with India to solve the Island's ethnic problems. 'India is a powerful country and we cannot fight India, but if India intends to invade us we will not give in', he adds.

9 May 1984

In two separate statements at the APC, the TULF and the All Ceylon Tamil Congress (ACTC) denounce the conference as an exercise in futility and accuse the government of dragging its feet in efforts to seek a negotiated settlement.

18 May 1984

Jayewardene tells delegates attending the APC that more emphasis should be placed on widening opportunities in education, employment and exercise of language rights than on the devolution of power.

2 June 1984

President Jayewardene concludes his talks with Mrs. Gandhi. He makes a plea that India should urge the TULF to participate in the deliberations of the two committees of the APC in their search for a just solution to the ethnic crisis. He adds that Mrs. Gandhi has 'entirely agreed' with his view that the Tamil problem is an internal issue to be settled by the Sri Lankan people themselves.

26 June 1984

Amrithalingam says that he will abide by any decision Mrs. Gandhi and the Government of India take after talks with the Sri Lankan President, and will place it before the Sri Lankan Tamils for ratification.

27 June 1984

The External Affairs Minister of India, P.V. Narasimha Rao, has discussions with the Sri Lankan Minister, Athulathmudali, on the modified proposals sent by Jayewardene which envisage the creation of some kind of an over-arching second chamber to be elected by the Tamil majority districts, and the regrouping of the district councils.

28 June 1984

The LTTE asks for recognition as a political force rather than as a group of terrorists before arriving at any settlement at a round table conference.

30 June to 2 July 1984

President Jayewardene has talks in New Delhi with Mrs. Gandhi and her cabinet colleagues.

23 July 1984

President Jayewardene places before the plenary sessions of the APC a six-point memorandum containing new proposals to resolve the Tamil problem. The highlight of the proposals is the creation of a second chamber of members representing the 25 districts.

16 August 1984

The Minister of State for External Affairs, Ram Niwas Mirdha makes a statement in Lok Sabha on the Sri Lankan situation. India stands for Sri Lanka's unity and integrity, and is against all forms of violence. Steps are taken to curb activities that may be directed against Sri Lanka, from the Indian side. Induction of foreign security agencies by Sri Lanka would aggravate matters.

16 November 1984

Rajiv Gandhi conveys to the Sri Lankan Government that India is committed to genuine and lasting friendship between the two nations.

11 December 1984

Rajiv Gandhi appeals to the Sri Lankan Government to take immediate steps to defuse the violent situation and give a lead at the APC on December 14 to achieve a viable political settlement.

22 December 1984

Amrithalingam rejects the draft bills presented by the Sri Lankan President to the APC to solve the ethnic problem in Sri Lanka as they fall far short of his party's acceptable minimum for regional autonomy as an alternative to Eelam.

28 January 1985

The UNP working committee accuses India of a de facto invasion of the Island using Tamil guerrillas and some members of the Tamil political parties as troops.

16–18 February 1985

Athulathmudali in New Delhi pleads that G. Parthasarathy be ignored. He secures the release of Sri Lankan arms cargo seized by Indian customs. Militant boats full of arms have been seized (29 March 1985).

27–29 March 1985

Foreign Secretary Romesh Bhandari in Colombo for talks, pleads for cessation of all acts of violence and resumption of political dialogue. JR offers general amnesty and security forces in barracks if militants agree to a cease-fire.

29 April 1985

The Minister of State for External Affairs, Khurshid Alam Khan makes a statement in the Lok Sabha. A Special Advisory Group is set up by the Indian Prime Minister to monitor implications of the Sri Lankan situation. Discrimination against Tamils and Muslims is denounced. Khurshid Alam Khan objects to Jayewardene's statement given on Kashmir during his visit to Pakistan.

10–17 May 1985

Strong Sri Lanka reactions to Khurshid Alam Khan's statement.
Sri Lanka refuses to participate in the SAARC Ministerial meeting at Thimphu.
Esmond Wikramsinghe, Sri Lankan leader of SAARC delegation to Thimphu, visits Delhi on his way back to Colombo to defuse the situation.

27 May 1985

Sri Lanka calls on India to implement a new anti-terrorist law against Tamil militants in Tamil Nadu.

28–30 May 1985

Foreign Secretary Romesh Bhandari in Colombo to pave the way for President Jayewardene's visit to New Delhi.

1–3 June 1985

President Jayewardene arrives in New Delhi for talks with the Indian Prime Minister to end the ethnic carnage in Sri Lanka. Both agreed to defuse the situation and create a conducive atmosphere for finding a political solution. Together they also visit Dhaka.

18 June 1985

The five major separatist guerrilla groups in Sri Lanka agree to stop hostilities for 12 weeks.

8–13 July 1985

The first Thimphu talks between Tamils and Sri Lankan government commence, under the auspices of the Indian Government, in Thimphu, the capital of Bhutan.

The first Thimphu talks conclude while a considerable gap remains between the proposals put forth by the Sri Lankan delegation and the Tamil groups. But prospects of negotiation are kept open with an agreement to reconvene the meeting on 12 August.

15 July 1985

Prime Minister Rajiv Gandhi says that India will play only the limited role of mediation and does not wish to give instructions. He also says that India does not wish to support Eelam and that he does not expect Tamil areas to be given more power than that enjoyed by the Indian states.

6 August 1985

The Sri Lankan President says that the Tamils' demand for an amalgamation of Northern and Eastern Provinces would mean a division of the country.

8 August 1985

The Indian Foreign Secretary, Romesh Bhandari, holds talks with Sri Lankan government leaders and others on arrangements and proposals for the second Thimphu talks.

11 August 1985

Rajiv Gandhi said that India will not support any linkage of Northern and Eastern Provinces because of the population imperatives of the latter.

12–17 August 1985

Phase II of the Thimphu talks collapses as the Tamil groups walk out in protest against the killings of Tamils in Vavuniya and Trincomalee. Earlier, Hector Jayewardene, the leader of the official Sri Lankan delegation, starts off on the wrong foot by tabling on the opening day of the talks a harsh statement rejecting the four cardinal principles of the Tamil delegation. Also he makes a *faux pas* by characterizing the Tamil delegation as 'representing the interests of certain Tamil groups', which immediately leads to polemical duels and diversions from substantive issues.

23 August 1985

The Government of India issues deportation orders against three Sri Lankan Tamil leaders—A.S. Balasingham, S.C. Chandrahasan and N. Satyendra—for their alleged involvement in sabotaging the second Thimphu talks.

24 August 1985

Jayewardene warns that he is prepared for war if the Tamil militants are not willing to resolve the Island's ethnic crisis by peaceful means. 'If it is peace, it is peace, if it is war, it is war', he declares.

31 August 1985

The Sri Lankan delegation, led by Hector Jayewardene, formulates a draft proposal in consultation with the Indian Government officials which would form the basis for further talks with the Tamil leaders. It envisages constitution of a provincial council in each province within 30 days of reaching an agreement with the Tamil leaders.

10 September 1985

The Tamil Eelam Front urges India to send a peace-keeping force to be stationed in North and East Sri Lanka to prevent any further massacre of Tamils by Sri Lankan security forces and the Sinhalese.

13 September 1985

Indian and Sri Lankan officials conclude their discussions on the working paper drafted by Hector Jayewardene in consultation with the Indian government, paving the way for a fresh round of consultation between the Indian team and the Tamil militants of Sri Lanka.

16 September 1985

The Sri Lankan government extends the 12-week old cease-fire between its security forces and the Tamil militant groups for a further period while expressing 'deep interest over India's efforts to help resume the peace talks'.

17 September 1985

Representatives of the Eelam National Liberation Front convey to Rajiv Gandhi their apprehension that the draft proposals evolved by the Sri Lankan government will not meet the aspirations of the Tamils. They plead, 'if any proposals were worked out which did not meet their approval, they should be kept out of the accord. No such accord should be thrust down their throats'.

28 September 1985

Broad agreement is reached on an interim cease-fire between the government and militants following Romesh Bhandari's talks in Colombo and Madras. Both the parties agree that there will be no cease-fire violations provided there is no provocation from the other side.

28 October 1985

Rajiv Gandhi says: 'We are interested in one united Sri Lanka, in the form of a government that the people of Sri Lanka want. We do not want any disintegration or break-up of Sri Lanka.'

15 November 1985

Expressing his confidence in Rajiv Gandhi, Sri Lankan Prime Minister, Premadasa says, 'whether the Indian Prime Minister will succeed or not—his goodwill and genuine approach are beyond question . . . . I feel very strongly that we have established the ground work for a good relationship.'

20 November 1985

Prime Minister Rajiv Gandhi urges Sri Lankan Tamil groups to come forward with their proposals for resolving the ethnic problem.

3 December 1985

The TULF puts forward a comprehensive alternative proposal for devolution of powers to the Tamil people in Sri Lanka, envisaging a constitutional and political structure based on the federal principle.

28 December 1985

President Jayewardene indicates to the Government of India that he is prepared to consider sympathetically the TULF proposals for greater autonomy, but that he is totally opposed to the demand for a merger of the Northern and Eastern Provinces and the plea for appointment of Governors to head the provinces.

15 January 1986

India and Sri Lanka agree to resolve the problem of stateless Tamils of Indian origin. This is the result of S. Thondaman's talks with Rajiv Gandhi in Bombay during November 1985, and Indian High Commissioner Dixit's talks with Sri Lankan ministers in January 1986.

20 February 1986

Jayewardene announces nine conditions to be complied with in the implementation of any agreement to end the ethnic crisis. They include: abandonment of separate state demand, cessation of hostilities and closing down of training camps, surrender of arms by the Tamil militants, lifting of emergency in the Tamil areas, general amnesty to the militants, etc. The Sri Lankan Tamil leadership rejects the conditions set by Jayewardene.

10 March 1986

The Indian Prime Minister suggests that the Sri Lankan government should talk to the Tamils directly. He comes out strongly in favour of a political solution to the ethnic problem.

22 March 1986

Rajiv Gandhi says it is becoming difficult for India to understand what exactly the Sri Lankan government wants for resolving the ethnic problem in the Island Republic.

23 March 1986

The Indian Prime Minister informs the Sri Lankan President that he is prepared to send Romesh Bhandari to Colombo for a final round of talks if the Sri Lankan government will end the killings and come forward with concrete proposals for resolving the Tamil problem.

16 April 1986

Sri Lankan Foreign Minister, A.C.S. Hameed, hands over to the Indian Prime Minister a letter from Jayewardene containing his new proposals for settling the Tamil problem.

29 April 1986

A high-level Indian delegation led by P. Chidambaram leaves for Colombo in a fresh initiative by the Indian government to find a peaceful settlement of the Sri Lankan ethnic crisis. The delegation holds talks with the Sri Lankan government on its latest proposals, which envisage devolution of power to the extent prevailing in the Union Territories in India, an autonomous police force for each provincial council and adoption of English as the link language.

13 May 1986

Lalit Athulathmudali conveys to the Indian High Commissioner, J.N. Dixit, that the Sri Lankan government will be willing to discuss with the TULF any package of proposals that might emerge from the current Indo–Sri Lankan talks.

19 May 1986

Rajiv Gandhi regrets that proposals to solve the ethnic problem in Sri Lanka have been diluted, and urges the Sri Lankan government not to move towards a military solution.

22 May 1986

India threatens to withdraw its good offices in resolving Sri Lanka's ethnic problem if the Island's government continues with the current military offensive in the Northern peninsula.

27 May 1986

Lalit Athulathmudali says that Colombo is ready to begin informal discussions with Tamil militant leaders to settle the ethnic conflict on lines similar to the Geneva proximity talks between Pakistan and Afghanistan.

1 June 1986

Jayewardene sends a letter to Rajiv Gandhi assuring him that he is ready to resume the dialogue with the Tamil leaders. He wants India to get together a representative group of Tamil leaders to discuss the proposed settlement on the basis of the broad framework for devolution emerging from the talks in Colombo with the Indian delegation.

1 July 1986

New proposals of the Sri Lankan government on devolution of powers to the provincial councils (borrowed heavily from the Indian Constitution) aim at transferring the subjects under the state and concurrent lists in the seventh schedule to the provincial councils. While the demand for the merger of Northern and Eastern Provinces has not been conceded, a concession has been made to create a suitable constitutional arrangement for consultations between the provincial council and also permit them to act in coordination of matters of mutual interest and concern.

12 July 1986

Yogi, leader of the LTTE, says that they will welcome whatever action is taken by the Government of India for finding a political solution and will not be a hindrance to any other party which engages in a negotiated settlement or peace process.

13 July 1986

The militant leaders say that the proposals from the Sri Lankan government cannot form the basis for settlement of the ethnic problem in the Island. They insist on the acceptance of their four-point charter for any meaningful dialogue.

2 August 1986

An improved draft of the legislation to devolve powers to the Tamil provinces in Sri Lanka is finalized with the help of Indian constitutional experts incorporating the federal aspects of the Indian Constitution.

10 August 1986

Jayewardene says that if necesssary, the government can hold negotiations with the militants directly to find a solution and consider giving them amnesty to bring them back to the democratic way of life.

The Sri Lankan President calls upon the Indian government to sign with his government an agreement to cover the implementation of a peace accord on the ethnic crisis in the Island, holding of elections to the proposed provincial councils, and action against terrorism.

18 August 1986

Foreign Secretary A.P. Venkateswaran holds talks with leaders of five

Tamil militant groups to persuade them to join negotiations between Sri Lankan government and the TULF in Colombo.

21 August 1986

A high-level team of Indian ministers meets militant groups in Madras to propose a month's cease-fire.

2 September 1986

The Sri Lankan government makes three suggestions to solve the ticklish issue of merger of the Northern and Eastern Provinces. They are: a referendum in the Eastern Province to find out whether the people want a merger, setting up of a boundary commission to demarcate the Tamil areas and setting up zonal councils to provide a link between the two provinces.

4–6 September 1986

Indian and Sri Lankan Prime Ministers have talks during the Non-Aligned Summit at Harare. A 'nasty letter' addressed by Premadasa to Rajiv Gandhi annoys the latter.

Rajiv Gandhi says that India is not too eager to continue its mediatory role if Sri Lanka is not keen on resolving the Island's ethnic tangle soon.

13 September 1986

Premadasa in a statement in Sri Lankan Parliament accuses Rajiv Gandhi of weak leadership and urges him to stop Tamil rebel activities in Southern India.

29 September 1986

In yet another round of hectic discussions with Indian constitutional experts, TULF leaders finalize their counter-proposal to the latest draft formulations of the Sri Lankan government.

15–18 November 1986

Indo–Sri Lanka talks on ethnic issue during Bangalore SAARC Summit. Tamil Nadu Chief Minister M.G. Ramachandran is also involved. LTTE delegation of Prabhakaran, Balasingham and Thilakar are kept waiting for any possible consultations.

19 November 1986

India and Sri Lanka resume ministerial level talks in New Delhi to work out a more comprehensive and acceptable set of proposals for a political solution to the ethnic problem.

21 November 1986

Sri Lankan government submits its reply to the latest formulations submitted by India to solve the Island's ethnic crisis.

23–24 November 1986

Indian Ministerial delegation in Colombo for talks.

The latest round of Indo–Lanka talks fails to bridge gap on the issue of 'Tamil homeland'. The Sri Lankan delegation led by Jayewardene does not favour the idea, apparently mooted by India, of either merging or linking the proposed Tamil provinces, and proposes splitting the Eastern Province into three to provide for a Tamil province in the Batticaloa district.

15 December 1986

Indian ministers, P. Chidambaram and K. Natwar Singh hold talks with Tamil militant leaders in Madras.

17–19 December 1986

The two Indian Ministers of State, P. Chidambaram and K. Natwar Singh, meet Jayewardene to bring about an amicable settlement to the ethnic crisis.

A proposal emerges as a result of three rounds of talks with the Sri Lankan President by the two Indian ministers. It envisages carving out a Tamil linguistic entity of the existing eastern Amparai electorate from the existing boundaries of the Eastern Province.

24 December 1986

The LTTE takes strong exception to Lalit Athulathmudali's statement that it is important to build the goodwill brought about by the exchange of prisoners between the LTTE and Colombo further so that Sri Lankans may resolve their disputes without the assistance of outsiders. It says that remark amounts to insulting India's bid to find a solution to the problem. The LTTE also reiterates its faith in India's mediatory role and Rajiv Gandhi's integrity, saying that it will pledge its continued support to India's peace efforts.

27 December 1986

A four-member informal delegation of the Sri Lankan government headed by Vincent Perera and a Tamil businessman Jayabalasingham, a ruling party M.P., holds 'lengthy peace talks' with the most powerful of the Tamil militant groups, the LTTE, thus breaking new ground in the search for a solution to the Island's ethnic crisis.

5 January 1987

Indian High Commissioner in Colombo, J.N. Dixit, meets President Premadasa and cautions him against exercising the military option in Jaffna.

8 January 1987

Athulathmudali tells Parliament that the government has no intention of derailing the Government of India's good offices from the on-going process of negotiation towards peace. He feels, however, that Sri Lankans do not need anybody's permission to talk to Sri Lankans, although when brothers fight, outsiders can help to bring about peace.

12–13 January 1987

Gamini Dissanayake in New Delhi to reiterate Colombo's commitment to the proposals. But there is ambiguity in Colombo.

Dixit also meets Jayewardene and expresses concern on Colombo's vacillations from the 19 December proposals.

India conveys its disappointment to Sri Lanka over delay in finding political solution to the ethnic problem after a meeting of the Political Affairs Committee of the Cabinet on 7 January 1987.

22 January 1987

Gamini Dissanayake, Land Minister, says: 'If India has certain geo-political perspectives about the region and feels that Sri Lanka should support them, we should be willing to look at it and come to an understanding with India on the vital perspectives of their concern.'

7 February 1987

India urges the Sri Lankan President to declare publicly and unequi-vocally that he stands by the 19 December 1986 proposal for retaining the Eastern Province as a Tamil majority area after slicing off Amparai district. If he makes such a declaration, followed by a termination of the economic blockade of the Jaffna peninsula and a suspension of the military operations both in the Northern and Eastern Provinces, India will get in touch with the Tamil militants and prevail upon them to accept the 19 December proposal as a good basis for a negotiated settlement.

9 February 1987

Rajiv Gandhi sends a tough message that if Colombo does not (a) stop military operations against Tamils; (b) lift the economic blockade of Jaffna; (c) accept the 19 December proposals, then India will suspend its mediation effort and Sri Lankan 'conflict will prolong and escalate'.

24 February 1987

India suspends its mediation between the Sri Lankan government and Tamil militants in finding a political solution to the ethnic crisis. K. Natwar Singh tells the Rajya Sabha that India will not resume its good offices unless it receives a clear indication that Colombo is firm in its commitment to the 19 December 1986 proposals as a basis for resuming negotiations.

14 March 1987

Dinesh Singh visits Colombo as Rajiv Gandhi's special envoy. Meets Jayewardene and asks for the lifting of economic blockade of Jaffna.

Sri Lankan government relaxes fuel embargo on Jaffna on 17 March.

24 March 1987

Addressing a press conference at Sriharikota, Rajiv Gandhi says that India will have to take unilateral decisions in finding a solution to the ethnic problem in Sri Lanka if Tamil militants do not accept the 19 December 1986 proposals.

27 March 1987

Indian ministers Natwar Singh and Chidambaram talk to Balasingham and Thilakar.

The LTTE and EROS tell the Indian mediators that Sri Lanka should first stop all hostilities against the Tamils and lift the blockade of the Jaffna peninsula. They refuse to go into the merits of the 19 December proposals until these two conditions are met.

2 April 1987

Rajiv Gandhi sends a message to Jayewardene indicating that if Colombo ceases military operation. LTTE will participate in efforts for peace.

4 April 1987

The TULF urges the Indian Prime Minister to initiate 'independent action' to bring an end to the sufferings of the Tamils. 'The Island government has failed to honour any assurance it may have given to India regarding suspension of military offensive and lifting of the fuel and communications embargo on Tamil areas', the TULF says.

21 April 1987

Sri Lanka declares unilateral cease-fire. But LTTE does not respond. 127 Sinhalese shot dead on 17 April.

Bomb explosion at Colombo's Central Bus Stand.

23 April 1987

Prime Minister Premadasa's strong statement in Sri Lankan Parliament saying peace first, proposals for solution of ethnic issue later. He says that any friend who asks us for a political settlement will be considered an enemy. India should handover terrorists to the Sri Lankan government.

25 April 1987

India describes as 'extraordinary' the statement made by the Sri Lankan

Prime Minister in Parliament on 23 April that 'any friend who now asks us to find a political solution will be considered the biggest enemy'.

Chidambaram says that another initiative is under discussion.

27 April 1987

M.G. Ramachandran gave Rs. 4 crores to LTTE and other Tamil militants.

Rajiv Gandhi warns Sri Lanka not to seek a military solution to its ethnic conflict and stop its current offensive against Tamil militants.

28 April 1987

Jayewardene says India's policy towards Sri Lanka is 'Hitlarian'. He rules out talks with terrorists unless they laid down arms.

Jayewardene sends an *aide memoire* to India on Tamil Nadu's interference in Sri Lanka in the form of relief supplies to Jaffna.

2 May 1987

Jayewardene objects to M.G. Ramachandran giving money to Tamil militant groups.

13 May 1987

Dissanayake reiterates that there has been no vacillation on the Sri Lankan President's part as regards the 19 December proposals. He is only trying to be honest and keep India informed of his problems; the objections from the Muslims. But he has no intention of resiling from them and in fact is determined to try his best to persuade the Muslims to accept, in the interest of an overall solution.

26 May 1987

Sri Lankan forces launch 'Operation Liberation' in the North.

India's Minister of State for External Affairs K. Natwar Singh warns in New Delhi that this would have tragic consequences and that the Sri Lankan military move indicates the influence of external forces.

27 May 1987

Lalit Athulathmudali says the objective of the Lankan military offensive in the Jaffna peninsula is to get the terrorists to the negotiating table. 'I feel that there is no solution to this problem by means of violence . . . this can be resolved only by talks.'

Rajiv telephones Jayewardene but is rebuffed.

28 May 1987

Rajiv Gandhi administers a stiff warning to Sri Lanka against continuing the massacre of unarmed civilians in Jaffna. 'The time to desist from a military occupation of Jaffna is now. Later may be too late', he says.

Rajiv Gandhi indicates that the phase of New Delhi's good offices and bilateral dealings for a settlement of the ethnic issue is over. 'While India is patient and painstakingly working towards political solution, it is apparent now that the Sri Lankan government was buying time for pursuing the military option', he said.

1 June 1987

Sri Lankan Foreign Minister Hameed sends a message to UN Secretary General saying that his country is facing a potential external 'threat to its independence, sovereignty and territorial integrity'.

Indian High Commissioner Dixit meets Sri Lankan Foreign Minister A.C.S. Hameed and conveys India's decision to send twenty unarmed boats carrying foodstuff and vital medicines to the beleaguered Jaffna peninsula.

2 June 1987

Prime Minister Premadasa describes India's decision to send relief supplies as 'provocative' and warns that it could lead to grave consequences and 'violence hitherto undreamt of' on the Island. He informs Parliament that the President has ordered the army, the navy and the air force to protect the Island and its territorial waters

3 June 1987

The 20-boat Indian flotilla which sails out of Rameswaram in a bid to reach relief supplies to the beleaguered Jaffna peninsula returns after being stopped by Sri Lankan naval ships which refuse to allow it to enter Sri Lankan territorial waters.

4 June 1987

The Indian Air Force carries out a mission when it flies into the wartorn Jaffna peninsula of Sri Lanka to provide relief to the suffering people of Jaffna peninsula. The Sri Lankan government lodges a strong protest against the air-dropping of supplies by India in the Jaffna peninsula. It terms the action as 'a naked violation of our independence. We have no military or other means of preventing this outrage. It is an unwarranted assault on our sovereignty and territorial integrity. We shall hold India responsible for all consequences', the protest note says.

5 June 1987

The Minister of State for External Affairs, K. Natwar Singh, indicates that India is looking forward to discussions with Sri Lanka on the modalities for organizing and delivering further relief supplies to Jaffna peninsula.

9 June 1987

Jayewardene urges India to give up 'violence and bullying' and says Sri

Lanka will never fight its giant neighbour. He calls India's violation of his country's airspace as the seventeenth invasion of Sri Lanka from Indian soil in the Island's 2,500 year history.

15 June 1987

India and Sri Lanka agree on the modalities for the supply of relief items to the people of Jaffna.

19 June 1987

A.C.S. Hameed has intensive discussions with Indian leaders in New Delhi on resumption of talks on the ethnic issue. He says, India's mediation is valid and necessary and the 19 December 1986 proposals could be the basis for negotiations.

20 June 1987

Rajiv Gandhi says that India is awaiting a firm response from Sri Lanka on the political solution to the ethnic problem in the Island in view of the contradictions in the latter's approach. 'The ball is clearly in Sri Lanka's court. Our options can come only when we know their direction', he says.

1 July 1987

Dixit meets Jayewardene to give Rajiv's message.

In his message to Jayewardene, Rajiv Gandhi says, 'we did not convey any suggestion or specific ideas, but took note of the fact that the December 19 proposals provided a basis, as acknowledged by all parties concerned, for discussions and that Sri Lanka could build on it to end the Island's tragic problem.'

7 July 1987

India expresses concern over the killings of Sri Lankan soldiers by the LTTE.

16 July 1987

In what is regarded as 'quite extraordinary meeting', the Indian High Commissioner, J.N. Dixit, on an invitation from Jayewardene, meets 12 senior cabinet ministers to discuss certain proposals being formulated by the President to resolve the Tamil problem. He explains that Amparai should not be sliced off from the proposed North–East Province and that the merger of North–East should precede the referendum rather than follow it. In return to this accommodation by Sri Lanka, he says, India will send all the Tamil militants to Sri Lanka.

18 July 1987

Jayewardene's message to Rajiv Gandhi says, 'the merger of the Northern and Eastern provinces is not a new idea. The merger had been accepted by the Donoughmore Commission in 1931, appointed by the British to consider the demand by the people of Ceylon for universal franchise in legislative councils' elections and other administrative reforms.'

21 July 1987

Rajiv Gandhi sends his emissary to Madras with the latest proposal of Jayewardene for holding discussion with the Tamil groups. Although an outright merger of the two provinces is not on the agenda of the latest proposal, Jayewardene is prepared to have a regional provincial council with a common Governor and Chief Minister. If the proposals are acceptable, Jayewardene wants India to underwrite the accord.

23 July 1987

Sri Lanka Broadcasting Corporation announces that the accord is being finalized and will be signed on 29 July 1987.

27 July 1987

Annoncing the rejection of the accord, V. Prabhakaran describes it as an act of betrayal and affirms his resolve to continue the armed struggle in Sri Lanka. Describing Gandhi's decision to sign the accord, as 'disappointing and shocking', the LTTE chief says that it amounts to 'a stab in the back of the Tamils'. He says that the accord will remain only on paper as it has been drawn up ignoring the Tamils' aspirations.

29 July 1987

India and Sri Lanka sign an agreement that provides for a set of mechanisms to safeguard the interests of the Tamil minority, envisages a role for India in its implementation and, most important of all, takes into account the security concerns of India in the region.

Source: Compiled by the author from newspapers and other published sources.

Appendix II

Annexure 'C'

In terms of paragraph six of the President's statement of 1 December 1983, the following proposals which have emerged as a result of discussion in Colombo and New Delhi are appended for consideration by the All-Party Conference. These proposals are in the context of the unity and integrity of Sri Lanka and will form a basis for formulating the Agenda of the All-Party Conference.

1. The District Development Councils in a province be permitted to combine into one or more Regional Councils if they so agree by decisions of the Councils and approved by referendum in that district.
2. In the case of the District Councils in the Northern and Eastern Provinces respectively, as they are not functioning due to the resignation of the majority of members, their union within each province to be accepted.
3. Each region will have a Regional Council if so decided. The convention will be established that the leader of the party which commands a majority in the Regional Council would be formally appointed by the President as the Chief Minister of the region. The Chief Minister will constitute a Committee of Ministers of the region.
4. The President and the Parliament will continue to have overall responsibility over all subjects not transferred to the regions and generally for all other matters relating to the maintenance of the sovereignty, integrity, unity and security and progress and development of the Republic as a whole.
5. The legislative power of the region would be vested in the Regional Councils which would be empowered to enact laws and exercise executive powers in relation thereto on certain specified listed subjects including the maintenance of internal law and order in the region, the administration of justice, social and economic development, cultural matters and land policy. The list of subjects which will be allocated to the regions will be worked out in detail.
6. The Regional Councils will also have the power to levy taxes, cess

or fees and to mobilize resources through loans, the proceeds of which will be credited to a consolidated fund set up for that particular region to which also will be credited grants, allocations or subventions made by the Republic. Financial resources will be apportioned to the regions on the recommendations of a representative Finance Commission appointed from time to time.

7. Provision will be made for constituting High Courts in each region. The Supreme Court of Sri Lanka will exercise appellate and constitutional jurisdiction.

8. Each region will have a Regional Service consisting of (*a*) officers and other public servants of the region and (*b*) such other officers and public servants who may be seconded to the region. Each region will have a Regional Public Service Commission for recruitment and for exercising disciplinary powers relating to the members of the Regional Service.

9. The armed forces of Sri Lanka will adequately reflect the national ethnic position. In the Northern and Eastern regions, the police forces for internal security will also reflect the ethnic composition of these regions.

10. A Port Authority under the Central Government will be set up for administering the Trincomalee port and harbour. The area which will come under the administration of the Port Authority as well as the powers to be assigned to it will be further discussed.

11. A national policy on land settlement and the basis on which the Government will undertake land colonization will have to be worked out. All settlement schemes should be based on ethnic proportions so as not to alter the demographic balance subject to agreement being reached on major projects.

12. The Constitution and other laws dealing with the official language Sinhala and the national language, Tamil, be accepted and implemented as well as similar laws dealing with the national flag and anthem.

13. The conference should appoint a committee to work out constitutional and legal changes that may be necessary to implement these decisions. The Government would provide its secretariat and necessary legal offices.

14. The consensus of opinion of the All-Party Conference will itself be considered by the United National Party Executive Committee and presumably by the executive bodies of the other parties as well, before being placed before Parliament for legislative action.

Appendix III

Cease-fire Framework before the Thimphu Talks

At the instance of the Government of India, the following four-phase plan for a cease-fire between the Sri Lankan government and the Tamil militants took effect on the 18 June 1985. However, although the cease-fire agreement had envisaged that 'secret talks' between the parties would commence only in Phase IV, in the event, again, at the instance of the Government of India, the talks commenced at Thimpu, Bhutan, on 8 July 1985. The text of the regional agreement was as follows:

In order to create a congenial atmosphere for an accetable political solution to the ethnic question in Sri Lanka, certain steps need to be taken by the Government of Sri Lanka on the one hand and the Tamil militants on the other.

The following series of steps should be implemented by the Government of Sri Lanka on the one hand and the Tamil militants on the other as indicated, over periods shown against each step (viz.):

Phase I: Start on 18 June for Three Weeks

Action to be taken by Sri Lankan Government	Reciprocal steps by the Militants
1. Government will lift restrictive legislation on use of roads and vehicles and suspend enforcement of prohibited zone.	Stop using the prohibited zone for carrying men and material!
2. New settlements will be suspended.	Stop attacks on civilians— both Sinhalese and Tamils— in the North, East and elsewhere.
3. Security forces will carry out cordon and searches and operations	Cease attacks in the North, East and elsewhere on government offices,

in the presence of
local officials and
magistrates.

4. Lift of surveillance
zone, stop infusion of
further resources to
armed services and
police establishments.

economic targets and
private property.

Stop induction of men
and material to affected
areas from outside
Sri Lanka.

Phase II: Three Weeks

1. Security forces will
suspend raids and
suspend curfew

Cease attacks in the North
directed against convoys
of security forces including
police establishments, mining
of roads, rail tracks and
bridges. Stop carrying of arms.

Phase III: Two Weeks

1. Observe cease-fire.

2. Police stations which had
been closed down will be
reopened and the law and
order function will be
carried out by the police.

3. Amnesty will be declared
and those in custody against
whom charges have not been
filed will be released.
(Those who have been
charged will be released
after the conclusion of
successful discussions).

Observe cease-fire.

Phase IV

Secret talks on substantive issues for reaching a political settlement to
take place between the emissaries of the Government and representatives
of the Tamil political leadership and the Tamil militant groups. The venue
of these talks could be a third country acceptable to both sides. Every
effort should be made to maintain the secrecy of these talks and in any
case, of the course of the discussions. The search for a solid foundation for

a political solution must be completed within a period of three months from the date of declaration of cease-fire and amnesty. Depending on the result of these secret talks, open and direct dialogue between the Government and the representatives of the Tamils can commence as soon as the necessary groundwork is considered to have been laid.

Appendix IV

Text of the Indo-Sri Lanka Agreement to Establish Peace and Normalcy in Sri Lanka, Colombo, 29 July 1987*

The Prime Minister of the Republic of India, His Excellency Mr. Rajiv Gandhi and the President of the Democratic Socialist Republic of Sri Lanka, His Excellency Mr. J.R. Jayewardene having met at Colombo on 29 July 1987.

Attaching utmost importance to nurturing, intensifying and strengthening the traditional friendship of India and Sri Lanka and acknowledging the imperative need of resolving the ethnic problem of Sri Lanka, and the consequent violence, and for the safety, well-being and prosperity of people belonging to all communities in Sri Lanka.

1. Having this day entered into the following Agreement to fulfil this objective.

    1.1 desiring to preserve the unity, sovereignty and territorial integrity of Sri Lanka;

    1.2 acknowledging that Sri Lanka is a multi-ethnic and a multi-lingual plural society consisting, inter alia, of Sinhalese, Tamils, Muslims (Moors), and Burghers;

    1.3 recognising that each ethnic group has a distinct cultural and linguistic identity which has to be carefully nurtured;

    1.4 also recognising that the Northern and the Eastern Provinces have been areas of historical habitation of Sri Lankan Tamil speaking peoples, who have at all times hitherto lived together in this territory with other ethnic groups;

    1.5 conscious of the necessity of strengthening the forces contributing to the unity, sovereignty and territorial integrity of Sri Lanka, and preserving its character as a multi-ethnic, multi-lingual and multi-religious plural society, in which all citizens can live in equality, safety and harmony, and prosper and fulfil their aspirations;

2. Resolve that:

    2.1 Since the Government of Sri Lanka proposes to permit adjoining Provinces to join to form one administrative unit and also by a

* *Foreign Affairs Record*, July 1987, pp. 252–57.

Referendum to separate as may be permitted to the Northern and
Eastern Provinces as outlined below:

2.2 During the period, which shall be considered an interim period
(i.e.) from the date of the elections to the Provincial Council, as
specified in para 2.8 to the date of the Referendum as specified in
para 2.3, the Northern and Eastern Provinces as now constituted,
will form one administrative unit, having one elected Provincial
Council. Such a unit will have one Governor, one Chief Minister
and one Board of Ministers.

2.3 There will be a Referendum on or before 31 December 1988 to
enable the people of the Eastern Province to decide whether:

(A) The Eastern Province should remain linked with the
Northern Province as one administrative unit, and continue
to be governed together with the Northern Province as
specified in para 2.2, or

(B) The Eastern Province should constitute a separate administrative unit having its own distinct Provincial Council
with a separate Governor, Chief Minister and Board of
Ministers.

The President may, at his discretion, decide to postpone
such a Referendum.

2.4 All persons who have been displaced due to ethnic violence, or
other reasons, will have right to vote in such a Referendum.
Necessary conditions to enable them to return to areas from
where they were displaced will be created.

2.5 The Referendum, when held, will be monitored by a committee
headed by the Chief Justice, a member appointed by the President,
nominated by the Government of Sri Lanka, and a member
appointed by the President, nominated by the representatives of
the Tamil speaking people of the Eastern Province.

2.6 A simple majority will be sufficient to determine the result of the
Referendum.

2.7 Meeting and other forms of propaganda, permissible within the
laws of the country, will be allowed before the Referendum.

2.8 Elections to Provincial Councils will be held within the next three
months, in any event before 31 December 1987. Indian observers
will be invited for elections to the Provincial Council of the North
and East.

2.9 The emergency will be lifted in the Eastern and Northern Provinces by 15 August 1987. A cessation of hostilities will come into
effect all over the Island within 48 hours of the signing of this
Agreement. All arms presently held by militant groups will be
surrendered in accordance with an agreed procedure to authorities
to be designated by the Government of Sri Lanka. Consequent to

the cessation of hostilities and the surrender of arms by militant groups, the army and other security personnel will be confined to barracks in camps as on 25 May 1987. The process of surrendering of arms and confining the security personnel moving back to barracks shall be completed within 72 hours of cessation of hostilities coming into effect.

2.10 The Government of Sri Lanka will utilise for the purpose of law enforcement and maintenance of security in the Northern and Eastern Provinces the same organisations and mechanisms of Government as are used in the rest of the country.

2.11 The President of Sri Lanka will grant a general amnesty to political and other prisoners now held in custody under the Prevention of Terrorism Act and other emergency laws, and to combatants, as well as to those persons accused, charged and/or convicted under these laws. The Government of Sri Lanka will make special efforts to rehabilitate militant youth with a view to bringing them back to the mainstream of national life. India will cooperate in the process.

2.12 The Government of Sri Lanka will accept and abide by the above provisions and expect all others to do likewise.

2.13 If the framework for the resolutions is accepted, the Government of Sri Lanka will implement the relevant proposals forthwith.

2.14 The Government of India will underwrite and guarantee the resolutions, and cooperate in the implementation of these proposals.

2.15 These proposals are conditional to an acceptance of proposals negotiated from 4.5.1986 to 19.12.1986. Residual matters not finalised during the above negotiations shall be resolved between India and Sri Lanka within a period of six weeks of signing this Agreement. These proposals are also conditional to the Government of India cooperating directly with the Government of Sri Lanka in their implementation.

2.16 These proposals are also conditional to the Government of India taking the following actions if any militant group operating in Sri Lanka does not accept this framework of proposals for a settlement, namely:

   (A) India will take all necessary steps to ensure that Indian territory is not used for activities prejudicial to the unity, integrity and security of Sri Lanka.

   (B) The Indian Navy/Coast Guard will cooperate with the Sri Lanka Navy in preventing Tamil militant activities from affecting Sri Lanka.

   (C) In the event that the Government of Sri Lanka requests

the Government of India to afford military assistance to implement these proposals the Government of India will cooperate by giving to the Government of Sri Lanka such military assistance as and when requested.

(D) The Government of India will expedite repatriation from Sri Lanka of Indian citizens to India who are resident there concurrently with the repatriation of Sri Lankan refugees from Tamil Nadu.

(E) The Governments of India and Sri Lanka will cooperate in ensuring the physical security and safety of all communities inhabiting the Northern and Eastern Provinces.

2.17 The Government of Sri Lanka shall ensure free, full and fair participation of voters from all communities in the Northern and Eastern Provinces in electoral processes envisaged in this Agreement. The Government of India will extend full cooperation to the Government of Sri Lanka in this regard.

2.18 The official language of Sri Lanka shall be Sinhala. Tamil and English will also be official languages.

3. This Agreement and the annexure thereto shall come into force upon signature.

In witness whereof we have set our hands and seals hereunto. Done in Colombo, Sri Lanka, on this the twenty-ninth day of July of the year one thousand nine hundred and eighty-seven, in duplicate, both texts being equally authentic.

Rajiv Gandhi
Prime Minister of the Republic of India

Junius Richard Jayewardene
President of the Democratic Socialist Republic of Sri Lanka

ANNEXURE TO THE AGREEMENT

1 His Excellency the Prime Minister of India and His Excellency the President of Sri Lanka agree that the Referendum mentioned in paragraph 2 and its sub-paragraphs of the Agreement will be observed by a representative of the Election Commission of India to be invited by His Excellency the President of Sri Lanka.

2. Similarly, both Heads of Government agree that the elections to the Provincial Council mentioned in paragraph 2.8 of the Agreement will be observed by a representative of the Government of India to be invited by the President of Sri Lanka.

3. His Excellency the President of Sri Lanka agrees that the Home
Guards would be disbanded and all paramilitary personnel will be
withdrawn from the Eastern and Northern Provinces with a view to
creating conditions conducive to fair elections to the Council.

   The President, in his discretion, shall absorb such paramilitary
forces, which came into being due to ethnic violence into the regular
security forces of Sri Lanka.

4. The Prime Minister of India and the President of Sri Lanka agree
that the Tamil militants shall surrender their arms to authorities
agreed upon to be designated by the President of Sri Lanka. The
surrender shall take place in the presence of one senior representative
each of the Sri Lankan Red Cross and the Indian Red Cross.

5. The Prime Minister of India and the President of Sri Lanka agree
that a joint Indo–Sri Lankan observer group consisting of qualified
representatives of the Government of India and the Government of
Sri Lanka would monitor the cessation of hostilities from 31 July
1987.

6. The Prime Minister of India and the President of Sri Lanka also
agree that in terms of paragraph 2.14 and paragraph 2.16(C) of the
Agreement, an Indian Peace Keeping contingent may be invited by
the President of Sri Lanka to guarantee and enforce the cessation of
hostilities, if so required.

Prime Minister of India
New Delhi
29 July 1987

Excellency,

Conscious of the friendship between our two countries stretching over
two millennia and more, and recognising the importance of nurturing this
traditional friendship, it is imperative that both Sri Lanka and India
reaffirm the decision not to allow our respective territories to be used for
activities prejudicial to each other's unity, territorial integrity and security.

In this spirit, you had, during the course of our discussions, agreed to
meet some of India's concerns as follows:

(i) Your Excellency and myself will reach an early understanding
about the relevance and employment of foreign military and intelligence personnel with a view to ensuring that such presences will
not prejudice Indo–Sri Lankan relations.

(ii) Trincomalee or any other ports in Sri Lanka will not be made
available for military use by any country in a manner prejudicial
to India's interests.

(iii) The work of restoring and operating the Trincomalee oil tank farm will be undertaken as a joint venture between India and Sri Lanka.

(*iv*) Sri Lanka's agreement with foreign broadcasting organisations will be reviewed to ensure that any facilities set up by them in Sri Lanka are used solely as public broadcasting facilities and not for any military or intelligence purposes.

In the same spirit, India will:

(*i*) Deport all Sri Lankan citizens who are found to be engaging in terrorist activities or advocating separatism or secessionism.

(*ii*) Provide training facilities and military supplies for Sri Lankan security forces.

India and Sri Lanka have agreed to set up a joint consultative mechanism to continuously review matters of common concern in the light of the objectives stated in para 1 and specifically to monitor the implementation of other matters contained in this letter.

Kindly confirm, Excellency, that the above correctly sets out the agreement reached between us. Please accept, Excellency, the assurances of my highest consideration.

Yours sincerely,

(*Rajiv Gandhi*)

His Excellency
Mr.J.R. Jayewardene

President of Sri Lanka
29 July 1987

Excellency,

Please refer to your letter dated the 29th of July 1987, which reads as follows:

Excellency,

1. Conscious of the friendship between our two countries stretching over two millennia and more, and recognizing the importance of nurturing this traditional friendship, it is imperative that both Sri Lanka and India reaffirm the decision not to allow our respective territories to be used for activities prejudicial to each other's unity, territorial integrity and security.

2. In this spirit, you had, during the course of our discussions, agreed to meet some of India's concerns as follows:

(*i*) Your Excellency and myself will reach an early understanding about the relevance and employment of foreign military and intelligence personnel with a view to ensuring that such presences will not prejudice Indo–Sri Lankan relations.

(*ii*) Trincomalee or any other ports in Sri Lanka will not be made available for military use by any country in a manner prejudicial to India's interests.

(*iii*) The work of restoring and operating the Trincomalee oil tank farm will be undertaken as a joint venture between India and Sri Lanka.

(*iv*) Sri Lanka's agreements with foreign broadcasting organisations will be reviewed to ensure that any facilities set up by them in Sri Lanka are used solely as public broadcasting facilities and not for any military or intelligence purposes.

3. In the same spirit, India will:

(*i*) Deport all Sri Lankan citizens who are found to be engaging in terrorist activities or advocating separatism or secessionism.

(*ii*) Provide training facilities and military supplies for Sri Lankan security forces.

4. India and Sri Lanka have agreed to set up a joint consultative mechanism to continuously review matters of common concern in the light of the objectives stated in para I and specifically to monitor the implementation of other matters contained in this letter.

5. Kindly confirm, Excellency, that the above correctly sets out the agreement reached between us.

Please accept, Excellency, the assurances of my highest consideration.

Yours sincerely,

(*Rajiv Gandhi*)

His Excellency
Mr. J.R. Jayewardene
President of the Democratic Socialist Republic of Sri Lanka, Colombo

This is to confirm that the above correctly sets out the understanding reached between us. Please accept, Excellency, the assurances of my highest consideration.

(*J.R. Jayewardene*)
President

Appendix V

Agreement between the Indian High Commissioner in Sri Lanka and the LTTE

1. A list of those present is at Annexure attached.
2. The High Commissioner informed Mr. V. Pirabhakaran that President Jayewardene has agreed to establish an Interim Administrative Council for the Northern and Eastern Provinces, as per the following composition:

    (a) Chief Administrator/Administrator in Council—One of the three persons included in the list submitted by the LTTE to be appointed.

(i) LTTE	5
(ii) TULF	2
(iii) Muslims	2
(to include one nominee of LTTE)	
(iv) Sinhalese	2
Total	12

3. Mr. Pirabhakaran agreed to the composition of the Interim Administrative Council as indicated above.
4. The High Commissioner Shri J.N. Dixit informed Mr. V. Pirabhakaran that President Jayewardene had agreed to delegate his executive powers, as envisaged in paras 10.1 and 10.2 of the Bangalore proposals to the Administrator in Council during the interim period i.e., till elections to the provincial councils are held.
5. The Administrator in Council would accordingly be responsible for the maintenance of law and order and other responsibilities as outlined in the relevant paragraphs.
6. It was agreed that the establishment of an Interim Administration would facilitate the fulfilment of the five demands put forward by the LTTE in its resolution conveyed on 13 September '87 to the High Commissioner.
7. Mr. Pirabhakaran said that the LTTE would fully cooperate in the implementation of the Indo–Sri Lanka Agreement subject to assurances given to him by the Prime Minister of India in July 1987.

8. Mr. Prabhakaran said that the LTTE would surrender the remaining arms i.e., other than the personal arms for the security of their leaders once conditions of security for their leaders and cadres are created.

9. Mr. Pirabhakaran agreed that the LTTE will cooperate fully and ensure smooth functioning of all aspects of the civil administration, including the functioning of the police force.

10. Mr. Pirabhakaran agreed that free and fair elections to the provincial council will be held and that the LTTE will cooperate fully in the process.

11. High Commissioner Shri Dixit and Mr. Pirabhakaran agreed that the LTTE and the Indian official media would desist from mutual criticism.

12. In view of agreement having been reached on paras 2 to 11 above, the Sri Lanka Government will announce the establishment of the Interim Administrative Council within 48 hours of the signing of the Agreed Minutes.

13. It was also agreed that the Governments of India and Sri Lanka will formally announce the salient points of the Agreement.

14. Upon this being done, the LTTE would make an announcement about the withdrawal of its agitation and fasting unto death campaigns.

Signed	Signed
(Ms PURI)	(K MAHENDRA RAJA)
First Secretary (Political)	Dy Leader LTTE

HIGH COMMISSION OF INDIA
COLOMBO
28 September 1987   28 September 1987

Appendix VI

Letters Exchanged between Prime Minister of India, Rajiv Gandhi and the President of Sri Lanka, R. Premadasa on the Question of IPKF Withdrawal from Sri Lanka

1. Letter from the President of Sri Lanka to the Indian Prime Minister handed over in New Delhi by Bernard Tilakaratna, Foreign Secretary & Special Envoy of the President

2 June 1989

My dear Prime Minister,

I am writing to you on some matters of urgent importance. The most immediate matter relates to the presence of Indian Forces in Sri Lanka. After I assumed the Presidency of Sri Lanka, the Government of India initiated the withdrawal of troops. We are grateful for your prompt action in this regard.

One of the important campaign pledges made by me at both the Presidential and Parliamentary Elections was the withdrawal of the IPKF on being elected to office. I assumed the office of President of Sri Lanka on the 2nd of January 1989. Five months have elapsed since then. The complete withdrawal of the IPKF, will, hopefully, contribute to stabilizing the situation in Sri Lanka, where the presence of the IPKF has become a deeply divisive and resentful issue. It is also in keeping with your often expressed sentiments that the IPKF will be withdrawn when requested by the President of Sri Lanka.

I am thankful for the efforts of the IPKF during the time it has been in our country. I have often paid tribute to the bravery of the many officers and men who lost life and limb in the discharge of their duties. The tragedy of violence has not only affected your soldiers, it has destroyed many Sri Lankans as well. Our Armed Forces and large numbers of civilians, innocent and uninvolved, have suffered beyond description. Their sacrifices must not be in vain. I am confident that a complete withdrawal of the IPKF will enable me to secure the trust and confidence of my people. Therefore, I would like all IPKF personnel to be withdrawn from Sri Lanka by July 31st 1989.

The withdrawal of the IPKF will also enable Sri Lanka to host the SAARC Summit in November this year in a climate of tranquillity. As you are aware, we could not undertake our obligation to do this in 1988. You will appreciate how difficult it is to hold a regional gathering of this nature with foreign forces on our soil. Our people are most enthusiastic about welcoming leaders of our own region, particularly our closest neighbours. However, their anxieties must also be satisfied, especially in relation to their deep patriotic and nationalist sensitivities.

In this context, we have submitted several proposals regarding an Indo-Lanka Friendship Treaty. I believe that, in the long term, such an agreement will further strengthen relations between India and Sri Lanka. I await your response to our proposals in this regard.

We have always appreciated your sincere interest in the unity and the territorial integrity of our country. Our own efforts to this end need the understanding and goodwill of our neighbours. I believe, that your people and you yourself, share these objectives and will contribute to their realization.

I have just seen the Aide Memoire which was handed over to me by your High Commissioner this evening. As the Aide Memoire refers to the need for consultations between our Governments, I am designating my Foreign Secretary to personally clarify our position on these matters.

With assurances of my high consideration and esteem,

Yours sincerely,

Sgd. R. Premadasa

His Excellency Shri Rajiv Gandhi
Prime Minister of India
Prime Minister's Office
New Delhi.

2. Letter from the Prime Minister of India to the President of Sri Lanka

New Delhi,
20th June, 1989

Dear Mr. President,

I have your letter of the 2nd June, which was handed over to me by your Special Envoy, Foreign Secretary Tilakaratna.

India is committed to preserving the unity and integrity of Sri Lanka, under the terms of the Indo-Sri Lanka Agreement. It was as a result of

this commitment and our responsibility as a guarantor for the implementation of the Indo-Sri Lanka Agreement that we responded to the request
of the government of Sri Lanka to send the IPKF. This was at a time when
the situation seemed headed inexorably towards the break-up of Sri
Lanka. During its presence, the IPKF has striven, with considerable
success but at heavy cost to itself, to prevent such an outcome and
safeguard the unity and integrity of Sri Lanka. Three successive elections
have been held peacefully despite threats of terrorist violence in the
North-East, and all Tamil groups, barring one, have joined the democratic
process. All the Tamil groups, barring one, had given up the demand for
Eelam. If the process of devolution of powers to the Provincial Council
had been implemented in time and had the deliberate attempt by the Sri
Lankan Government to alter the population balance in the Tamil areas by
the continued State-sponsored colonisation of Tamil areas been stopped,
the extremists would have been further isolated and marginalised, and the
violence ended.

As you have yourself stated, we had started the withdrawal of the IPKF
even before you requested for it. A broad time frame for the IPKF's
withdrawal was also discussed at our initiative based on which your
Foreign Minister had made a statement in your Parliament on the 31st
March, 1989. All this was being done on the basis of assurances given by
the Sri Lankan Government and the assumption that the implementation
of the Indo-Sri Lanka Agreement—especially the devolution of powers to
the Provincial Councils—would proceed simultaneously, so that the legitimate aspirations of the Tamils could be met within the framework of the
unity and integrity of Sri Lanka. It is pertinent to recall that it was
precisely because these aspirations were not being met that a situation was
created which threatened the unity and integrity of Sri Lanka.

I have always maintained that the IPKF will not stay in Sri Lanka a day
longer than necessary. But we cannot be unmindful of the responsibilities
and obligations of the two countries under the Indo-Sri Lanka Agreement.
Tamil militant groups were persuaded to support the Indo-Sri Lanka
Agreement and to join the democratic process within the framework of a
united Sri Lanka only on the basis of assurances that the Tamil majority
North-Eastern Province will be given substantial devolution of powers.
Our two Governments are, therefore, morally and legally bound to ensure
that the Tamils are given the autonomy they were promised, both in the
13th Amendment to the Sri Lankan Constitution, as also in the additional
areas promised in the Agreement signed between former President Jayewardene and myself on 7 November, 1987. Failure to do so will only
lend credence to the claims made by some Tamil groups that Tamils
cannot expect justice within a united Sri Lanka. We have to be fully
conscious of the dangers of a return to a situation which may be worse
than that prevailing prior to the Indo-Sri Lanka Agreement.

We believe that, in the spirit of traditional friendship between our two countries, we must jointly draw up a mutually agreed schedule for the full implementation of the Indo-Sri Lanka Agreement and the complete withdrawal of the IPKF. The two have to be joint, parallel exercises.

We have no objection to your proposal for a Friendship Treaty. I had told your Special Envoy that we could set dates for commencing discussions with a view to finalising the text of the proposed treaty.

Yours sincerely,

Sgd. Rajiv Gandhi

His Excellency
Mr. Ranasinghe Premadasa
President of the Democratic Socialist
Republic of Sri Lanka
Colombo.

3. Telex message from the President of Sri Lanka to the Indian Prime Minister on 28th June, 1989.

Excellency,

I am glad to inform you that the LTTE has announced a complete cessation of hostilities against the Sri Lanka Government with immediate effect.

The LTTE which is no longer a proscribed group has in the course of recent discussions with the Government of Sri Lanka agreed to settle whatever problems they have through a process of negotiation.

Under the circumstances it will be appreciated if your Excellency will ensure that the IPKF does not take any offensive action against the LTTE which will tend to prejudice the negotiations that are currently in progress.

Accept Excellency the assurances of my highest consideration.

R. Premadasa

President

4. Letter from the President of Sri Lanka to the Indian Prime Minister

30 June 1989

Dear Prime Minister,

I am in receipt of your letter of 20 June in reply of my letter of 2 June 1989.

I thank you for reiterating India's commitment to preserve the unity, sovereignty and territorial integrity of Sri Lanka as was stated in the Indo-Sri Lanka Agreement.

We appreciate the assistance given by the Indian Government in providing the personnel to assist in the acceptance of arms surrendered by the militants as envisaged by Article 2.9 of the Agreement. We are also thankful for the assistance provided at our request, in terms of Article 2.16(c) of the Agreement and paragraph 6 of the Annexure in affording military assistance to ensure the cessation of hostilities.

I am unable however to accept the contention that the implementation of the Indo-Sri Lanka Agreement, including the devolution of powers to the Provincial Councils, is in any way linked with the withdrawal of the Indian Armed Forces. They had been invited to Sri Lanka for the specific purpose of guaranteeing and enforcing the cessation of hostilities. The Indo-Sri Lanka Agreement does not provide for continued military activities by the Indian Armed Forces in Sri Lanka after a request has been made by me to have them withdrawn. Continuation of such military activities would also be a violation of peremptory norms of international law.

The Indian Peace Keeping Force came to Sri Lanka at the request of the President of Sri Lanka. Due to the circumstances that arose thereafter the IPKF was requested by the President to afford military assistance to ensure the cessation of hostilities. The only condition that should be satisfied for the withdrawal of the Indian Armed Forces is a decision by the President of Sri Lanka that they should be withdrawn. The request made by me to withdraw the Indian Armed Forces has satisfied this condition. It is therefore incumbent on the Government of India to withdraw the Indian Armed Forces from Sri Lanka.

The proposals for the political settlement of the ethnic problem negotiated from 04.05.1986 to 19.12.1986 as well as the residual matters to be finalised between the Government of Sri Lanka and the Government of India have all been accepted and incorporated in the relevant amendments to our Constitution and the Provincial Councils Act. The delay in giving effect to certain proposals within the time frame envisaged by the Agreement had been occasioned by the inability of the Indian Armed Forces to ensure a cessation of hostilities and violence in the North and the East.

The actual functioning of the Provincial Councils in the new system of administration is applicable not only to the North and the East but to all the Provinces of Sri Lanka. This is entirely a political process in which the military has no role whatsoever. You will no doubt agree that it has been an experience common in many other jurisdictions that the establishment of an entirely new structure of administration based on devolution, is essentially a long term process. There is neither a legal nor any other rational basis for the presence of any military force to ensure that the administrative structure is fully in place in any Province of Sri Lanka. I have, in consultation with the Ministers of the Cabinet and Chief Ministers of the Provincial Councils, taken all steps to ensure that the administrative structure necessary for the effective exercise of devolved powers is in place as expeditiously as possible.

As I have already intimated to you in my letter of 2 June 1989, one of the important pledges made by me both at the Presidential and at the Parliamentary Elections was to ensure the withdrawal of the Indian Forces. To quote the Manifesto:

> We will seek a Friendship Treaty with India on the lines of the Indo-Soviet Friendship Treaty. If by the time our candidate is elected President the Indian Forces have not left, we will ensure that they are withdrawn.

The main Opposition Party, the Sri Lanka Freedom Party, in the election manifesto had stated that the Indo-Sri Lanka Agreement would be abrogated and the Indian Forces asked to leave. Thus it will be seen that over 95 per cent of the voters clearly mandated the withdrawal of the Indian Force. The majority approved the UNP proposal for the conclusion of a Friendship Treaty with India.

I would also like to mention a most significant development, which may not have been brought to your notice, namely that the majority of the people of all three communities in the North and the East demand the immediate withdrawal of the Indian Forces.

In your letter you have mentioned that there has been a deliberate attempt by the Government of Sri Lanka to alter the population balance in Tamil areas by continuing state-sponsored colonisation. I must emphatically refute this. There has been no colonisation whatsoever in these areas since the signing of the Indo-Sri Lanka Agreement.

The ground is now set for the Government to resolve any outstanding issues relating to the ethnic problem on the basis of consultation, compromise and consensus with all communities and groups concerned. As I already informed you, the LTTE has announced the cessation of hostilities against the Government of Sri Lanka. They have also resolved to settle any outstanding issues through negotiations and discussions. It is in this context that I have requested you to issue the necessary instructions to the Indian Armed Forces to refrain from offensive operations against the LTTE. The LTTE has already expressed its willingness to put an end to such activities against the Indian Armed Forces on a reciprocal basis. The withdrawal of the Indian Forces within the time frame visualised by me is an essential condition for the Government to proceed with the consolidation of a political settlement.

Far from being of any assistance in the complete resolution of ethnic problem, the presence of the Indian Forces is now a serious impediment. In this connection, I must bring to your notice an alarming development that has been taking place in the Northern and Eastern Provinces. There are complaints that youths mostly of tender age are being forcibly conscripted by certain political groups and are being trained at the hands of the Indian Forces. I need not elaborate on the possible consequences that will follow if this is not checked forthwith.

Therefore, in consideration of all these circumstances, I again earnestly request an immediate recommencement of the withdrawal of the Indian Armed Forces and an acceleration of this process.

I am glad at your favourable response to my proposal for a Friendship Treaty with India. We have already given our draft to the Minister of External Affairs in New Delhi. I would request the discussions should commence without delay, so that this Treaty could give concrete and expeditious expression to the traditional bonds of friendship between our two countries.

Yours sincerely,

Sgd. PRESIDENT

His Excellency Shri Rajiv Gandhi
Prime Minister of India
Prime Minister's Office
New Delhi

5. Message from the Indian Prime Minister to the President of Sri Lanka on 30th June, 1989.

Dear Mr. President,

I have your message of the 29th June sent through your High Commissioner.

The Indo-Sri Lanka Agreement provides for a cessation of hostilities between the Tamil militant groups and the Sri Lanka Forces, and also for the Sri Lanka Forces to stay in barracks in the North East Province. Both these were achieved on the 30th July, 1987. Thus there has already been an effective cessation of hostilities between the Sri Lanka Forces and the LTTE. I am glad that the LTTE has now formally conceded this reality.

We hope that the formal agreement of the LTTE to cease hostilities clearly implies their commitment to the unity and integrity of Sri Lanka and to renounce violence and to respect democratic processes. We trust that, consequent to giving up violence, the LTTE will resume surrender of arms through the Sri Lanka Government—a process which had started on the 5th of August, 1987 and is not yet complete. Unless the LTTE have undertaken to hand over their arms and to renounce violence not only towards the Sri Lanka Government but towards the other citizens of the North Eastern Province, their announcement of cessation of hostilities would be meaningless.

Since the IPKF has a mandate in terms of India's role as a guarantor, for ensuring the physical safety and security of all communities of the North Eastern Province, I would appreciate clarifications on the points I have mentioned above. These clarifications will facilitate an immediate decision on the IPKF's cessation of offensive action to disarm the LTTE. The earlier we receive your response, the quicker will be the process of initiating suitable action.

Yours sincerely,

Sgd/- Rajiv Gandhi

6. Telex Message from the President of Sri Lanka to the Indian Prime Minister on 4th July, 1989.

Dear Prime Minister,

I have your message of 30th June sent through your High Commissioner in response to my message requesting you to ensure that the Indian Armed Forces in Sri Lanka do not take any offensive action against the LTTE. Such action or any intensification of operations is liable to prejudice the negotiations currently in progress and prolong the armed conflict.

Your statement that cessation of hostilities took place on 30th July, 1987 does not accord with facts. The LTTE ceased hostilities against the Sri Lanka Security Forces only for a few days but resumed violence on 2nd August, 1987 and continued until they announced a cessation of hostilities in June, 1989. During the interim 148 service and police personnel were killed and 80 were wounded, 481 civilians were killed and 115 were injured.

The LTTE announced a cessation of hostilities only in June this year after the commencement of the dialogue with the Government. This cessation covers not only the Government but also the people in the North and the East and in fact the people in the whole of Sri Lanka. At the same time the LTTE reiterated its commitment to resolve all outstanding problems through negotiation and discussion and indicated their readiness to enter the democratic process.

As stated in your message you have been seeking to disarm the LTTE for the past two years and this process is not yet complete nor have you been able to bring them to the negotiating table. I am confident that I will be able to ensure that the LTTE gives up their arms after the Indian Armed Forces have been withdrawn.

The political solution which I seek to provide will not only be within the framework of our Constitution but must also preserve the sovereignty of our people, the unitary character and the territorial integrity of our country.

The responsibility of providing safety and security for its citizens within Sri Lanka is solely the responsibility of the Government of Sri Lanka. The Indo-Sri Lanka Agreement does not and indeed cannot in international law provide a mandate for the Government of India or its Armed Forces to assume any responsibility for this function otherwise than at the express request of the Sri Lanka Government. In any event during the past two years when the Indian Armed Forces were operating in the Northern and Eastern Provinces they were unable to prevent the killings of a number of civilians and the displacement of an even larger number from their homes, beside the casualties referred to above.

Any interpretation of the agreement which seeks to provide a mandatory role for the Government of India or its armed forces within Sri Lanka otherwise than at the express request of the Government of Sri Lanka would constitute a serious interference in the internal affairs of a friendly sovereign country and a gross violation of the peremptory norms of international law. I am sure that such is not your intention.

I trust these clarifications will enable you to ensure that the Indian Armed Forces do not continue any offensive operations against the LTTE.

Yours sincerely,

R. Premadasa
President

7. *Letter from the Prime Minister of India to the Sri Lankan President handed over in Colombo by the Principal Secretary to the Prime Minister & Special Envoy Mr. B.G. Deshmukh.*

New Delhi
July 11, 1989

Dear Mr. President,

I have your letters of 30th June and 5th July.

I do not wish to enter into a debate on various interpretations of mutual obligations assumed by our two sovereign nations. These are quite clear. I also do not wish to go into the validity of assertions like the LTTE having resumed violence on 2nd August, 1987 whereas the arms surrender started and the amnesty letter was handed over by the Sri Lanka Government to the LTTE three days later. We should let facts speak for themselves.

There is an Agreement between our two countries. This Agreement is meant to preserve the unity and integrity of Sri Lanka and to ensure the safety, security and legitimate interests of the Tamils. Nearly a thousand Indian soldiers have made the supreme sacrifice in fulfilment of India's obligations as a guarantor of this Agreement. Since the signing of the Agreement, not only have the Provincial Council elections been held, but also the Parliamentary and Presidential elections. The situation in the North-Eastern Province is far more settled and peaceful than elsewhere in Sri Lanka. Despite all this, the devolution package promised to the Tamils has not been implemented. These are incontrovertible facts.

Both of us agree that the IPKF should be withdrawn. Both of us agree that we had commenced the withdrawal even before you asked for it. A broad time frame of IPKF's withdrawal had in fact been discussed. Discussions of finalising the details were proposed by your Foreign Minister at Harare only a few days prior to your unilateral announcement of 1st June.

I have repeatedly said that the IPKF's withdrawal schedule should be worked out through joint consultations along with a simultaneous schedule for the implementation of the Indo-Sri Lanka Agreement. We are willing to resume discussions on this subject at any time and place of your convenience. Your colleague, the Honourable Mr. Thondaman, who met me here, would have conveyed to you our desire for friendly relations and our willingness to resolve any misunderstandings through mutual consultations. If, however, discussions for this purpose are not acceptable to you, we will have to decide the details of IPKF's withdrawal unilaterally consistent with our responsibilities and obligations under the Indo-Sri Lanka Agreement.

While I reiterate the Government of India's willingness to cooperate with your Government to resolve pending issues, I must emphasise to Your Excellency that India has traditionally been mindful of the sanctity of the Agreements it signs with other countries and of commitments solemnly undertaken under such Agreements. India will under no circumstances deviate from this policy affecting our concerns.

It has been our practice to maintain the confidentiality of official correspondence, particularly between Heads of State or Government unless otherwise agreed upon. However, the gist of your message to me was more often than not made available to the media before it reached me. Now I find that all our recent correspondence has been officially made public by the Sri Lanka Government. I may thus be constrained to depart from tradition by authorising this communication being made public, after you receive it.

Yours sincerely,

Sgd/- Rajiv Gandhi

8. Letter from the President of Sri Lanka to the Prime Minister of India

12th July, 1989

Dear Prime Minister,

I am in receipt of your letter of 11th July 1989 which was handed to me by your Special Envoy. I thank you for the courtesy of sending him to Sri Lanka in an attempt to resolve the issues regarding the withdrawal of the Indian Armed Forces.

I explained to your Special Envoy and his delegation my position with regard to the withdrawal of the Indian Armed Forces from Sri Lanka. I informed them that the discussions can continue based on the four premises set out below.

Firstly, the Indian Armed Forces arrived in Sri Lanka as a peace-keeping force to assist in restoring peace. They came at the request of the President of Sri Lanka and were under his command as the Commander-in-Chief of the Armed Forces. Their invitation was in terms of Item 6 of the Annexure to the Indo-Sri Lanka Agreement which says 'that an Indian Peace keeping Contingent may be invited by the President of Sri Lanka to guarantee and enforce the cessation of hostilities if so required.' The fact that the President of Sri Lanka is the Commander-in-Chief of all Armed Forces in Sri Lanka has been recognised by the Government of India.

Secondly, the Agreement was between the Government of Sri Lanka and the Government of India. There were no other parties to the Agreement. In fact the LTTE protested that they were left out of the Agreement and in fact their leaders had been confined for a duration of time leading up to the signing of the Agreement.

Thirdly, the presence of the Indian Armed Forces and the devolution of powers to the Provincial Councils are totally unconnected. I have explained this to you at great length in my earlier communications. I have told your delegation that the devolution of power by the Sri Lanka Parliament is entirely an internal matter. No foreign agency can oversee the implementation of legislation enacted by or compel the Parliament of a sovereign State to enact any particular provision of law. In any case, as stated in my earlier letter of 30th June 1989 you would appreciate that devolution is essentially a long term process. There is neither any legal nor any other rational basis for the presence of any military force to ensure that the process of devolution is complete. It would therefore be incorrect and unrealistic to contend that the Indian Armed Forces were expected to remain in Sri Lanka till the process of devolution is completed.

Fourthly, the Government of India undertook not to permit Indian territory to be used for activities prejudicial to the unity, integrity and security of Sri Lanka. I was constrained to point out to your delegation that Mr. Padmanabha and others who are campaigning to keep the Indian Armed Forces in Sri Lanka have not only been permitted to publicly express their intention of making a unilateral declaration of Eelam whilst being on Indian soil but also to publicise such declaration on Indian national television.

I explained further to them that the invitation extended to the Indian Armed Forces was based on assurances contained in the Agreement that the time frame required for cessation of hostilities was 48 hours from the signing of the Agreement and for the surrender of arms was 72 hours from the cessation of hostilities. You would also appreciate that the decision to invite an Indian Peace Keeping Contingent was in the context of the resolve that a solution to the ethnic problem should be through negotiation and not by the use of military force. As such, the invitation could not have been interpreted as being one for the Indian Peace Keeping Contingent to engage itself in the prolonged use of force.

The reassurance with which I noted the withdrawal of Indian forces when I assumed office turned to disappointment when I observed that the withdrawal was not being effected as expeditiously as possible. After careful consideration I decided that the 31st July 1989 was the suitable deadline for the withdrawal of the Indian Armed Forces from Sri Lanka.

The President of Sri Lanka could under Article 2.16(c) of the Agreement obtain Indian military assistance when he thinks such assistance is necessary. In my Election Manifesto I promised to solve the problem, not by the use of force but by a process of consultation, compromise and consensus. The people of this country endorsed this manifesto. The dialogue initiated under this mandate has already borne fruit. The LTTE once the most intractable of the militant groups has ceased hostilities not only against the Government, but against all the people of the North and the East and indeed against all the people of Sri Lanka. They have agreed to join the democratic process and are now committed to settling problems by negotiation. In this context continued military action by the Indian armed forces is not only unnecessary but also prejudicial to a settlement by discussion and negotiation.

Action by the Indian armed forces is also gravely prejudicial to a political settlement with the LTTE who assert their need to carry arms as long as they are being attacked by the Indian forces and other militant groups who reportedly enjoy the support of the Indian forces. Further the very presence of the Indian armed forces in Sri Lanka has made it difficult for me to enter into any dialogue with other political groups. In the meantime, certain groups in other parts of the country are resorting to violent activity on account of what they claim to be the inability of the Government to ensure the withdrawal of the Indian armed forces. The continued presence of the Indian armed forces is driving these groups to escalating their violence to crisis proportions.

My officials will be holding discussions based on these basic premises. I shall be replying to the other issues including the statement attributed to my Foreign Minister raised in your letter of 11th July 1989 at the conclusion of the discussions between your delegation and my officials.

Yours sincerely,

PRESIDENT

9. Letter from the President of Sri Lanka to the Prime Minister of India

19 July 1989

Dear Prime Minister,

Further to my letter of 12th July, 1989 I wish to clarify certain matters referred to in your letter of 11th July, 1989.

I agree that we should not enter into a debate. The terms of the Agreement are clear. The events leading up to that Agreement and the subsequent developments are fresh in our minds.

In regard to the cessation of hostilities by the LTTE, it is a fact that the Indian Armed Forces in Sri Lanka had not been able, even after two years, to ensure such cessation and complete disarming the militants. At the time of the signing of the Agreement it was envisaged that this process would not take more than five days.

I also agree with your assertion that the Agreement involves the acceptance of mutual obligations by two sovereign and friendly nations. The objective of this Agreement was to resolve the ethnic problem and to end the violence that was a threat to the unity and territorial integrity of Sri Lanka. The Agreement also sought to ensure the physical security and safety not only of the Tamil ethnic community but of all communities inhabiting the Northern and Eastern Provinces.

I must thank you once again for the assistance provided by the Indian Forces in response to Sri Lanka's request for military assistance to guarantee and enforce the cessation of hostilities. We are sad that over a thousand Indian lives have been lost.

Sri Lanka for her part has discharged all her obligations under the Agreement and in particular taken all effective and meaningful steps towards the devolution of power.

Sri Lanka has amongst other things, amended the Constitution, enacted legislation necessary to establish Provincial Councils, temporarily merged the Northern and Eastern Provinces, implemented the Official Languages policy, held the Provincial Council Elections, set up the infrastructure and provided the personnel and finances necessary for effective functioning.

I wish to reiterate that I have at all times held the view that the problems of the Tamil linguistic groups in Sri Lanka should be resolved, not by the use of force but by the process of consultation, compromise and consensus.

Firm in this belief, I, as the Presidential candidate, incorporated in my manifesto a pledge to secure the withdrawal of the Indian Armed Forces as a necessary prelude to political negotiations and a durable settlement. I did so in October/November 1988. The people of Sri Lanka by an overwhelming majority endorsed this principle, both at the Presidential and Parliamentary elections.

The events of the past months have proved the wisdom of my approach. The LTTE once the most intractable of groups has now agreed to eschew violence and join the mainstream of political democracy.

You state that 'the situation in the North-Eastern Provinces is far more settled and peaceful than elsewhere in Sri Lanka.' If this be so, there would be a lesser need for offensive action by the armed forces in these areas.

Furthermore, the substantial grievance over which the other Provinces began fomenting unrest, is the continued presence of the Indian Armed Forces in Sri Lanka. As you are aware, the agitation commenced with the signing of the Agreement and continued to escalate due to the presence of the Indian Armed Forces. So that, whichever way it is looked at, the continued presence of the Indian Armed Forces is an obstacle to the restoration of peace and normalcy in Sri Lanka.

Whilst we are both agreed that the Indian Armed Forces in Sri Lanka should be withdrawn, I cannot, for the reasons more fully set out in the annex hereto, agree that the terms of the Agreement do, or can in law be interpreted to mean, that the withdrawal of the Indian Armed Forces is in any way linked with or preconditioned upon the implementation of the process of devolution, or for that matter, the performance of any other obligation cast upon Sri Lanka by the Agreement.

The continued presence of the Indian Armed Forces or the conduct of any operations by such forces within Sri Lankan territory, is conditional only upon the concurrence of the Sri Lanka Government. It would therefore by unlawful for the Government of India to continue to maintain her Armed Forces within Sri Lankan territory in the absence of such concurrence.

It would be incompatible with the sovereignty of a State to concede a right for any alien armed force to operate within its territory contrary to the wishes of the Head of State who is also the Commander-in-Chief of its forces—from whom such alien armed force is not taking orders.

You would also appreciate that any continued offensive action against a section of my people who have publicly announced a cessation of hostilities against the Government and all the people of Sri Lanka would amount to the unlawful taking of civilian lives.

As already intimated to you, with the recommencement of the withdrawal process it will be possible to set in motion consultations to accommodate any logistical constraints which may arise.

You have stated that my Foreign Minister has discussed a broad time frame for the withdrawal of the IPKF. According to him the former Indian High Commissioner in Colombo had intimated that some of the IPKF would be withdrawn by 30th of June and the rest by 31st of December. It appears that this had been a tentative proposal made by your former High Commissioner and I must emphasise that we have not at any time agreed to such a time frame.

I continue to receive reports of the forcible conscription of young people in the Northern and Eastern Provinces and their training at the hands of the Indian Forces. Since I wrote to you on this matter on 30th June, the situation has been aggravated. There is now an exodus of young people from the Northern and the Eastern Provinces fleeing from this conscription. A sizeable number is being accommodated in camps in Colombo.

I am thankful for the assurance in your letter that India has traditionally been mindful of the sanctity of the principle of observing the obligations of Agreements entered into by India. I wholly endorse the principle that Agreements should be observed. In this regard I invite your attention to the express provision in the Indo-Sri Lanka Agreement that the provision of military assistance by the Government of India is 'as and when requested' by the Government of Sri Lanka.

It should also be noted that the Agreement contemplates that the Indian Armed Forces will assist the Government of Sri Lanka and not be operating on their own initiative.

However, if it is your view that the Agreement should be construed as creating an obligation for the Indian Armed Forces to remain in Sri Lankan territory without the concurrence and against the express wishes of the Sri Lanka Government, I as the President of an independent sovereign Republic, would have no option but to treat the Agreement as being inimical to Sri Lanka's sovereignty and national interests.

Yours sincerely,

PRESIDENT

ANNEXURE

The entry into and the continued presence of Indian Armed Forces on Sri Lankan territory can be lawful only upon the express concurrence of the Government of Sri Lanka.

It is a peremptory norm of international law, that the presence of, or the conduct of operations by, any foreign armed force within the territory of a sovereign state, otherwise than with the express concurrence of the Government of that state amounts to an act of aggression. Such acts of aggression have not only been recognized as unlawful, but unequivocally condemned by the community of civilized nations. This principle has also been reiterated in several United Nations instruments.

In the Indo-Sri Lanka Agreement several acts of co-operation are obligated upon the Government of India. The provision of military assistance is one such act of co-operation.

An examination of the structure of the Agreement makes it clear, that the Agreement contemplated implementation without the use of force, that the Government of India agreed to underwrite and guarantee the acceptance of the Agreement by the militant groups, who would then cease hostilities and surrender their arms.

The Government of Sri Lanka undertook to confine its Armed Forces to barracks and to grant an amnesty to the militants who were in custody.

The rendering of military assistance is governed by Article 2(c) which clearly stipulates that the affording of military assistance is 'as and when' requested by the Government of Sri Lanka.

This Article makes it clear beyond argument, that the basic provision of international law regarding the necessity of the concurrence of the government of the domestic state in the entry of foreign armed forces into its territory has been recognized and observed.

With the release of the militants from custody and the confining of the Armed Forces to barracks by Sri Lanka, and the failure to disarm the militants or to ensure cessation of hostilities, there was resumption of the violence, which necessitated the request for Indian military assistance. Accordingly the invitation to the Indian Armed Forces was, as unequivocally stated in clause 6 of the Annexure, 'to guarantee and enforce the cessation of hostilities'.

Any attempt to construe this invitation as providing a mandatory right for the Armed Forces so invited to 'protect' minorities or to oversee the devolution of power would be an untenable construction of the Agreement.

Such a construction would neither accord with the clear understanding stated in the Agreement nor with the peremptory norms of international law.

Appendix VII

Indo–Sri Lanka Agreements on the IPKF Withdrawal

VIIA: Joint Communique issued simultaneously by the Government of India and the Government of Sri Lanka on 28th July 1989.

The President of Sri Lanka has requested the Prime Minister of India to recommence the withdrawal of the IPKF. The withdrawal will recommence on the 29th of July 1989. The High Commissioner of India reiterated the invitation of the Minister of External Affairs of the Government of India to the Foreign Minister of the Government of Sri Lanka to visit India to discuss the time schedule for the withdrawal of the remaining IPKF contingent in Sri Lanka. The invitation has been accepted. This opportunity will be used to review the implementation of the Indo-Sri Lanka Agreement. During the visit of the delegation the question of cessation of offensive military operations by the IPKF and the safety and security of all communities in North Eastern Province of Sri Lanka will also be discussed.

(The text was signed by the High Commissioner for India in Sri Lanka, Mr. L. Mehotra and the Foreign Secretary of Sri Lanka, Mr.Bernard Tilakaratna).

Source: *Sri Lanka News Letter*, Vol. IX. No. 4/89, New Delhi, p. 19.

VIIB: Press Statement issued by Sri Lanka Delegation at the conclusion of talks in New Delhi on 4th August 1989

1. A delegation led by Hon. Ranjan Wijeratne, Foreign Minister of Sri Lanka and comprising Hon. A.C.S. Hameed, Minister of Higher Education, Science and Technology and senior officials of the Government of Sri Lanka visited New Delhi from July 29 to August 4, 1989 at the invitation of the Minister of External Affairs of India, His Excellency Shri P.V. Narasimha Rao.
2. During their stay in Delhi, the delegation called on the Prime Minister of India, His Excellency Shri Rajiv Gandhi. The delegation had two

rounds of talks with the Prime Minister of India and several discussions with the Minister of External Affairs, His Excellency Shri P.V. Narasimha Rao and the Minister of Defence, His Excellency Shri K.C. Pant. The talks were held in a cordial and friendly atmosphere.

3. The discussions centered around the regular and expeditious withdrawal of the IPKF, the cessation of offensive military operations by them and the security situation in the Northern and Eastern Provinces and other relevant issues. During the discussions, both sides presented their proposals for resolving the issues involved.

4. The Sri Lanka delegation leaves for Colombo today and will submit their report to His Excellency President R. Premadasa for his consideration and decision.

Source: *Sri Lanka News Letter*, Vol. IX, No. 4/89, New Delhi, p. 19.

VIIC: Text of Joint Communique on IPKF Withdrawal

Colombo, September 18. The following is the text of the joint communique issued simultaneously by the Government of India and the Government of Sri Lanka today.

In pursuance of the communique signed in Colombo on July 28, 1989, by Mr. L.L. Mehrotra, the High Commissioner of India, and Mr. Bernard Tilakratne, Secretary, Ministry of Foreign Affairs of Sri Lanka, three rounds of consultation were held by the two Governments.

A Sri Lankan delegation, led by the Foreign Minister, Mr. Ranjan Wijeratne, visited India from July 29 to August 4, 1989. Mr. Bradman Weerakoon, Special Envoy of the President of Sri Lanka, held further discussion in New Delhi from August 15 to 17, 1989. A final round of talks was held between Mr. Rajiv Gandhi, Prime Minister of India, and Mr. Ranjan Wijeratne, Foreign Minister of Sri Lanka, during their visit to Belgrade from September 4 to 7, 1989.

Cordial, friendly: The talks were held in a cordial and friendly atmosphere. They covered bilateral issues, including the de-induction of the remaining IPKF contingents in Sri Lanka, the implementation of the Indo-Sri Lanka Agreement, and measures to ensure the safety and security of all communities of the North-Eastern Province of Sri Lanka.

The implementation of the Indo-Sri Lanka Agreement was reviewed in depth by the two sides. The Sri Lankan side briefed the Indian side on the progress made and the further steps taken by them for the expeditious implementation of the devolution process, such as establishing of the provincial police force and facilitating the effective functioning of the North-Eastern Provincial Council, and the establishment of an adequate administrative structure for that purpose. The Lankan side also informed the Indian side that it would institute all measures to strengthen the civil administration as early as possible which would ensure peace and normalcy in the North-Eastern Province.

Peace committee: The Sri Lankan side informed the Indian side of their decision to set up a peace committee on September 20, 1989, to afford an opportunity to all political and ethnic groups in the North-Eastern Province to come together to settle their differences, through a process of consultation, compromise and consensus, and to bring all groups into the democratic process, thereby ending violence and improving conditions for the physical safety and security of all communities. This would help restore normalcy and contribute to the effective functioning of the North-Eastern Provincial Council. The first meeting of the peace committee will be held within three weeks of the setting up of this committee. This decision was welcomed by the Indian side.

It was decided to set up a security coordination group comprising the Sri Lankan Minister of State for Defence, the Chief Minister of the North-Eastern Province, the Sri Lankan Defence Secretary and the GOC of the IPKF, with a view to avoiding any adverse impact on the law and order situation in the North-Eastern Province and to suggest measures to ensure the safety and security in the North-Eastern Province as the phased de-induction of the IPKF and the strengthening of the civilian administration of the North-Eastern Province of Sri Lanka proceed. This group will keep in view the recommendations of the peace committee relating to the safety and security of the inhabitants of the North-Eastern Province.

In view of the above, the process of de-induction of the IPKF, which recommenced on July 29, 1989, will be continued on an expeditious schedule. All efforts will be made to accelerate the de-induction of the IPKF to complete de-induction by December 31, 1989.

The Indian side stated that the suspension of offensive military operations by the IPKF will come into effect at 6 a.m. on September 20, 1989. An observer group consisting of the Sri Lanka Army Commander and the GOC of the IPKF will report any violations of the cessation of hostilities and immediate consequential action taken, and recommend further remedial action to the President of Sri Lanka—PTI.

Sd/-   Sd/-
L.L. Mehrotra   B.P. Tilakaratne
High Commissioner   Secretary to the Ministry of
for India   Foreign Affairs of Sri Lanka

Source: *The Hindu*, 19 September 1989.

Appendix VIII

Security Co-ordination Groups' Decisions Regarding the Security of the Tamils

VIII A: Minutes of Security Co-ordinating Group

Meeting—8th October, 1989

Members Present:

(1) Hon'ble Ranjan Wijeratne—Minister of Foreign Affairs and Minister of State for Defence; (2) Hon. A. Varatharajaperumal, Chief Minister; (3) Gen. D.S. Attygalle, Secretary, Ministry of Defence; (4) Lt. Gen. A.S. Kalkat, GOC, IPKF.

Also Present:

(5) Gen. S.C. Ranatunga, Secretary, Ministry of State for Defence;
(6) Dr. S. Jaishankar, Political Adviser to GOC IPKF;
(7) Brig. L.J.I. Fernando, Secretary.

The Charter of the S.C.G. was formalised as per para 5 of the September 18 Joint Communique between Governments of India and Sri Lanka. This covered four points as follows:

(a) Avoiding any adverse impact on law and order situation in North-Eastern Province.

(b) Suggesting measures to ensure safety and security in North-East Province.

(c) Strengthen civilian administration in North-East Province.

(d) Keep in view recommendations of Peace Committee relating to safety and security in North-East Province.

1. Gen. Kalkat informed that the Report of the Observer Group on violations of the conditions for suspension of offensive military operations by the IPKF in the North-East up to 4th October, 1989 was submitted to H.E. the President on 6th October 1989. Gen. Kalkat stated that the Report showed that there had been a reduction of militancy since suspension of offensive Mil Ops, by the IPKF. However, there had been a slight increase in acts of terrorism and extortion by the LTTE against the other Tamil parties, and civilian

population. By and large the condition for suspension of Mil Ops is holding.

2. The Chief Minister said that there had been an increase of violation by LTTE and harassing of EPRLF, ENDLE and TELO members, their families and supporters. The Chief Minister also stated that extortion and hijacking of vehicles have shown an increase.

3. GOC IPKF informed that the IPKF was in a position to commence de-induction from 15th October 1989. The first area to be vacated would be Amparai district. He requested that SCG address itself to its charter in terms of para 5 of the Joint Communique and confirm that all arrangements to ensure law and order for security of all people in the area had been completed so that there is no vacuum, after which he would inform the Government of India and then confirm the dates of commencement of de-induction to the Sri Lanka Government.

4. The Hon'ble Minister of State for Defence expressed his satisfaction and stated that the following steps must be taken in the four polling divisions of Amparai, Kalmunal, Potuvil and Sammanthurai.

Reactivate Policy

1. Police Stations in the Amparai district will be brought up to full strength with at least 100 policemen per Police Station as early as possible. Of 1,500 Citizen Volunteer Force personnel, sufficient numbers as decided by the IGP and DIG in consultation with Hon. Chief Minister are to be inducted into the Reserve and Regular Police Force to fill vacancies. Ethnic balance in recruitment within the Province will be maintained.

2. Law and order will be maintained by the Chief Minister through the police with the assistance of the CVF. The DIG will be responsible to and under control of the Chief Minister for maintenance of law and order.

3. The Chief Minister is of the view that the Police personnel and CVF in North-East Province should be adequately and properly armed to meet any eventuality.

4. The Chief Minister is keen to get the CVF expanded. The numbers required for the CVF for Police and Armed Forces will be worked out by Secretary/Defence, Army Commander, Inspector-General of Police and Chief Minister. The strength of the CVF is to be determined by the above Committee. The final decision will be discussed and decided by the Security Co-ordinating Group.

5. *Deployment of Sri Lanka Armed Forces*

1. After the de-induction of the IPKF fully from the area, the Sri Lanka Army will vacate public buildings such as schools, hospitals etc. and will be relocated, for which, the Chief Minister will provide suitable areas acceptable to the Commander of the Army in consultation with the Minister of State for Defence.
2. The Sri Lanka Army will not be called out for military operations except with the consent of H.E. the President and the Chief Minister, if there is such a requirement.

6. *Civil Administration*

1. The Civil Administration must function again as soon as possible. Mr. W.T. Jayasinghe has been appointed to liaise with State Officials in North-East Province to resolve problems of devolution and report to H.E. the President.
2. The usage of the term 'Provincial Government' was discussed. Sri Lanka Government documents were produced to prove that the term was in use from 1985 to 1986. The Hon'ble Minister of State for Defence said that he would have it examined.

7. *General*

1. *Recruitment to the Police Force in the North-East Province*
   Vacancies to the Police Force will be filled from among the CVF personnel. The ethnic balance within the Province will be maintained. Depending on qualifications and experience, these personnel may be absorbed into the Police Reserve or Regular Police. Educational qualifications may be waived in regard to the Police Reserve as approved by H.E. the President.
2. *National and Pronvincial Police Commissions*
   The legislation for the Provincial Police Commission will be taken up in Parliament shortly. The question of appointing one or two DIGs to the North-East Province will be discussed with H.E. the President in consultation with the Attorney-General, as the Chief Minister is of the view that there should be only one Provincial Police Division for North-East Province. All 54 Police Stations in the North-East Province will be brought up to full strength with at least 100 policemen for each Police Station as early as possible. Additional Police personnel may be required for static duty in the main towns.
3. *Recruitment to the Armed Forces*
   Recruitment to the Armed Forces should be carried out to ensure that the Armed Forces reflect the ethnic ratio within a specified time frame. Initially, personnel of the CVF will be absorbed into

the Armed Forces Volunteer Units irrespective of educational qualifications for services in the North-East Province.

8. Chief Minister and Secretary/Defence will inform Minister of State for Defence that the above decisions have been complied with.

9. *Next Meeting*

The next meeting of Security Co-ordinating Committee will be at 17.30 hrs. on 19th October 1989 at Operational Headquarters, Ministry of Defence.

Sd/-

Brigadier L.J.I. Fernando

Secretary

VIII B: Minutes of the Security Co-ordination Group Meeting

Held on 19th October 1989 at OP HQ MOD

Present:

Hon. Ranjan Wijeratne, Minister of Foreign Affairs and Minister of State for Defence; Hon. A. Varatharajaperumal, Chief Minister, North-East Province; Gen. D.S. Attygalle, Secretary, Ministry of Defence; Lt. Gen. A.S. Kalkat, GOC, IPKF.

In Attendance:

Lt. Gen. H. Wanasinghe, Commander of the Sri Lanka Army; Mr. E.E.B. Perera, Inspector General of Police; Dr. S. Jaishankar, Political Advisor to GOC, IPKF; Dr. K. Vigneswaran, Secretary to the Chief Minister, North-East Province; Lt. Col. C. Seneviratne, Secretary.

1. The Chief Minister's letter to the Minister of State for Defence dated 16 October 1989 was discussed by the Group. Steps taken on matters referred to in the letter are as follows:

   (a) It was decided that SSP Mr. T.E. Anandarajah would be appointed to function under the Chief Minister as the DIG Police of the North-Eastern Range.

   (b) The Group was informed that the Police in Amparai District had already been brought under the purview of the DIG Police, North-Eastern Range.

   (c) The Group was informed that the Bill for the establishment of the National and Provincial Police Commissions has been referred to the Supreme Court as an urgent bill and will be placed before Parliament at the next session due to commence on 7 November 1989.

2. The GOC-IPKF informed that Amparai District will be vacated by the IPKF by 24 October 1989. The final contingent from Amparai District would be sailing home from Trincomalee on 25 October 1989.

3. The IGP informed the SCG that he is in the process of bringing up to full strength 13 Police stations in Amparai District. The CVF would be inducted where necessary.

4. The requirement of automatic weapons for the CVF and Police Reservists was discussed. Due to non-availability of weapons with the Sri Lanka Police, the Sri Lanka Government made a request to the GOC–IPKF for the IPKF to provide weapons on loan to enable the Chief Minister to meet the situation. The GOC–IPKF said that he would refer the request to his Government and advise the Group shortly. Meanwhile the Chief Minister and the Inspector General of Police would work out the requirement of weapons and inform the GOC–IPKF.

5. The Chief Minister, the Secretary to the Ministry of Defence, the Commander of the Army and the Inspector General of Police will meet as a Committee at the Ministry of Defence on 21 October 1989 at 1000 hours, to discuss the expansion of the CVF as per paragraph 4 (4) of the minutes of 8th October 1989 and to work out the number of weapons required by the CVF and the Police Reservists deployed in the North-East Province.

6. The SCG noted that Mr. W.T. Jayasinghe had not yet met the state officials of the North-East Province to resolve problems of devolution as per paragraph 6 (1) of the minutes on 8 October 1989. This should be expedited.

7. It was decided to move the STF platoons out of Amparai District. In its place, the Sri Lanka Army will be deployed only where necessary.

8. The GOC–IPKF will inform the SCG of the next de-induction after reviewing the situation in Amparai District on vacation.

9. The next meeting of the SCG will be at 1500 hours on 1 November 1989 at OP HQ MOD.

Secretary

sd/-

VIII C: Minutes of the Security Co-ordination Group Meeting

Held on 1 November 1989 at OP HQ MOD

Present:
   Hon. Ranjan Wijeratne, Minister of Foreign Affairs and Minister of
State for Defence; Hon. A. Varatharajaperumal, Chief Minister, North–
East Province; Lt. General A.S. Kalkat, GOC IPKF; General S.C. Rana-
tunge, Acting Defence Secretary.
In Attendance:
   Lt. General Hamilton Wanasinghe, Commander of Sri Lanka Army;
Mr. E.E.B. Perera, Inspector General of Police; Dr. K. Vigneswaran,
Secretary to Chief Minister, North-East Province; S. Jaishankar, Political
Adviser to GOC–IPKF.

1. Progress on implementation of SCG Minutes of 8 and 19 October
   was reviewed:
   (a) It was confirmed that SSP Mr. Anandraja had been appointed
       DIG of North-East Police range and that police in Amparai
       District had been brought under his purview. (Reference
       paras 1 (a) and (b) of October 19 minutes).
   (b) CM drew attention to the Bill on National and Provincial
       Police Commissions not being included in the order papers
       of the Parliament. Minister agreed to look into the matter
       and rectify the situation. (Reference para 1 (c) of October 19
       minutes).
   (c) On Devolution, CM indicated that SLC officials had sought
       more time to study the position papers of Devolution which
       had been given to them by him. Discussions as envisaged
       with Mr. W.T. Jayasinghe had still to take place. (Reference
       para 6 of October 19 minutes and 6 (1) of October 8 minutes).
       Minister agreed to expedite matters.
   (d) On STF it was pointed out that they had yet to move out
       fully from Amparai District. (Reference para 7 of October
       19 minutes). Minister directed immediate action to complete
       their de-induction.

2. On enquiry by the Minister regarding request of Government of Sri
   Lanka for loan of automatic rifles for CVF, CCC IPKF intimated
   that Government of India had agreed to the request in principle.
   CM intimated that the IGP had indicated immediate initial requirement of 5,000 rifles. SCC requested that these be quickly provided.

GOC–IPKF advised that since IPKF does not possess automatic rifles, his Government was making arrangements to provide the same. He would get it expedited.

3. On the expansion of CVF (Reference para 5 of October 19 minutes and para 4 (4) of October 8 minutes) CM intimated that he had held discussions with Defence Secretary and IGP. However, agreed minutes had to be finalised. It was decided that the Sub-Committee should meet on 3rd November at 0900 hours to finalise the minutes and report to the SCG.

4. GCC–IPKF informed the SCG that the next area to be vacated by IPKF is Batticaloa District. Readjustments and preparations for this are under way. The SCG should examine the adequacy of law and order arrangements. The exact date of vacation will be intimated thereafter.

5. CM stated that he could confirm adequacy of arrangements only after the decisions arrived at during the Sub-Committee meeting of 21 October vide para 5 and the arrangements for arming the CVF vide para 4 of the SCG meeting of 19 October had been implemented. The Minister asked for these to be expedited and in the meanwhile directed that Sri Lankan Police should take necessary steps to man its police stations in Batticaloa District as had been done in Amparai District. IGP intimated that police stations in Batticaloa District had been brought to full strength. The Minister also directed that STF should deinduct completely from Batticaloa District.

6. The SCG would reconvene on 3rd November at 1030 hours.

sd/-
(Secretary)

VIII D: Minutes of the Security Co-ordinating Group

Meeting Held on 3 November 1989

Present:

Hon. Ranjan Wijeratne, Minister of Foreign Affairs and Minister of State for Defence; Hon. A. Varatharajaperumal, Chief Minister, North-East Province; Gen. D.S. Attygalle, Secretary, Ministry of Defence; Lt. Gen. A.S. Kalkat, GOI–IPKF.

In Attendance:

Lt. Gen. H. Wanasinghe, Commander of the Sri Lanka Army; Mr. E.E.B. Perera, Inspector General of Police; Dr. K. Vigneswaran, Secretary to Chief Minister, North-East Province; S. Jaishankar, Political Adviser to GOC-IPKF.

1. The SCG considered and approved the minutes of the Special Committee meetings held on 21 October and 3 November 1989. These minutes are at Annexure A.

2. The Minister assured the Chief Minister that the bill to establish Police Commissions would be introduced in Parliament on 7 November 1989 and passed within a few days.

3. The Chief Minister complained of extortion by the LTTE. The Minister ordered DIG North-East Province to get the CVF to take necessary measures to stop this immediately.

4. The Chief Minister produced letters mailed by the LTTE to North-East Province officials threatening them. The letters were dated 26th October 1989. About 40 letters were given by the Chief Minister who directed Secretary, Defence to take this matter up with the LTTE.

5. The Chief Minister drew attention to the occupation of Komari and Thandiyadi camps by the LTTE, which were formerly occupied by the IPKF. The Minister ordered that the CVF should take action to evict the LTTE and that the Sri Lankan Army should assist the CVF if required.

6. The Minister stated that he would propose a Cabinet paper to relax the educational qualifications in the recruitment to the Police and Armed Forces.

7. The Chief Minister raised the issue of convening a Peace Committee meeting as its recommendations are to be considered by the SCG. The Minister said that the LTTE had raised the issue of forced conscription of youths, for its non-participation in the Peace Committee meetings. The Chief Minister pointed out that this was an afterthought on the part of the LTTE and it is clear that the LTTE is avoiding to come into the democratic process on one pretext or the other. He reported that an early meeting of the Peace Committee was necessary. The Minister stated that he would take up this matter with H.E. the President.

8. The Chief Minister requested the Minister to take up the matter on devolution of power to the Provincial Councils with H.E. the President, with a view to expediting the devolution process.

9. The next meeting of the SOG was planned for 16th November 1989 at 1830 hours.

                                              Sd/-
                                          Secretary

ANNEXURE 'A'

Minutes of the Special Committee Appointed by the Security Coordinating Group to Discuss the Details and the Numbers Required for the Citizens Volunteer Force, Provincial Police and the Armed Services

1. In view of the directions given in para 4 of the minutes signed by the Security Coordinating group on 8 October 1989, the following persons met to make representations for a final decision by the SCG:

   Chief Minister, North-East Province; Secretary, Ministry of Defence; Inspector General of Police; Secretary to the Chief Minister, North-East Province; Mr. Anandarajah, DIG North-East Province.

2. *Present Strength of the CVF*

   The CVF was raised under the command of the IGP, pending the formation of the Provincial Police Division in the North-East Province. The number of persons officially approved by the Ministry of Defence and intimated to the IGP was 3,000. This number was increased by a further 365 to provide security to Provincial Council members, over and above the 3,000. Funds are available only up to 31 December 1989 for the payment of this number, namely 3,865.

3. *Expansion of CVF*

   The CVF which has a current strength of 3,000 will be increased to 7,000 in the same manner as the earlier 3,000 were regularised.

4. *Absorption to the North-East Provincial Police*

   Once the Provincial Police Division is established, personnel of the CVF who have the requisite qualifications as laid down by the National Police Commission, will be absorbed to the North-East Provincial Police Division. The Chief Minister will recommend to the National Police Commission to lower educational standards for recruitment to the Police Force for a limited period to enable the absorption of CVF personnel into the Provincial Police. This has become necessary due to the extraordinary situation that prevailed in the North-East Province during the past several years.

   All Police Reservists and CVF personnel presently deployed in the North-East Province will be properly and adequately armed with automatic weapons for the present.

   All CVF personnel will be entitled to the very same financial benefits as the Police Reservists deployed in the North-East Province.

5. *Ethnic Proportions of Armed Services*

   As agreed by the SCG, the Provincial Police will be recruited in accordance with the ethnic proportion of the North-East Province. The National Police Division, the regular Armed Forces and the

Volunteer Forces of the three Armed Services, will reflect the national ethnic proportion.

Secretary/Defence informed that the present approved cadre of the Security Forces is as follows:

Army	Regular	2,000	Officers	32,000	Other Rank
	Volunteer	775	"	18,529	-do-
Navy	Regular	569	"	6,940	-do-
	Volunteer	100	"	1,000	-do-
Air	Regular	583	"	7,919	-do-
Force	Volunteer	150	"	2,100	-do-

Of the total sanctioned strength of 72,665 Security Personnel, Tamils and Muslims do not constitute even 1 per cent. Immediate steps should be taken to ensure that the Army, Navy and Air Force reflect the ethnic composition of the country both among the Regulars and the Volunteers. In order to maintain the ethnic ratio, a time frame of three years would be necessary with a significant input in the first year.

6. *Ethnic Proportions of Police Force*

The sanctioned cadre is 27,000 Regulars and 17,000 Reservists totalling 44,000.

Similar arrangements have to be made to achieve Divisional and National ethnic ratio.

7. *Short Term Arrangements*

The Chief Minister expressed the view that in the first year 50 per cent of the total number of Tamils and Muslims required to maintain the ethnic proportion in the Armed Forces should be recruited. Secretary/Defence expressed the view that it may not be practicable to recruit such a number in the first year. Additionally, there would be financial constraints in such recruitment. In all recruitments, the normal administrative procedure will be followed. In the meantime action will be taken to fill all vacancies in the Forces resulting from retirements during the next three years, with Tamil and Muslim personnel. Education qualifications may have to be lowered for a limited period to enable youth from the North-East Province to join the Forces. This is necessary due to the extraordinary situation that prevailed in the North-East Province over the past several years.

VIII E: Position Paper on Implementation of Decisions

of Security Co-ordination Group

Introduction

The Charter of the SCG was formulated as per paragraph 5 of the Joint Communique of 18 September 1989 between the Governments of India and Sri Lanka. This covered four points as follows:

(a) Avoiding any adverse impact on law and order situation in the North-East Province of Sri Lanka;

(b) Suggesting measures to ensure safety and security in the North-East Province;

(c) Strengthen the civilian administration in the North-East Province; and

(d) Keep in view recommendations of the Peace Committee relating to the safety and security in the North-East Province.

The Security Coordination Group comprised of the following members: (1) Hon. Ranjan Wijeratne, Minister of Foreign Affairs and Minister of State for Defence; (2) Hon. A. Varatharajaperumal, Chief Minister, NEP; (3) Gen. D.S. Attygalle, Secretary, Ministry of Defence; (4) Lt. Gen. A.S. Kalkat, GOC–IPKF.

Though the SCG met several times since October 1989, the Government of Sri Lanka did not make genuine efforts to implement the decisions. The following schedule indicates the present position:

Date of meeting	Important decisions taken	Positons regarding implementation
8.10.1989	1. Deinduction of IPKF to commence in the Amparai District from 15.10.1989	Deinduction completed in Amparai by 25.10.1989 Law and order under control of Police, CVF and addtional personnel trained for absorption into CVF
	2. Law and order will be maintained by the Chief Minister through the Police with the assistance of the CVF	Chief Minister in control of law and order for about 10 days only, as Sri Lankan Security Forces together with LTTE mounted attacks on CVF personnel
	3. Sufficient number of	Not implemented

(Continued)

Date of meeting	Important decisions taken	Positons regarding implementation
	CVF personnel to be inducted into the Reserve and Regular Sri Lanka Police Force to fill vacancies	
	4. DIG to be responsible and be under control of the Chief Minister for the maintenance of law and order	Though the DIG has been appointed with the concurrence of the Chief Minister, he gets directions from the IGP of the Sri Lanka Government
	5. After the deinduction of the IPKF, the Sri Lanka Army will vacate public buildings and will be relocated in suitable areas provided by the Chief Minister and acceptable to the Commander of the Army, in consultation with the Minister of State for Defence	Being violated by the Sri Lanka Government
	6. The Sri Lanka Army will not be called out for military operations except with the consent of the President and the Chief Minister	Being violated by the Sri Lanka Government
	7. Mr. W.T. Jayasinghe, Adviser to the President, to liaise with State Officials of the North-East Province to resolve problems of devolution and report to the President	Not implemented
19.10.1989	1. Bill for the establishment of National and Provincial Police Commissions to be placed before Parliament at sessions	Action delayed and Bill placed before Parliament in late December 1989

(Continued)

Date of meeting	Important decisions taken	Positons regarding implementation
	2. Special Task Force platoons to be moved out of Amparai District	Implemented only in late November 1989. Subsequently STF moved into other Districts of the Province
3.11.1989	1. The current approved strength of 3,000 of the CVF to be increased to 7,000, in the same manner as the earlier 3,000 were regularised	Not implemented
	2. Once the Provincial Police Division is established, personnel of the CVF to be absorbed into the North-East Police Division	Provincial Police Division yet to be established
	3. All Police Reserve and CVF personnel in North-East to be properly and adequately armed with automatic weapons	Not implemented
	4. The National Police Division and the Provincial Police Division to reflect the respective ethnic ratios	Not implemented
	5. As Tamil-speaking persons do not constitute even 1 per cent of the total sanctioned strength of 72,665 of the armed forces personnel in Sri Lanka, immediate steps to be taken to ensure that the Army, Navy and Air Force reflect the ethnic composition of the country, both among the Regular and	Not implemented

(Continued)

Date of meeting	Important decisions taken	Positons regarding implementation
	Volunteers, within a time frame of 3 years with half the intake during the first year	
	6. The Chief Minister drew the attention of the occupation of Komari and Thandiyadi camps in Amparai District by the LTTE, which were formerly occupied by the IPKF. It was decided that the CVF should take action to evict the LTTE and that the Sri Lanka Army should assist the CVF, if required	The LTTE, operating from these camps, attacked two nearby CVF camps with the support of the special Task Force (STF) of the Sri Lanka Government
	7. The Chief Minister raised the issue of convening the Peace Committee meeting as its recommendations are to be considered by the SCG. The Minister of State for Defence stated that he would take up this matter with the President	No outcome
	8. The Chief Minister requested the Minister to take up the matter of devolution of powers with the President with a view to expediting the devolutionary process	No outcome

Conclusions

The Security Coordination Group had been made ineffective by the deliberate acts of omissions and commissions of the Sri Lanka Government. Had the decisions of the SCG been sincerely implemented by the Sri Lanka Government, the safety and security of the Tamils of Sri Lanka could have been ensured to a great degree.

Index

INDEX